Learn Romani

Das-dúma Rromanes

Learn Romani

Ronald Lee

University of Hertfordshire Press

First published in Great Britain in 2005 by
University of Hertfordshire Press
College Lane
Hatfield
Hertfordshire AL10 9AB
Reprinted in 2017

British Library Cataloguing in Publication Data
A catalogue record for this book is available from the British Library

ISBN 978-1-902806-44-0 paperback

Design by Geoff Green Book Design
Cover design by John Robertshaw
Printed in Great Britain by Hobbs the Printers Ltd

Waso Russel Demitro

Ka múrro phúro amal thai wuchitêli, O Káko Wáso Demítro. Kakya buki sas amáro súno. Te thas tele ánde ram, amári shib, te sikyon, amáre terne, pêngi Rrómani shib ánde l' gesa te aven. Dem túke múrri solax te kámas-kerav kakya buki. Akana me kerdem e ángluni pártya. Te del o Del te kerav o dúito pártya, amári swatonêngi-búkfa. Te soves mishto Káko, zhi-ka dikhav tu mai yêkh dáta ándo amáro Rromano Raiyo.
Te Trayil Romanestan!

To my old friend and mentor, Elder Waso Russel Demitro. This work was our dream. That we put down in writing, our language, that our young people might learn their Romani language in the days to come. I gave you my sacred oath that we would accomplish this work. Now I have completed the first part. May God grant that I complete the second part, our dictionary. May you sleep well, Uncle, until I see you again in our Romani heaven.
May the Romani nation yet live!*

Akana sikyovas te das-dúma Rromanes
Now we shall learn to speak Romani
Te aven baxtale
May you be fortunate

* The reality of the Roma as a non-territorial nation.

Notes

Songs, poems, proverbs and folk tales

These examples of recorded Romani are not part of the lessons. They do not have to be learned nor fully understood as the student advances through the course, and are included to show samples of the language. Some contain words and grammatical rules which have not been covered up to that point and these will be explained in footnotes. The reason for including them is simple. Unlike the situation in Europe where newspapers, magazine articles and even books are appearing in various Romani dialects, there is no written material in the dialect covered by this course, so these songs, poems, proverbs and folk tales show the language recorded from native speakers. When all the lessons have been completed, the student can then refer back to these as examples of recorded Romani. For those who wish to proceed quickly through the course, these samples can be bypassed and returned to later with a better understanding of the language.

On grammatical and linguistic terminology

Donald Kenrick and I originally designed this course in the early 1970s to enable Romani people who may have lost their ancestral language and who may not have had the advantage of much formal education to relearn it. Grammatical terms were kept to a minimum and explained in simple English. The edited course has now been upgraded to a higher level and more grammatical terms have been employed with explanations in parentheses (brackets) and other aids retained for ease of understanding, however, overall grammatical and linguistic terminology has been kept to a minimum. Those interested in this area of Romani linguistic studies can consult the sources listed in the bibliography. This course is designed to help students learn basic Kalderash-Romani.

Contents

Foreword by Ian Hancock

Director, The Romani Archives and Documentation Center
The University of Texas at Austin

Throughout the Seventies, the journal *Roma*, edited by the late Padmashri Weer R. Rishi at the Indian Institute of Romani Studies (IIRS) in Chandigarh, Panjab, published a series of Romani lessons written by Ronald Lee and edited by Donald Kenrick. They provided the first access ever to the language for speakers of English. *Roma*, however, was not a widely accessible journal, and even when the IIRS combined all of the eighteen lessons into a single volume available for purchase separately, its availability remained nevertheless limited. It is with considerable satisfaction, therefore, that we now find this enlarged and corrected version of those lessons made available by the University of Hertfordshire Press, itself gaining a worldwide reputation as a publishing house specialising in Roma-related topics.

Rather than consisting simply of an overview of Romani grammar (e.g. Hancock, 1995, 2003) or a general discussion of the language (e.g. Bakker et al., 2000), the present volume is an actual learning tool aimed at providing a basic usable knowledge of Romani through a series of carefully graded lessons. While a number of proposed writing systems exist for Romani, the present volume wisely employs an orthography based on English, aimed in particular at English speakers, including those Roma in North America who have lost the language and who would like to regain it. Such an orthography, which has no necessary accent marks, is also most easily used in email correspondence.

The author has deliberately selected Vlax- (Vlach, Danubian) Romani as the dialect of choice, since this has the greatest number of speakers worldwide, and is the most widely spoken geographically. Most of the existing dictionaries and other linguistic treatments of Romani deal with Vlax, and the Kalderash variety of Vlax, in particular. Vlax dialects are those most widely spoken in North and South America, where it has perhaps between one and two million speakers. Even more live throughout Europe and the rest of the world.

Ronald Lee is in the process of compiling a separate dictionary to accompany the present book; at this time Vlax-English dictionaries are practically non-existent, but Demeter (1990) has a useful English to Kalderash-Romani cross-index, as does Gjerdman and Ljungberg (1963) and Boretzky and Igla (1994), though this latter includes other dialects besides Vlax.

Introduction

Romani has many dialects and no standard written form. This course is based on the language as spoken by the Kalderash Roma in the US, Canada, Latin America and Europe. A native speaker of any Kalderash dialect can usually converse fluently with any other speaker. Differences between Kalderash dialects are slight and consist mainly of words borrowed from non-Romani languages, which are common only to specific groups of speakers in a given country, and in pronunciation – roughly parallel to colloquial British English and American English or Mexican Spanish and Castillian Spanish. Since Kalderash Roma travel widely and intermarry in different countries, these non-Romani loan words find their way to Kalderash communities all over the world. A specific speaker may not use a certain loan word in his or her particular dialect but may be familiar with it, having heard it from other speakers.

Kalderash-Romani also belongs to a number of related dialects spoken by groups such as the Lovári, Machwáya, Churári, Mashári, Tsolári and others. All these dialects belong to the Vlax-Romani group, which means that the speakers evolved these dialects in Wallachia, Moldavia, Transylvania (and other geographical areas where the surrounding language was Romanian) over a period of many generations and then carried them by migration to other regions of central, eastern and western Europe, the Americas and elsewhere. There are an estimated three million Roma in the Americas, a large number of whom continue to speak Kalderashítska or Machwanítska and related Vlax-Romani dialects. An unidentified number, estimated at two to three million or more Vlax-Roma still live in Romania and other Balkan countries, and there are others in Russia plus eastern, central and western Europe. How many speak Romani is unknown but large numbers do, including children. Speakers of Vlax-Romani dialects far outnumber speakers of any other Romani dialect and they have the widest geographical distribution of any Romani group.

A knowledge of Kalderash-Romani will also help conversation with speakers of non-Vlax-Romani dialects since core language (thematic) words are the same or close to the Romani words in other dialects. It is the loan words or athematic items and sometimes certain grammatical rules that differ. Kalderash and other Vlax-Romani dialects have a large input of loan words derived from Romanian while non-Vlax-Romani dialects have a large input of borrowed words from other languages such as Turkish, Albanian and/or the Slavic languages.

Some groups of Romani speakers such as the Sinti in western Europe, the English Romanies, Finnish Kaale and others, speak kinds of Romani that are very different from Kalderash, but there are still a large number of words that are the same in all Romani dialects. To help your rapid progress, only a few variations of Kalderash or related Vlax-Romani dialects have been introduced, mainly in songs, until Lesson eleven so you will have to be patient if the Romani you hear around you is not exactly the same as that used prior to this point. Some variations between different speakers of the dialect in this course will be explained in the notes and these variant forms should not be learned, but are there simply to show the variations that might be heard from speakers of the Kalderash dialect.

All Romani speakers also use non-Romani words and expressions from the surrounding non-Romani language and, when these are not English, they can confuse the English-speaking student. Typical North American-Kalderash might appear as: **De lêske** (few dollars) **te zhal ka o** (supermarket) **te kinel pêske** (ice cream) which translates as 'Give him a few dollars so he can go to the supermarket and buy himself ice cream'. Mexican-Kalderash on the other hand might say: **O Frúnka si buntash,** (*un hombre muy malo*)**, xav lêske shoro** which is 'Frúnka is a troublemaker, a very evil man, I'll destroy him'. Of course, the Romani words for the English and Spanish in these two examples could easily be used. This mixing of two languages is common in all Romani dialects and when speaking Romani, native speakers will often fall back on a word in the non-Romani language and bring this into their sentence as a loan word. A typical example is in Canadian-Kalderash: **Musai te zhas ka o dukáto te (sain)is (afid)évito** 'You must go to the lawyer and sign an affidavit'. More formal speech between elders, between strangers and foreign Roma and during the Romani tribunal (**Kris-Rromani**) usually employs all Romani words.

Some grammatical and linguistic terms have been used in the lessons and are explained in plain English for students unfamiliar with them. This course is not designed for trained linguists, although they may find it useful, but for non-Romani people in general who want to become familiar with Romani and for Romani people who wish to relearn their ancestral language in its most useful modern form. Vlax-based Romani functions as the language of communication between Romanies from many countries who have no non-Romani language in common. It is used at international conferences, appears in print and during radio broadcasts and many speakers of other Romani dialects have adopted it in order to be able to converse with Romanies from other countries.

Romani is rapidly evolving in today's world and this Vlax-based international Romani is evolving and becoming the most widely spoken and written form of the language. The various related dialects are levelling and new words and new meanings for old words are constantly entering this international dialect as Roma who speak related dialects find new ways to express modern concepts and inventions. Typical examples include **mobílo** 'mobile phone', **sinzizáto** 'synthesiser', **sistéma-sônóri** 'sound system', **Bôrdo-Dirêktórya** 'Board of Directors', **komputêri** 'computer', **maimúnka** 'computer mouse', **lumiyáki-miriyázha** 'internet, World Wide Web', **filástra** 'window, computer screen', **azilantomos** 'refugee status', **krisi** and **tárdyulash** 'refugee case hearing', **shêltèri** 'shelter for refugees', **phandayimos** 'detention centre', **shingale** 'immigration officials', **báldo** 'ball, dance', **stipênda** 'stipend', **djulêshi** 'organisational business meeting', **zhútso** 'wire, news service', **tonomáto** 'jukebox', plus hundreds of others.

Pronunciation (phonetic system)

There is no standard pronunciation of Kalderash-Romani that can be said to be used by all speakers, any more than there is a standard pronunciation of English vowels and consonants that would assist non-English speakers to understand English speakers in various regions of the British Isles, North America, Australia, New Zealand, South Africa, the Caribbean Commonwealth countries and anywhere else where English serves as the native language. The pronunciation of Romani differs because of migrations, isolation in specific regions by some groups, influences from the surrounding non-Romani language(s) also spoken by the speakers and other factors. These minor differences will be discussed in Lesson eleven.

The pronunciation given is based on my own. I learned Canadian-Kalderash-Romani from my peers in my early teens after returning to Canada from Britain where I spent my childhood years. This was augmented in my late teens and early twenties by a close association with French-Kalderash speakers living in Canada, as the work partner of Ványa Kwiek (**O Ványa le Dâtchèsko**) and by collaborating with Waso Russel Demitro (**O Wáso le Mitásko**), a Canadian-Kalderash elder, who assisted me in compiling the first English-Kalderash-Romani lexicon (as yet unpublished) in the early 1960s in Montreal. I have been speaking, writing and reading published works in Romani ever since. The alphabet (phonetic system) used in this course is based on one I devised in the 1960s and have been using with many other Romani people, in personal correspondence and in my published works. Anything else could create errors in the course because of both my long familiarity with the original system and the fact that I have found it to work well with Romani speakers who also speak and write English.

Since the end of Communism, large numbers of Vlax-Romani speakers have arrived in Canada as refugees from persecution in central and eastern Europe, with whom I have been conversing on a daily basis due to my involvement in the Roma Community Centre (RCC) in Toronto, an NGO which assists Romani refugees in Canada with immediate issues of immigration, social settlement and other needs. By using the Romani in this course, I have been able to speak almost daily in Romani with Kalderash speakers and speakers of closely related Vlax-Romani dialects from Romania, Bulgaria, Hungary, the former Yugoslavia, the Czech Republic and elsewhere. I have also found this

Romani very useful in communicating with non-Vlax-Romani speakers whose dialects are different but who are able to understand me fairly well because of common words and a basically similar grammar, for example, the Czech/Slovak Roma who speak the Rromúngero dialect of Romani; the Pólska Rróma, a Polish non-Vlax-Romani group; Roma from Kosovo and Bosnia who mostly speak a Yérli-Romani dialect or the Gurbéti and Chergári-Romani dialects.

The alphabet (phonetic system) used in this course is based on English and designed for English speakers. This way, it avoids the use of accents used in Romani alphabets on computers with foreign-language keyboards. It has been successfully used by Romani speakers in the RCC and Canada in general who need to write Romani on a standard keyboard. It is also used for Romani which appears in the RCC magazine, *Romano Lil*. The stress accents used in this course do not have to be used by Romani speakers and they have been used to assist the student to pronounce the Romani in the lessons. In a course of this type it is impossible to give all the variations of sounds, especially vowels, that might be encountered from Kalderash or Vlax-Romani speakers in general. Those interested in this area should consult the following: Hancock, Ian. *A Handbook of Vlax Romani*. New York: Slavica Publishers, Inc., 1995, which is listed in the bibliography of useful sources. However, the following pronunciation guide designed for this course will enable the student to be understood in Kalderash-Romani and to understand it when it is spoken if he or she follows the guidelines indicated. For further assistance, the cassette tape and course created by Père A. Barthélémy entitled *Żanés Romanés?* is currently available in Canada and is also listed in the bibliography with details of how to order. In addition there is a CD of Romani folk music in various dialects, *Homage to Kali Sara*, produced by my wife and I, which includes most of the North American-Kalderash and East European-Romani songs which appear among samples of Romani in the lessons in this course. This too is listed in the bibliography.

Even though I speak fluent Kalderash-Romani, all words given as examples of pronunciation and many examples of sentences, idioms, songs, proverbs and other material in this course have been recorded from native speakers of Kalderash since the 1950s and are contained in a series of notebooks and on tape. This has been augmented, when necessary, by cassette tapes, CDs and published material by native speakers. Some European examples of Romani in the lessons and in some of the reading material were contributed by Donald Kenrick who is an acknowledged scholar in the area of Romani and its dialects.

I also wish to compliment Mr Kenrick for a truly excellent job of structuring the lessons into a logical developmental sequence for the original course upon which this revised version has been based. I am also indebted to Victor A.

Friedman of the University of Chicago, whose support and critique have been greatly appreciated, and to Dr Ian Hancock of the University of Texas, whose advice and assistance in the area of Romani linguistics has been invaluable. Finally, but certainly not least, I owe thanks to my patient and long-suffering wife, Giannina Bottaccini, who has lived with the creation of this course since I began the final editing in 2003 and who has been my systems engineer, computer expert and alter ego.

Vowels

a Most like Spanish *mañana* but the **< a >** in English 'father' is close. **< A >** is longer when it is stressed than when it is not. Examples: **dad** 'father', **azilánto** 'male refugee', **akana** 'now'.

â A short **< a >** sound as in English 'hat'. Example: **ânchépo** 'smelling salts, snuff'.

ã The **< aw >** sound as in English 'awful'. Example: **kwãsa** 'scythe'. This sound occurs only in a few words.

e As in French *allé* or English **< A >** when reciting 'A,B,C' or the **< ai >** sound in English 'pain'. Examples: **rakle** 'non-Romani boys', **bale** 'pigs'.

ê Between the **< e >** in English 'bed' and Spanish *huevo*. Examples: **amên** 'us', **mênshiya** 'ball'.

i Like the **< ee >** sound in English 'seem'. Examples: **iv** 'snow', **rakli** 'non-Romani girl', **Ivropáno** 'European man'.

î Close to the **< i >** sound in English 'tin'. Example: **tînzhíri** 'skillet'.

o A long **< o >** sound like English 'home' or French *eau*. Example: **raklo** 'non-Romani boy'.

ô Close to English 'hot, pot, got' or Spanish *hombre*. Example: **drôm** 'road'. Americans should be careful with this sound which is closer to British English. Many Americans pronounce this short **< o >** like a short **< a >** as in the English word 'hot' which sounds more like 'hât'. Even American-Kalderash use this sound so that Romani **shôto** 'bigshot' actually sounds like **shâto.**

u A long **< oo >** sound as the **< ou >** sound in English 'you', Spanish *luna* or French *vous*. Examples: **tu** 'you', **manush** 'male person, human being, elderly man, Sir'.

û A very short vowel sound something like the **< u >** in English 'under'. It is a centralised and unrounded vowel sometimes represented in Romani by **< ï >** with an umlaut as a diacritic (pronunciation) mark. Examples: **zûn** 'saddle', **atvtsûn** 'steel'. It must be heard to pronounce it correctly. See also Hancock, Ian, 1995, p.45.

y   When **< y >** is used in this alphabet as a 'glide' or 'semi-vowel' it is a short **< y >** sound which regularly replaces the long **< ee >** sound in words like **bakri** 'ewe' or **sapní** 'female snake' when these singular nouns become plurals. Examples include **bakrya** and **sapnya** and other instances which will appear throughout the lessons.

Vowel stress

Kalderash-Romani and Vlax-Romani dialects in general place the stress on the last vowel in the word. When this occurs, no stress mark will be shown. When the stress falls on a vowel other than the last, it will be indicated as follows: **láda** 'trunk, chest' with the stress on the first vowel, **masári** 'butcher' (stress on the second vowel) or **barvalo** 'rich' where the stress falls on the last vowel and does not need to be indicated. Stress position can also change depending on where the word appears in a sentence. There can be sentences like: **Wo si manush barvalo** 'He is a wealthy man' (with the stress on the last vowel of **barvaló**) or **O bárvalo manush mulo** 'The wealthy man died'. In this second example the stress in **bárvalo** is on the first vowel not the last.

   When the diacritics **â, ã, ê, î, ô** and **û** are used to indicate vowel sound, the stress accents will be indicated even if the stress falls on the last vowel, as in **mômêlí** 'candle', unless the vowel marked with the pronunciation mark is to be stressed. For example: **mênshiya** 'ball' (stress falls on the first vowel), **pônyáva** 'carpet' (stress falls on the second vowel) and **drômorró** 'small, narrow road' (stress falls on the third or last vowel). In a very few words, all vowels in the word may be **â, ã, ê, î, ô** or **û** and, in this case, the vowel to be stressed will appear not with the accent **< ^ >** but with the French grave accent **< ` >**. An example is **vôrdòn** 'caravan' where the stress falls on the second **< o >**. More instructions about stress will be found in the lessons.

Double vowels (diphthongs)

ai   Similar to the sound of English 'high' or 'rye'. Example: **nai** 'finger'. When the word **nai** has a case ending added to it the diphthong becomes **< aiy >** with the case ending added. Example: **naiyêsa** 'with the finger'. The **< y >** is a glide between the diphthong and the case ending*. It is not pronounced **nai-êsa** but **nai-y-êsa**.

---

*   Case endings will be fully described in the course lessons. They can be ignored for now.

ei* Rarely used except as an interjection or in songs. It sounds like the **< ey >** in English 'hey!' Example: **Ei, shavále!** 'Hey, Romani boys!'

oi Close to the sound of English 'oyster' or 'boy'. Example: **gunoi** 'rubbish'. When words with this sound have case endings added the **< oi >** becomes **< oiy >** with the case ending added. Example: **gunoiyêsa** 'with the rubbish'.

ui A difficult sound for English speakers, like the **< ouille >** in French *ratatouille*. Example: **mui** 'mouth'. As with **< ai >** and **< oi >**, the **< ui >** becomes **< uiy >** when the word has a case ending added to it. Example: **muiya** 'mouths' (masculine plural ending in **< a >**).

Stress of diphthongs

When double vowels are stressed, the stress mark is shown on the first letter of the double vowel but the double vowel is stressed as a single sound. Example: **cháiniko** (**chái**-niko) 'teapot'. When not stressed, no stress mark appears. Example: **raikano** (rai-**kanó**) 'elegant' where the stress falls on the last **< o >**.

Consonants

Aspirated consonants

In the following pronunciation guide there are three aspirated consonants: **< kh >**, **< ph >** and **< th >**. These are pronounced as a hard **< k >**, **< p >** or **< t >** followed by a puff of air. The closest sound in English to this is the explosive sound of the standard British pronunciation of the **< kh >** in 'blockhouse.'

b Close to English **< b >**. Example: **balo** 'male pig'.

c Not used in this alphabet.

ch A hard **< ch >** sound not like English 'cheer' but more like 'chatter'.

d A dental **< d >** as in French or Spanish with the tongue touching the back of the top teeth. Examples: **dav** 'I give', **diwáno** 'meeting, discussion'.

dj Close to the **< j >** sound of English 'Jack'. Examples: **djédjêsh** 'train', **djéla** 'thing, matter', **djungalo** 'ugly'.

f Close to English. Examples: **fárba** 'paint', **fakalêtso** 'stooge, rolling pin'.

g Hard **< g >** as in English 'got'. Examples: **gitára** 'guitar', **galav** 'saddle bag'.

---

* In a few words like **shey** 'Romani girl, daughter' and **dey** 'mother' there is a **< y >** sound after the **< e >**. When these words take a case ending like **sheyan** (feminine plural accusative case) a definite **< y >** sound can be heard.

In Romani this sound should never be pronounced as in English 'George'.

h   Like English **< h >** in 'hammer'. Example: **harmasári** 'stallion'.

j   Not used in this alphabet except with **< d >** (see above **< dj >**).

k   Close to the English sound in 'poker'. A hard **< k >** sound, not like English 'kismet'. Example: **kukurúzo** 'Indian corn, corn on the cob'.

kh A harder **< k >** (aspirated), like the **< kh >** in 'workhorse'. Examples: **kher** 'house, home', **khaini** 'chicken'.

l   Closer to the English **< l >** in 'glue' than in 'lend'. Examples: **lav** 'I take', **alav** 'word'.

ly This is actually a single sound in Romani. Example: **raklya** 'non-Romani girls'. It is close to the **< ll >** in Castillian Spanish as in *llamar* or the **< gl >** in Italian *voglio*. The standard Canadian/American English **< li >** in 'valiant' or 'Valium' is close.

m   English value as in 'mother'. Examples: **mobíli** 'automobile', **mômêlí** 'candle'.

n   English **< n >** can be used here but in Romani it is a dental sound with the tongue touching the upper front teeth. Examples: **kána** 'when', **nanári** 'pineapple'.

ng When **< n >** and **< g >** appear together in a Romani word, they are pronounced as in English 'mango' and never like two sounds as in 'man go'. Examples: **mangav** 'I want', **lêngo** 'theirs', **bêng** 'devil'.

ny When **< n >** is followed by the 'glide' or 'semi-vowel' **< y >** it becomes one sound like the Spanish **< ñ >** in *mañana* or the combination of **< ny >** in English 'canyon'. Examples: **sapnya** 'female snakes' (plural of **sapni**) or in **sapnyánsa** 'with the female snakes'.

p   Like English **< p >** in 'spot'. Examples: **páni** 'water', **papíriya** 'documents, papers'.

ph Aspirated. This is a hard **< p >** sound followed by a puff of air. Somewhat like the sound in 'haphazard' in English rather than the **< p >** in Peter. Do not pronounce it as an **< f >** as in English 'phone'. Examples: **phúrdav** 'I blow, breathe', **phurt** 'footbridge'.

q   Not used in this alphabet.

r   Close to Spanish **< r >** as in 'Pedro' (not rolled). The **< r >** must be heard, not slurred, as is common in English. Examples: **rai** 'gentleman', **ródav** 'I seek, search'.

rr In some Kalderash dialects, for example, in Canada, the US, parts of Latin America, France and other countries of Europe, the Kalderash **< rr >** is pronounced from the throat (a guttural sound) like German *roust* or the Continental French **< r >** as in *rendez-vous*. It should sound like an uvular

< rr > made when a person gargles. Examples: **Rrôm** or **Rrom** 'Romani man or 'husband', **Rrômní** or **Rromni** 'Romani woman or wife', **rrai** 'switch, cane', **burr** 'bush, thicket'. Ask a native speaker to say **rai** 'gentleman' and **rrai** 'switch cane' for the difference in sound.

In some other Kalderash and Vlax-Romani dialects the **< rr >** sound is often retroflexed or trilled. The **< rr >** must be heard clearly and not slurred. It is not the same sound as the **< r >** given in this alphabet. For beginners, a clearly pronounced **< r >** will do for both until they can hear these sounds from native speakers or from a recorded source. In the UK, the Scottish **< r >** sound, while not exactly the Romani sound, would be better than the standard English **< r >** as in 'Robert'. Examples: **rroiyi** 'spoon', **rrátsa** 'duck'.

s Similar to English **< s >** in 'sea'. This is never slurred to become a **< z >** sound as it is in English, for example, the final **< s >** in 'strangers' or the **< s >** in 'business'. Examples: **sîm** 'I am', **sap** 'male snake', **skamin** 'chair'.

sh The English sound as in 'sheep' will be close enough. There are actually two different **< sh >** sounds in Romani, one as in **shîl** 'cold, flu' and a slightly differing one in **shêl** 'hundred'. In **shêl** the tongue is forward on the palate but in **shîl** it is curled backwards towards the throat, more like the **< sh >** in 'shoe'. Not all Romani speakers from different groups pronounce these two sounds the same and it is suggested that the **< sh >** in 'sheep' or 'shoe' be used for this sound since the related vowels in a given word will result in the right pronunciation in the alphabet for this course (which is based on English spelling) as in **shoshoi** 'rabbit' and **shîl** 'cold'. Other examples: **shib** 'tongue, language', **shoro** 'head'.

t A dental **< t >** sound and unaspirated like the English **< t >** in 'stop'. In Romani, however, the tongue should touch the back of the upper front teeth. Example: **tu** 'you'.

th A dental **< t >** and a hard, explosive sound suggesting a puff of air after the **< t >**. Something like the combination **< th >** in English 'hothouse' or the English **< t >** in 'top' but more aspirated (stronger puff). This sound should never be pronounced like **< th >** in English 'think' because this does not exist in Romani. Examples: **thud** 'milk', **thagar** 'ruler, king'.

ts This is a single sound in Romani like the **< ts >** in English 'itself' or in Italian *pizza*. Examples: **tsêra** 'tent', **tsigára** 'cigarette', **tsirratsítsa** 'pittance'.

v A soft **< v >** sound. Some speakers pronounce this almost like English **< w >**. A definite and clearly heard soft **< v >** appears in words like **voliv** 'I love' and **vórba** 'discourse'.

w A definite **< w >** sound. Examples: **wudar** 'door', **wúlitsa** 'street'.

x A guttural sound from the throat like the **< ch >** in Scottish 'loch' or

German *Achtung*. Examples**: xas** 'we eat', **xoxavel** 'he is lying'.

y   Pronounced like English 'yellow' when it is used as a consonant. Examples: **Yádo** 'Hades', **yalakráno** 'scorpion'.

z   Like English 'zeppelin'. Examples: **zalzáiro** 'acid', **zumin** 'soup'.

zh This sound is like the **< zh >** in 'Doctor Zhivago'. It exists in English but is shown by different letters, for example, the **< z >** sound in 'azure' or the **< s >** sound in 'pleasure'. Examples: **zhav** 'I go', **zhanav** 'I know'.

Lesson one

The present tense

Read the following table aloud and look carefully at the endings. The personal pronouns (words in brackets before the verb) do not need to be used but often are employed for emphasis or clarity, for example, **Mangav xabe** 'I want (some) food' is a simple statement of fact as compared to **Me mangav xabe!** '*I* want food!' or 'It's *me* who wants food!' with a greater emphasis. The verb conjugations (i.e. verb endings) are in italics in the table to clarify them and show who is doing the action. Romani has no infinitive like 'to want' in English, therefore the verb stem or root of a Romani verb will either be conjugated to one of its forms in the present tense, for example, **mangav** 'I want', or given as the verb stem **mang-** to which the appropriate conjugation must be added as shown below:

mang- (the verb stem or root)

(me)	mang*av*	I want
(tu)	mang*es*	you want (singular)
(wo)	mang*el*	he wants
(woi)	mang*el*	she wants
o Rrôm	mang*el*	the Rom wants
(ame)	mang*as*	we want
(tume)	mang*en*	you want (plural)
(won)	mang*en*	they want

You will notice the ending **< en >** has two meanings and usually the sense will be clear from the situation but, if not, use the personal pronoun **tume** or **won**.

There is also a long form of the verb i.e. **mangáva, mangésa, mangéla**, etc. This can be ignored for now as there is no change in meaning using the shorter form given in this lesson.

Test whether you have understood

If **beshav** means 'I sit, I am sitting' and comes from the verb stem **besh-**, what is the English for:

1.   **beshas**
2.   **beshes**

3.   **beshel**
4.   **beshen** (give two meanings)

If 'he drinks' is **piyel**, what is the Romani for:

5.   I drink
6.   they drink
7.   we drink
8.   you drink (singular)

Check your answers on the last page of this lesson and, if you made any mistakes, look carefully at the table above again.

The definite article: the word 'the'

There are only two genders in Romani: masculine and feminine. Nouns denoting inanimate objects (like table and chair) will either be masculine and take **< o >** or feminine and take **< e >**. For example:

o grast   the horse
e grasni   the mare
o lil   the letter
e ryat   the night

Most nouns ending in a stressed **< o >** like **balo** 'male pig' use **< o >** and most words ending in a stressed **< i >** like **bali** 'sow' use **< e >**. For other nouns ending in consonants you will have to consult the word lists in each lesson and eventually a dictionary.

   Learn these words with **< o >** or **< e >** in front of them. Learn 'letter' as **o lil** 'the letter' and **e yag** as 'the fire'.

Test

Test whether you have understood and again, check your answers on the last page of this lesson. If **manrro** is 'bread' and **bali** is 'sow', what is the Romani for:

9.   the bread
10.   the sow

The indefinite article: the words 'a' and 'an'

The English words 'a' and 'an' (indefinite articles) have no equivalent in Romani. For example, **lil** 'letter' or 'a letter' and **grast** 'horse' or 'a horse'. You will see that sometimes **< o >** and **< e >** are used where 'the' is not used in English. This happens in front of and with people's names:

E Mára avel	Mary is coming
O Stévo avel	Steve is coming
Kon avel?	Who is coming?

Here are a few more examples of statements in Romani:

(Wo) avel	He is coming
(Wo) lasharel o wudar	He repairs the door
E shey phutrel o lil	The girl opens (is opening) the letter

Questions are usually asked by raising the voice, as in English, or by turning part of the sentence round: **O shávo avel?** (with the voice rising) or **Avel o shávo?** 'Is the Romani boy coming?'

In Romani, the present tense translates the following English forms: I come, I am coming, I do come and, as in English, the present tense can be used to express the future as in 'I am coming tomorrow' or 'When I come tomorrow, I'll see you.'

Avav ages	I am coming today
Avav tehára	I am coming tomorrow

Word lists

These word lists give the words, including verbs, used in each lesson and may sometimes include words not used in the lesson when relevant. For example, if the word 'today' is used in the lesson the words for 'yesterday' and 'tomorrow' may also be given so that the student can make a basic list of important related words which can be learned together and interchanged in the sentences given in the lesson or used with native speakers for practice.

Words ending in **< o >** are always masculine and words ending in **< a >** and **< i >** can be considered feminine, however, if they are masculine this will be indicated by (m.) following the word in the list. Words ending in consonants like **skamin** 'chair' will also have the gender indicated in the word list as (m.) or (f.). Words which are plural like **love** 'money' also use **< le >** for the plural and the gender will be indicated as (m. pl.) masculine or (f. pl.) feminine.

ages	today
ánde	into, in
avav	I come

beshav	I sit
chi	not, do not (negative particle, for example, **Chi zhav** 'I am not going')
doháno	tobacco
Gazhi	non-Romani woman, wife of a non-Romani man
Gazho	non-Romani man, husband of a non-Romani woman
grasni	mare
grast	horse (referring to a gelding; **harmasári** 'stallion')
kerav	I do, make
kon?	who?
lasharav	I repair
lil (m.)	letter
mangav	I want
manrro	bread
na	no (in answer to a question)
phagav	I break
phandav	I close, tie
phutrav	I open
piyav	I drink (or **piyav doháno** 'I smoke tobacco')
rakli	non-Romani girl
raklo	non-Romani boy
ryat (f.)	night
Rrôm	Romani man, husband (if Romani)
Rrômní	Romani woman, wife (if Romani)
shávo	Romani boy (also heard as **shav** 'son, boy, young man' (if Romani), for example, **O shav avel** 'The young Romani man is coming')
shey	Romani girl
so?	what?
sóba	room
tehára	tomorrow
wudar (m.)	the door
ya	yes (also **áva** and **va**)

Spoken exercises

These should be done aloud, preferably with a partner or in a group.

1. Make up as many sentences as possible, choosing one item from each column. Think of the meaning as you say them:

e shey	(chi) mangel manrro
e Gazhi	piyel doháno
(wo)	phutrel o wudar
(woi)	beshel
o raklo	phagel
o Rrôm	mangel doháno
o shávo	lasharel

2. Answer the questions, firstly using **ya** 'yes' and then **na** 'no'. Cover the right-hand side and use it only to check your answers:

Manges manrro?	Ya, (me) mangav manrro
	Na, (me) chi mangav manrro
Phages o wudar?	Ya, (me) phagav o wudar
	Na, (me) chi phagav o wudar
Aves?	Ya, avav
	Na, chi avav
Piyes doháno?	Ya, (me) piyav doháno
	Na, (me) chi piyav doháno

3. Make up answers to these questions. Suggested answers are on the right-hand side:

Kon avel?	O shav avel
Kon beshel?	E Rrômní beshel
So mangel?	Mangel manrro

Written exercises

Translate into English:
1. **O Rrôm phandel o lil**
2. **E Gazhi chi piyel doháno**
3. **So lasharen won?**
4. **Manges manrro?**
5. **Avas**

Translate into Romani:

6. What are you (one person) doing?
7. Is the (Romani) man coming?
8. She is sitting
9. The (non-Romani) boy does not want bread
10. We are repairing the door

Check your answers at the end of the lesson.

Reading exercise

Read the poem aloud. In the text you will find words and grammatical formations not yet introduced in the lesson but these are explained in the notes and you will eventually come to them as the lessons progress. Do not attempt to learn them all at this point as the exercises are there simply to help you learn how to pronounce Romani.

A Canadian-Kalderash poem from Waso Russel Demitro, 1963

Sas-pe, Dévla
Tha shai te avel-pe
Yêkh piramno thai piramni
Yêkh ambrolin po drôm
Kon telal la, Dévla, kai beshel
Yêkh kamado thai kamadi
Kon kamel-pe thai chi mai lel-pe
Mek lel shtrángo te amblavel-pe.*

Translation

There was once, God,
And there may be again,
A lover and his sweetheart
A pear tree by the roadside
Who, God, is sitting under it
A lover and his lass

---

*　**Notes: sas-pe** 'there was once, once upon a time', **Dévla** 'God' (vocative case, used only in direct address with **Del** as the noun), **tha, thai** 'and, also', **shai te avel-pe** 'there might be again', **yêkh** there is no indefinite article in Romani as in English 'a man is coming' or 'I see a horse'. The word **yêkh** or **êkh** means the numeral 'one', for example, 'only one person knows'. **Yêkh** or **êkh** is sometimes used in Romani to express 'a' or 'an' in English and **yêkh** most often appears in Kalderash-Romani in songs, folk tales and poems. **Piramno** 'male lover who is courting a female', **piramni** 'female lover who is courted by a male', **ambrolin** 'pear tree' (from **(o) ambrol** 'pear'), **telal la** 'under, underneath it', **kamel-pe** 'he desires for himself' (**pe** or **pês** is a reflexive pronoun and means 'himself' or 'herself'), **shtrángo** 'rope, hangman's noose' ('rope' in general is **shelo** in Kalderash therefore **amblavel-pe** 'he hangs himself').

He who desires for himself
And does not take unto himself
Let him take a rope and hang himself.

A riddle

Kon avel ánde sóba thai chi pushel?
Who comes into the room without asking permission?

Thematic and athematic

It is very important to explain these terms at this point in order to simplify the Romani grammatical rules which will be presented throughout the following lessons. Rather than use 'regular' and 'irregular' to define which parts of speech follow the original grammar (thematic grammar) and which words do not (described as athematic grammar in this course) it will be better to introduce these two linguistic terms from the beginning.

Vlax Romani grammar may be treated in two categories: *thematic* and *athematic*. These have two different historical origins, and different surface morphology *(word formation)*. Thematic grammatical rules apply to words in the original stock, i.e. words of Indian origin, as well as to words acquired from all other languages the ancestors of the Roma met on the journey westwards before reaching Europe. These include items *(words)* from Persian, Kurdish, Ossetian, Armenian, Georgian and Byzantine Greek among others. Athematic grammatical rules apply to words acquired from other languages after crossing into Europe, including later Greek, South Slavic, Romanian, East Slavic, Hungarian, German, English and so on. It is their athematic lexicons *(groups or lists of loan words which differ from one Romani dialect to another)* which present the principal barrier to mutual intelligibility among speakers of the different Romani dialects.

Thematic items are almost always stressed on their final syllable, and athematic items are almost always stressed on other syllables, thus **shukar**, thematic *(with stress on the < ar >)* and **múndro**, athematic *(with stress on the first vowel or syllable < ú >)* which both mean 'beautiful'.*

---

*   Hancock, Ian. *A Handbook of Vlax Romani*. New York: Slavica Publishers, Inc., 1995, p.54. The words in italics in parentheses (brackets) have been inserted for clarity by the author.

To make the above more understandable, it has been said that Romani is a 'Balkanized Indian language'. This becomes very clear when we realize that the thematic vocabulary and grammatical rules were common to all Roma when they entered Europe. Once there, small groups left this population and made their way to central, eastern, western, southern and northern Europe. The vast majority, however, remained in the Balkans where their Romani gradually adopted batteries of loan words from Balkan languages. Because of centuries spent in Romanian-speaking regions, mainly under slavery, the Kalderash and other Vlax-Romani groups adopted a huge battery of Romanian loan words and other groups adopted words from other Balkan languages such Serbian, Bulgarian and other Slavic languages, Turkish, Greek and Albanian. These adopted loan words are athematic and have their own grammatical rules that differ somewhat from the thematic grammatical rules of the original common language often referred to as 'proto Romani'.

The first lesson in this course presents the thematic grammatical rules. The athematic grammatical rules are gradually introduced from Lesson two onwards but some athematic nouns have already appeared in the word list from Lesson one. The distinction between thematic and athematic grammatical rules will become clearer as the student progresses through the course from Lesson three onwards.

Answers to questions in this lesson

1.	we sit
2.	you sit (to one person)
3.	he sits, she sits
4.	you sit (to more than one person) or they sit
5.	**(me) piyav**
6.	**(won) piyen**
7.	**(ame) piyas**
8.	**(tu) piyes**
9.	**o manrro**
10.	**e bali**

Answers to the written exercises

1.	The Rom is closing the letter (closes the letter)
2.	The non-Romani woman is not smoking (doesn't smoke)
3.	What are they repairing?
4.	Do you want some bread?
5.	We are coming

6.	**So keres?**
7.	**Avel o Rrôm?**
8.	**Woi beshel**
9.	**O raklo chi mangel manrro**
10.	**Lasharas o wudar**

Answer to the riddle:

the wind (**e balwal**)

Lesson two

Word list

aswin (f.)	teardrop
bakro	sheep (ram)
balo (m.)	pig
baro	big, important
barvalya	rich
bikinas	we sell
bírto	tavern, bar
chorro	poor, miserable
das	we give
dikhav	I see
dui	two
fóro	city, town
hai	and (also **thai** and **tha**)
kai	where (interrogative and relative)
kalo	black
kher (m.)	house
love (m.pl.)	money
marel	he beats, hits
mulo	dead
parno	white
phuro	old
sap (m.)	snake
sastri (m.)	iron
savo	which
shinav	I cut
shuri	knife
so	what (interrogative and relative)
stagi	hat
terno	young, inexperienced
than (m.)	place, spot, location
tsino	small
turbáto	wild, mad

vôrdòn (m.)	caravan (horse-drawn) (also 'travel trailer', 'station wagon' or 'van' in modern Romani)
wudar (m.)	door
wêrsh (m.)	forest, bush
zhav	I go (**zhal** 'he, she goes'. See Lesson three for verbs in **< al >**)

Plural nouns

In Romani the following changes to plural nouns take place (athematic plural rules will be introduced in later lessons):

Masculine nouns ending in **< o >** change to **< e >**:

balo 'pig'	**bale** 'pigs'
Gazho 'non-Rom'	**Gazhe** 'non-Roma'

Masculine nouns ending in a consonant have an **< a >** added:

sap 'snake'	**sapa** 'snakes'
kher 'house'	**khera** 'houses'

For masculine nouns ending in a diphthong add **< ya >**:

rai 'gentleman'	**raiya** 'gentlemen'
rashai 'priest'	**rashaiya** and **rasha** 'priests'
xulai 'landlord'	**xulaiya** 'landlords'
shoshoi 'rabbit'	**shoshoiya** 'rabbits'
mui 'mouth'	**muiya** 'mouths'

Feminine nouns ending in **< i >** will change to a **< y >** and add an **< a >**:

shuri 'knife'	**shurya** 'knives'
bali 'sow'	**balya** 'sows'
rakli 'non-Romani girl'	**raklya** 'non-Romani girls'

Feminine nouns which end in a consonant will add an **< a >** but a very few feminine animate nouns will add **< ya >**:

bar 'fence'	**bara** 'fences'
dab 'blow'	**daba** 'blows'
asvin 'tear'	**asvina** 'teardrops'

but

phen 'sister'	**phenya** 'sisters'

To feminine nouns ending in a diphthong add **< ya >**:

goi 'sausage'   **goiya** 'sausages'

In a few cases, the form of both masculine and feminine nouns changes from the singular to the plural and this is called noun root inflection:

ryat 'night'   **rakya** 'nights' (feminine gender)
zhukel 'male dog'   **zhukla** 'male dogs' (masculine gender)

Test whether you have understood

Turn these words into the plural form:

1.   **Rrôm**
2.   **Rrômní**
3.   **wudar**
4.   **asvin** 'teardrop'

As usual, the answers are on the last page of the lesson.

Plural definite article

The word 'the' also changes when it refers to the plural and becomes **< le >** before all plural nouns:

o balo   'the pig'   **le bale** 'the pigs'
e shuri   'the knife'   **le shurya** 'the knives'

Thematic adjectives

Thematic adjectives like 'big', 'small' and 'red' change their endings in Romani depending on the word they describe. They end in **< o >** when used with masculine nouns:

o baro balo   'the big pig'
o baro lil   'the big (important) letter'

They end in **< i >** when used with feminine nouns:

e bari rakli   'the big girl'
e bari asvin   'the big teardrop'

They end in **< e >** when used with masculine or feminine plural nouns:

le bare lila   'the important letters'
le bare raklya   'the big girls'

The adjective also must change based on the gender and number of people speaking. If **bokhalo** means 'hungry', then:

me sim bokhalo	a man speaking (**sim** 'I am' which does not change for gender)
me sim bokhali	a woman speaking
ame sam bokhale	a group of people (**sam** 'we are' which does not change for gender)

Test

The adjective 'black' is **kalo**, **kali** or **kale**, depending on the gender and number of the noun it describes. It follows the same pattern as **baro**. Put the correct form in the space provided in the following phrases:

5.	**le … wudara**
6.	**o … balo**
7.	**e … Rrômní**

Thematic and athematic adjectives which do not end in a stressed **< o >** do not change their form when used with nouns in the nominative case* (the word as given in the word lists):

o shukar balo	the beautiful pig
e shukar bali	the beautiful sow
le shukar bale	the beautiful pigs
o turbáto raklo	the mad boy
e turbáto rakli	the mad girl
o dívlio balo	the wild pig
e dívlio bali	the wild sow

Unstressed adjectives like **turbáto** and **dívlio** are athematic and do not change for gender in the nominative singular. Other such adjectives are **múndro** 'wonderful', **xlútro** 'cunning' and **skúrto** 'short'. But **lúngo** 'long' is typical of the exceptions:

o lúngo drôm	the long road
e lúndji fíra	the long strand, thread
le lúndji bal	the long hair (**bal** 'hair' is plural)

---

*   A few exceptions to this rule occur in athematic unstressed adjectives ending in **< o >**, for example, there are some which end in **< go >**. These unstressed loan adjectives all appear in a table in Lesson seventeen.

o drágo grast	the beloved horse
e drázhi grasni	the beloved mare
le drázhi shave	the beloved children

Thematic Romani adjectives ending in a consonant like **shukar** 'beautiful' and **ivand** 'raw' do not change their form when used with nouns in the nominative:

o shukar grast	the beautiful horse
e shukar grasni	the beautiful mare
le shukar shave	the beautiful children

Athematic adjectives ending in **< me >** do not change for gender or plural:

volime	beloved
o volime Rrôm	the beloved Rom
e volime Rrômní	the beloved Romni
le volime Rroma	the beloved Roma

The adjective 'old'

Romani makes a distinction between 'old in age' for people and animals and for inanimate objects:

Phuro 'old in age' (people and animals)   **O phúro Rrôm avel**
The old Rom is coming

Phurano 'old' (made a long time ago)   **Dikhav phúrano kher**
I see an old house

Plus there is also:
Do-multano 'ancient, way back in the distant past, antediluvian'

Possessive pronouns

Possessive pronouns also have three forms like thematic adjectives, highlighted in the following table:

	Masculine nouns	Feminine nouns	Plural nouns
my, mine	**múrro shávo**	**múrri shey**	**múrre shave**
	múrro lil	**múrri shuri**	**múrre lila**
your, yours (sing.)	**tíro shávo**	**tíri shey**	**tíre shave**
	tíro lil	**tíri shuri**	**tíre lila**
our, yours (pl.)	**amáro shávo**	**amári shey**	**amáre shave**
	amáro lil	**amári shuri**	**amáre lila**

your (pl.)	tumáro shávo	tumári shey	tumáre shave
	tumáro lil	tumári shuri	tumáre lila

The stress on these words can change position depending on the sentence, as will be shown in later lessons, in songs and in sentences throughout this course. For example, **Kai si tíro dad?** 'Where is your father?', **Tíro mobíli si avri** 'Your car is outside' and **Godo si amaro** 'That is ours'. There is no hard-and-fast rule for this and different native speakers will change the stress in different ways. You will need to hear the language spoken to hear the various patterns. In general speech, when the pronoun (or adjective) comes before the thing possessed, it is stressed as follows: **Múrro dad avel** 'My father is coming' or **Amáre báre Rrom aven** 'Our important men are attending'. When the pronoun (or adjective) comes after the thing possessed or stands at the end of the sentence, it takes the stress on the last vowel, for example, **Kodo mobíli si murro*** 'That car is mine' or **Wo si amáro Rrôm o baro** 'He is our important Rom'. In grammatical terminology, when the possessive pronoun (or adjective) is used attributively it takes the penultimate stress (**múrro**) and when used predicatively takes the stress on the last or ultimate vowel (**murro**). But there is no iron-bound rule for this as the sentence marked with the asterisk (*) shows with **kodo** – a demonstrative adjective used attributively which has the stress on the last vowel. Romani is an oral, non-literary language and native speakers follow a rhythmic pattern common in folk tales and rhetorical Romani used in the **Kris-Rromani** (Assembley of Elders) which is almost impossible to define by textbook rules devised for literary languages.

Compare these endings:

o baro shávo   e bari shey   le bare shave   le bare sheya

and note that the adjective ending depends upon the object possessed:

múrri shuri	my knife (knife is feminine gender **e shuri**)
múrro balo	my pig (pig is masculine gender **o balo**)

It does not matter whether 'my' refers to a male or female speaker; it must agree with the noun it describes.

Test

Insert the correct form: **amáro, amári** or **amáre** in the space provided:

8.   ... **wudar**

9.   ... **stagi**

10.   ... **bakre**

Most Romani adjectives like **baro, barvalo, mulo,** etc. can also be used as nouns, just like adjectives in French or Spanish, so **baro** can also mean 'important man', **barvalo** can mean 'rich man' and **mulo** can mean 'dead man'. This applies to the feminine and plural forms as well, for example, **barvali** 'rich woman' or **barvale** 'rich men', 'rich women' or 'rich people'. These now become nouns and have singular and plural forms based on gender and number:

barvalo 'rich man'   plural **barvale** 'rich men'
barvali 'rich woman'   plural **barvalya** 'rich women'

They can then be modified by the definite article and adjectives according to the rules described previously:

o bokhalo barvalo 'the hungry rich man'   plural **le bokhale barvale** 'the hungry rich men'
e muli barvali 'the dead rich woman'   plural **le mule barvalya** 'the dead rich women'

Stress of adjectives

The instructions above for the stress of personal pronouns also apply to adjectives. The stress of adjectives can change depending on their position in the sentence. **Wo si o bárvalo Rrôm** 'He is the rich Rom' or **Wo si o Rrôm o barvalo** 'He is the Rom, the rich one'.

Spoken exercises

Make up answers following the pattern of the first sentence using words from each column:
Example:

So dikhes?	**Dikhav le shurya**	
Phutres?	**Phutrav**	**khera**
Phages?	**Phagav**	**vôrdôná**
		stagya
		wudara
So marel?*		**o sastri**
		o vôrdòn
So marel		**o sastri**

*   **So marel?** 'What is he beating/hitting?'

Kon aven?	le bale aven
Beshen	le sapa
Beshen	le bakre
	le sheya

Answer these questions with **ya** 'yes' following the examples given (note the final stress on **murro** and **tiro**):

Tiro balo avel?	Ya, murro balo avel
Tire bale aven?	Ya, murre bale aven
Dikhel tiri stagi?	Ya, dikhel murri stagi
Marel o sastri?	Ya, marel o sastri

Make up sentences choosing one item from each column:

o baro	balo	avel
	bakro	
e bari	shey	avel
	shuri	shinel
le bare	bakre	aven
	Gazhya	dikhen

Answer **na** 'no' to the following sentences:

Dikhes yêkh shuri?	Na, dikhav dui shurya
Dikhes yêkh kher?	Na, ...
Lashares yêkh vôrdòn?	
Avel yêkh balo?	
Beshel yêkh Rrômní?	
Avel yêkh shey?	Na, aven dui sheya

Written exercises

Translate into English:

1.   **O phuro Rrôm hai e phuri Rrômní aven**
2.   **Won lasharen o kalo vôrdòn**
3.   **Dikhav le bare stagya**
4.   **Avel tíri têrni shey?**
5.   **Savi shuri manges?**
6.   **Wo marel o sastri**

Translate into Romani:

7.   Our dead pigs (plural)

8.   The rich non-Roma are sitting
9.   Your knife does not cut (singular)
10.   My black hat
11.   The poor Rom repairs our small caravan

Then make up five other sentences using the words given in 7–11 above.

Reading exercise
Read aloud:

Ándo báro wêrsh me zhav
kána phúrdel e balval
Me akharav núma tu chi aves
Beshav me akana kai le chirikle chi gilaban.
Kothe me beshav hai rovav.*

Translation

Into the big forest I go, when the wind is blowing
I call you but you do not come
I sit now where the birds do not sing
Yonder, I sit and weep.

A song

Ka o fóro zhas	To the town we go
Sastri bikinas	Iron we sell
Hai but love las.	And much money do we get.
Ándo bírto zhas	Into the tavern we go
Thai mol piyas	And wine we drink
Amáre love das.	Our money we give.

A riddle

So zhal kai Lúndra, zhal, hai ashel ándo yêkh than?
What goes to London, goes and stays in one place?

---

*   **Notes: khothe** 'yonder, over there' as opposed to **othe** 'there', **núma** 'but', **gilaban** 'they sing' (this verb form ending in **< an >** is explained in Lesson three).

Answers to questions in this lesson

1.   **Rroma**. While most Kalderash speakers usually say **Rrôm**
          and **Rrômní** in the singular, in the plural these words are
          usually pronounced **Rroma** and **Rromnya** with the long
          < o > sound not the shorter **< ô >** sound. Speakers of
          North American-Kalderash usually use **Rrom** for both the
          singular and the plural, for example, **o Rrom** 'the Romani
          man' and **le Rrom** 'the Romani men'. However, both
          Rromnya and **Rrômnyá** are correct for the plural of
          Rrômní.
2.   **Rrômnyá**
3.   **wudara**
4.   **asvina**
5.   **le kale wudara**
6.   **o kalo balo**
7.   **e kali Rrômní**
8.   **amáro**
9.   **amári**
10.   **amáre**

Answers to the written exercises

1.   The old Romani man and the old Romani woman are
          coming
2.   They are repairing the black caravan
3.   I see (am looking at) the big hats
4.   Is your young daughter coming?
5.   Which knife do you want?
6.   He is beating the iron
7.   **Amáre mule bale**
8.   **Le barvale Gazhe beshen**
9.   **Tíri shuri chi shinel**
10.   **Múrri kali stagi**
11.   **O chórro Rrôm lasharel amáro tsino vôrdòn**

Answer to the riddle: the road (**o drôm**)

Lesson three

Word list

ambrol (m.)	pear
astarel	he catches
chirikli	female bird
chiriklo	male bird
dad	father
drôm (m.)	road
dur	far
farbol	he paints
gilabal	he sings
gili	song, poem
ginel	he reads, he counts
grasni	mare
grast	horse (gelding)
harmasári	stallion
hêrgléla	herd, herd of
iv (m.)	snow
katar	from where (interrogative and relative)
kána	when (interrogative and relative)
khaini	chicken, hen
kothe	yonder, there (far away)
marel	he hits
masho	fish
melalo	dirty
murtáno	tomcat
mútsa	female cat
núma	but
othe	there, right there (close by)
phabai (f.)	apple (plural **phaba**)
prindjarel	he recognizes
ramol	he writes
ródel	he seeks, looks for
Rromani gili	Romani song

Rromano	Romani (self-ascriptive adjective)
sap	male snake
serel	he reminds, remembers
te	that (as conjunctive – see the following lesson for more details)
than (m.)	place, spot, location
thol	he puts, places
thulo	fat (adjective)
tsino	small, little
volil	he loves
wuzho	clean
xal	he eats
zhal	he goes
zhukel	dog
zhukli	bitch
zhuvli	woman, female, wife (**Si mursh wórka zhuvli?** 'Is it male or female?')

Many animals in Romani have male and female forms like **grast** and **grasni**. The plural form for animals of both genders is the male form, as in **hêrgéla bakre** 'a flock of sheep', unless the plural is for an all-female group, for example, **O harmasári ingarel bari hêrgéla grasnya** 'The stallion is leading a big herd of mares'. Non-mammals like insects usually have only one gender which can be male or female, such as **makh** 'fly', which exists only in the feminine gender, or **yalakráno** 'scorpion', which exists only in the masculine gender.

The infinitive of the verb

There is no infinitive of the verb in Romani like the English 'to go', 'to come', etc. In Romani, the conjunction **< te >** is used with two or more conjugated verbs to form the equivalent of the infinitive in English, for example, **Mangav te avav** 'I want to come', which is literally translated as 'I want that I come'. Note that both verbs have their endings (conjugations) as 'I want' and 'I come' separated by **< te >**.

This use of **< te >** can be used with all verbs in all the forms of the present tense:

tu manges te aves	you want to come (you want that you come)
wo mangel te avel	he wants to come (he wants that he comes)
woi mangel te avel	she wants to come (she wants that she comes)

ame mangas te avas	we want to come (we want that we come)
tume mangen te aven	you want to come (you want that you come)
won mangen te aven	they want to come (they want that they come)

The use of **< te >** to form more complicated sentences in Romani is fully explained in Lesson fourteen.

Transitive and intransitive verbs

An intransitive verb does not take an object, for example:

sovel	he is sleeping
avel	she is coming

But a transitive verb requires an object:

Lasharav o vôrdòn	I am repairing the caravan

The object here is **vôrdòn**. When substantives (nouns) appear as the object of a transitive verb they are said to be in the accusative case.

The accusative case

The subject of an action is the nominative so, for example, 'the *man* is coming', whereas the object of an action is the accusative, for example, 'he hit the *man*'. When a person or living animal is the object of an action, the word usually takes a special form called the accusative.

Living animals include mammals, fish, birds, reptiles and amphibians but not insects. God and other deities and demons, spirits and other supernatural or mythological entities in Kalderash demonology and folklore also take the accusative. When a noun is inflected (moved) from the nominative 'the *man* is coming' to the accusative case 'he hit the *man*', it is said to be inflected to the accusative case. Inflection of nouns means giving them their proper case ending when required by the grammatical rules. The accusative case in Romani is also called the oblique stem. Five other case forms are made from this oblique stem. These will be fully explained in the relevant lessons in this course.

Examples

Raklo avel	A boy is coming (**raklo** is the nominative or the basic word as given in dictionaries and word lists.

	It is the subject of the action)
Dikhav raklês	I see a boy (**raklês** is the accusative, the object of the action. Boy is the object of the action of seeing and takes the ending **< es >** in the masculine singular accusative case ending)
Rakle aven	Boys are coming (**rakle** is the nominative plural)
Dikhav raklên	I see boys (**raklên** is the accusative plural, the object of the action)

Note on pronunciation

In accusative endings, the **< e >** in **< es >** and **< en >** is usually not the long **< e >** sound as in **bale** 'pigs' but the shorter **< e >** sound as in **< ê >** described in the alphabet, although sometimes the long **< e >** sound is heard. The phonemes (sounds) have been marked as they are commonly used in North American-Kalderash.

How to form the accusative (oblique stem)

To make the accusative in masculine and feminine forms it is necessary to make the following changes:

Masculine thematic nouns ending in a consonant simply add **< es >** in the singular and **< en >** in the plural:

phral 'brother'	becomes **phralês**	plural **phralèn**
Rrôm 'Rom'	becomes **Rrômès**	plural **Rrômèn**
Dikhav le Rrômès	I see the Romani man	
Dikhav le Rrômèn	I see the Romani men	

There are a few exceptions to this rule which are subject to noun root inflection. These, which include a few inanimate objects, will have to be learned individually from native speakers or from reliable grammars of Kalderash-Romani. The most important ones will appear throughout this course in the following lessons, tables, songs and poems. For example, as will be seen below, **Del** 'God' in the nominative takes the form **Devles** in the accusative singular and **Devlen** in the accusative plural:

Del 'God'	becomes **Devles**	plural **Devlen**
dji 'soul'	becomes **djes**	plural **djen**
muter 'urine'	becomes **mutrês**	plural **mutrên**
muter 'urine' (inanimate)		
zhukel 'male dog'	becomes **zhuklês**	plural **zhuklên**

Masculine thematic nouns for people and living things ending in a stressed **< o >** change to **< es >** in the singular and **< en >** in the plural:

bakro 'sheep'	becomes **bakrês**	plural **bakrên**
bêngorró 'male demon'	becomes **bêngorrès**	plural **bêngorrèn**
khuro 'colt'	becomes **khurês**	plural **khurên**
raklo 'boy'	becomes **raklês**	plural **raklên**

For masculine athematic nouns for people, living things and male names ending in an unstressed **< o >**, keep the **< o >** and add **< s >** in the singular and **< n >** in the plural:

xarápo 'cannibal ogre'	becomes **xarapos**	plural **xarapon**
Stévo	becomes **Stevos**	
streyíno 'stranger'	becomes **streyinos**	plural **streyinon**
Trífolo	becomes **Trifolos**	

When a man's name ends in **< a >** this becomes **< as >** in the accusative:

Frúnka	becomes **Frunkas**
Zúrka	becomes **Zurkas**

Masculine athematic nouns ending in **< a >** change as follows:

gázda 'boss, owner'	becomes **gazdes**	plural **gazden**
katána 'soldier'	becomes **katanes**	plural **katanen**

All athematic masculine nouns and most male names ending in **< i >** drop the **< i >** and add **< es >** in the singular and take **< en >** in the plural:

Bábi 'Bob'	becomes **Babes**	
harmasári 'stallion'	becomes **harmasares**	plural **harmasaren**
Nándi	becomes **Nandes**	
Râni 'Ron'	becomes **Rânès**	
wuchitéli 'teacher'	becomes **wuchiteles**	plural **wuchitelen**

Occasionally, a male name ending in **< i >** can take the following accusative form:

Ámdi	becomes **Amdiyês**

Thematic and athematic masculine nouns ending in a diphthong are irregular:

brashkoi 'bullfrog'	becomes **brashkos**	plural **brashkên**
pitsagoi 'male swallow'	becomes **pitsagoiyês**	plural **pitsagoiyên**
rai 'gentleman'	becomes **ras**	plural **ran** or **raiyên**

rashai 'clergyman'	becomes **rashas**	plural **rashên**
shoshoi 'male rabbit'	becomes **shoshês**	plural **shoshên**
Xóraxai 'Muslim'	becomes **Xoraxês**	plural **Xoraxên**
xulai 'landlord, host'	becomes **xulas**	plural **xulên**

Masculine thematic and athematic nouns ending in **< áko >** retain the **< o >** in the masculine singular and form their plural accusatives from the plural of the nominative. These include thematic and athematic nouns:

gindáko 'cricket'	becomes **gindakos**	plural **gindachên**
khuláko 'squalid person'	becomes **khulákos**	plural **khulachên**
wortáko 'partner'	becomes **wortakos**	plural **wortachên**

The above occurs because the plural of masculine thematic nouns ending in **< áko >** is **< ácha >**.

Masculine nouns ending in **< ash >** and **< ach >** add **< es >** in the singular and **< en >** in the plural:

birtash 'bartender'	becomes **birtashês**	plural **birtashên**
tolmach 'translator'	becomes **tolmachês**	plural **tolmachên**

A very few athematic masculine nouns ending in a stressed **< e >** take the following accusative form:

Alxire 'Pope'	becomes **Alxires**	plural **Alxiren**

Feminine nouns for people and living things ending in a stressed **< i >** drop the **< i >** and add **< ya >** in the singular and **< yan >** in the plural:

bakri 'ewe'	becomes **bakrya**	plural **bakryan**
bêngorrí 'female demon'	becomes **bêngorryá**	plural **bêngorryán**
khuri 'female foal'	becomes **khurya**	plural **khuryan**
phivli 'widow'	becomes **phivlya**	plural **phivlyan**
Rrômní 'Romani woman'	becomes **Rrômnyá**	plural **Rrômnyán**

Feminine nouns for people and living animals ending in a consonant add **< ya >** in the singular and **< yan >** in the plural. (These are very few since most feminine nouns denoting people or female animals end in a stressed **< i >**):

phen 'sister'	becomes **phenya**	plural **phenyan**

(This form is European-Kalderash but is better for this course unless the student is learning from North American-Kalderash speakers.)

Feminine nouns ending in **< ey >** are irregular. The forms are given below:

dey 'mother'	becomes **da**	plural **deyan**
phey* 'sister'	becomes **pheya**	plural **pheyan**
shey 'daughter, girl'	becomes **sheya** or **sha**	plural **sheyan**

When a feminine noun, especially a woman's name, ends in an unstressed **< a >** this **< a >** becomes stressed in the accusative singular and changes to **< an >** in the plural for feminine animates:

Djanéta 'Janet'	becomes **Djaneta**	
gazdínka 'female boss'	becomes **gazdinka**	plural **gazdinkan**
Mára 'Mary'	becomes **Mara**	
Mártya 'Angel of Death'	becomes **Martya**	

Some masculine and feminine words which have the same form for the nominative singular and plural, such as **grast** 'male horse, gelding', take the plural form of the accusative when they are plural:

O grast sovel	The horse is sleeping	**Kinav grastês**	I am buying a horse
Le grast soven	The horses are sleeping	**Kinav grastên**	I am buying horses

Other animates in this group are **chor** 'thief, thieves', **kak** 'uncle, uncles' and **Rrom** 'Romani man/men and husband/husbands if Romani'. When inflected (changed) to the accusative and other case forms, they must be inflected to their plural form:

Nominative:

O chor avel	The thief is coming
Le chor aven	The thieves are coming

Accusative (inflected noun):

Dikhav le chorês	I see the thief
Dikhav le chorên	I see the thieves

Examples of the accusative case ending

Rodel bakrês	He is looking for a sheep
Marel Gazhya	He hits a non-Romani woman

---

*   **phey** 'sister' is used in North American-Kalderash, in French-Kalderash and has been heard from many Kalderash-Romani refugees from eastern Europe.

Mangel phenya	He wants a sister
Ródel bakrên	He is looking for sheep
Kinel grastên .	He is buying horses
Chi mangel grasnyan	He does not want mares

Note that nouns referring to inanimate objects and dead animals do not change to the accusative:

Ródel shuri	He is looking for a knife
Xas masho	We are eating (cooked) fish

but

Astarav mashên	I am catching (live) fish

Definite article used with the accusative

The word for 'the' also changes when the singular nominative is changed to the accusative.

When referring to one male person or animal the form is **< le >**:

Ródav le raklês	I am looking for the non-Romani boy

When referring to a female person or animal it becomes **< la >**:

Maren la sheya	They are hitting the (Romani) girl

When referring to more than one person or animal (in the plural) the form is still **< le >**:

Astaren le mashên	They catch the fish
Dikhen le raklyan	They see the girls

There is an exception in the North American- and some European-Kalderash dialects when using the accusative pronoun with names of people. When used with verbs such as 'to recognise' or 'to know', they are not usually inflected (changed) to the accusative. When used with action verbs such as 'to hit', 'to insult', 'to kill', etc., they are inflected to the accusative. A few examples with the verbs 'to know' and 'to recognise' not using the accusative:

Zhanav o Stévo	I know Steve
Prinjarav o Yánko	I recognize Yanko
Zhanes e Mára?	Do you know Mary?

Examples with transitive verbs denoting physical action (all using the accusative):

Akushel le Stevos	He is insulting Steve
Marel le Yankos	He is hitting Yanko
Chumidel la Mara	He is kissing Mary

The adjectives also change and the endings follow a similar pattern to the forms for 'the':

bare	male persons and animals	**Ródav le bare raklês**	I look for the big boy
barya	female persons and animals	**Ródav la barya sheya**	I look for the big girl
bare	more than one person or animal	**Ródav le bare mashên**	I look for the large fish

Many Kalderash speakers, especially in Canada and the US, often do not change the nominative to the accusative case when used as the object of the sentence. A person might say **Dikhav le barvale Rrômès** 'I see the rich Rom' using the accusative, while the same person's brother or sister might say **Dikhav o bárvalo Rrôm**, thus using the nominative form instead. This is calquing (copying) from English and so be aware of it if it is heard from a native speaker in North America, but follow the rules given in this course since these rules are followed in European dialects of Kalderash and by older, more formal speakers in Canada and the US.

Test whether you have understood

Translate into Romani the words given in English:

1.	**O tsino raklo phagel o wudar**	**Me marav** (the small boy)
2.	**E terni Rrômní beshel**	**Me dikhav** (the young Romani woman)
3.	**Le bare sapa piyen**	**Ame astaras** (the big snakes)
4.	**Le phure khainya soven**	**Mangav** (the old hens)

Spoken exercises
Pattern drills

Take suitable items from each column and form sentences. Say each sentence aloud and think of its meaning:

Wo ródel	**le bare Gazhês**
	le tsine raklês
Le Gazhe róden	**le melale grastês**

Me marav	le wuzhe chirikês
Won astaren	le kale Rromên
Ame dikhas	raklên
Tume mangen	sheyan
	Gazhyan
	grasnyan
	la barya raklya
	la melalya Rrômnyá
	grasnya

Questions and answers

Make up an answer following the pattern of those given:

Ródes tu rakles?	Ya, ródav raklês
	Na, chi ródav raklês
Dikhes la shukar juvlya?	Ya, …
	Na, chi dikhav la shukarya* juvlya (núma dikhav le melale grastês)
Prindjares le bare manushês?	Ya, …
	Na, … (núma …)
Manges le bare grastês?	Ya, …
	Na, …
So ródel?	Ródel chiriklês
	le chiriklês
	le bare chiriklês
	le tsine sheya
So mangel?	Mangel grastês
	shuri (inanimate noun, no change)
	e shuri

---

* While **shukar** does not change its ending in the singular or plural when the noun it modifies is in the nominative, it does change when the noun is in the accusative. Examples: **Dikhav le shukare raklês** 'I see the handsome boy', **Dikhav la shukarya raklya** 'I see the beautiful girl', **Dikhav le shukare raklên** 'I see the handsome boys', **Dikhav le shukare raklyan** 'I see the beautiful girls'. There are only a few other adjectives like **shukar,** which are **dopash** 'half', **gogiaver** 'wise, intelligent', **ivand** 'raw', **kuch** 'dear, expensive', **nasul** 'evil, bad' and **tang** 'narrow'. The general rule is that any Romani adjective ending in a consonant will behave like **shukar.**

More about unstressed adjectives ending in < o >

Athematic adjectives which end in an unstressed **< o >** like **prósto** 'common, ordinary' or **lúngo** 'long' also have special forms when used with the accusative. These are highly irregular and must be studied in detail. They are listed in a table in Lesson seventeen. **Múndro** 'wonderful' has the following forms which are commonly used but beware of the numerous exceptions, especially with those which end in **< go >** and **< to >** such as **ântrégo** 'entire, whole, complete', **drágo** 'dear, beloved', **krúgo** 'round', **lúngo** 'long' and **skúrto** 'short'. Different dialects of Kalderash can also employ different forms of these loan adjectives and often have some adjectives of this kind which are not used in North American-Kalderash.

Nominative form		Accusative form
O múndro raklo avel	The wonderful boy is coming	**Dikhav le múndrone raklês**
E múndro rakli avel	The wonderful girl is coming	**Dikhav la múndronya raklya**
Le múndri rakle aven	The wonderful boys are coming	**Dikhav le múndrone raklên**
Le múndri raklya aven	The wonderful girls are coming	**Dikhav le múndrone raklyan**

Colours

Thematic adjectives and athematic adjectives following the rules of thematic adjectives

These follow the rules given for thematic adjectives for gender and number, even though **melaxno** and **zeleno** are athematic and are better declined like **gálbeno**:

kalo	black
lolo	red
melaxno	brown
narandjáko	orange
parno	white
rupuno	silver, silvery
sumnakuno	gold, golden
zeleno	green

Athematic adjectives

Masc. & fem. nominative		Plural nominative	Masc. & pl. oblique*	Fem. oblique
chêdníla	purple	chêdnili	chêdnilone	chêdnilonya
gálbeno	yellow	gálbeni	gálbone	gálbonya
wúnato	blue	wúnatsi	wúnatone	wúnatonya

Verb conjugations

Thematic and athematic verbs

Thematic verbs follow the **< av >** conjugations illustrated below by **dikav** and **xav**. These consist of two groups. Those like **dikhel** take the ending **< el >** and those like **xal** take the **< al >** conjugation in the third person singular of the present tense. Athematic verbs follow the conjugations in **< iv >** and **< ov >** illustrated below in **voliv** and **farbov**:

	< a > conjugations		< i > conjugation	< o > conjugation
(me)	**dikhav** (I see)	**xav** (I eat)	**voliv** (I love)	**farbov** (I paint)
(tu)	dikhes	xas	volis	farbos
(wo)	dikhel	xal	volil	farbol
(ame)	dikhas	xas	volis	farbos
(tume)	dikhen	xan	volin	farbon
(won)	dikhen	xan	volin	farbon

Note that **xas, volis** and **farbos** can be the **tu** or **ame** forms.

From this lesson onwards the **wo** 'he' conjugation (third person singular) will be used in the word lists and it should be remembered that it is the same form to be used with **woi** 'she'. This will show clearly which conjugation the verb belongs to. **Azhukerel** 'he waits' will follow the **< el >** conjugation like **dikhel,** while **asal** 'he smiles' will follow the **< al >** conjugation like **xal**. **Ramol** 'he writes' will follow the conjugation of **farbol**, and **gindil** 'he thinks' will follow the conjugation of **volil** in the above table of verb conjugations.

Athematic loan verbs with the **< il >** conjugations are still being added to by Kalderash and other Vlax-Roma in Europe and the Americas, and include many modern verbs dealing with modern technology, for example, **imeylíl** 'he sends by email'. The athematic loan verbs ending in **< ol >** have become embedded in

---

* Oblique means the form of the adjective when used with the accusative and all other inflected case endings.

the language and very few, if any, new ones are appearing. New loan verbs almost always take the **< il >** endings.

Examples of verbs like **xal** which have the **< al >** conjugations:

Le chirikle gilaban	The birds sing (**gilabal** 'he sings')
Won asan	They are smiling/laughing (**asal** 'he smiles, laughs')

Also note the following:

O iv bilal	The snow is melting (**bilal**)
rrongyal	thunder peals
shtrafyal	lightning flashes

Test whether you have understood

If **zhal** means 'he goes' and **ramol** is 'he writes', then what is the Romani for:

5.   they go
6.   you write (singular)

What is the English for:

7.   **ramov**
8.   **ramon**

The verb 'to be'

'I am', 'you are' and so on (the present tense of 'to be') are irregular. Note the special forms for 'is not', 'they are not' and 'there is no, there is not' in the list below:

I am	**sim**	I am not	**chi sim**
you are	**san**	you are not	**chi san**
he, she is	**si**	he, she is not	**nai**
we are	**sam**	we are not	**chi sam**
you are	**san**	you are not	**chi san** (more than one person)
they are	**si**	they are not	**nai**
there is	**si**	there is no, not	**manai**
there are	**si**	there are no, not	**manai**

Examples

Khino sim	I am tired (a male speaker)
Khini sim	I am tired (a female speaker)
Khine sam	We are tired (plural for both genders)
Rrôm san?	Are you a Romani man?
Che cháso si?	What hour (time) is it?
Le bakre si melale	The sheep are dirty
Won nai Rrômnyá	They are not Romani women
Si love?	Is there (any) money?
Manai love	There is no money
Si bakre kothe?	Are there sheep there?
Manai	There aren't any (sheep)

Written exercises

Translate into English:

1. **Le terne rakle ramon thai ginen**
2. **O zhukel prindjarel la grasnya**
3. **Tumáro vôrdòn nai wuzho**
4. **Sim tíro phral, tu san múrri phen**
5. **Le chirikle róden tsine mashên**

Translate into Romani:

6. The young man is my brother
7. They are singing a Romani song
8. Our mare is not dirty
9. He hits the poor horse
10. They eat the fat hens

Reading exercises

Romani proverbs

Kon ródel, arakhel He who seeks, finds
Kon daral, te na* ródel zhuklên He who is afraid, let him not look for dogs

---

*   **na** is used as the negative in this type of expression using **te. Mangav te na avel** I don't
     want him to come (I want that he doesn't come)

Excerpt in Romani from a song adapted by Ron Bankley, a Canadian *Roman-itchel* songwriter and guitarist, from a poem by the author in his novel *Goddam Gypsy,* Montreal, Tundra Books, 1969, and first performed live in Toronto at the Plaza Flamingo on College Street for the first International Romani Day celebrations on 8 April 1999:

O drôm si baro
Thai zhal dur.
Si amên tan te zhas
Thai ame zhanas (twice)
Kána aresas.
Serel amên
O than kátar tradilyam*

This is the chorus and the verses are in English. The entire song plus other poems in Romani, Spanish and English appear in the booklet edited by Sijercic, Hedina et al, *Kanadáke-Romane Mirikle, Canadian-Romani Pearls,* Toronto, The Roma Community and Advocacy Centre, 1999. www.kopachi.com.

Translation

The road is long
It goes far
We have a destination
And we will know when we arrive
It will remind us of the place we were driven away from.

A prisoner's song by V.M. Pasquale (adapted)

Pash múrri filástra yêkh tsino chiriklo gilabal.
Múrro yilo rovel,
Dikhav yêkh lulugi po práxo.
Dui asvina den la o tráyo.
Me sim sar tu, lulugíyo†
Dur katar e zéleni mal, merav.

---

*   **tradilyam** 'we were exiled from'. This type of verb construction is fully explained in Lesson nine.

†   **lulugi** 'flower' but **lulugíyo** 'oh flower', a vocative form used only in direct address to a person and in poems, songs and folk tales to objects like flowers, stars, trees, etc. The rules for the vocative are explained in Lesson five.

Translation

By my window
A little bird sings.
My heart weeps.
I see a flower in (on) the dust.
Two tears give it life.
I am like you, oh flower
Far from the green field I die.

Answers to questions in this lesson

1.	**le tsine raklês**
2.	**la ternya Rrômnyá**
3.	**le bare sapên**
4.	**le phure khainyan**
5.	**zhan**
6.	**ramos**
7.	I write
8.	they write, you write

Answers to the written exercises

1.	The young (non-Romani) boys write and read
2.	The dog recognizes the mare
3.	Your caravan is not clean
4.	I am your brother, you are my sister
5.	The birds are looking for small fish
6.	**O terno manush si múrro phral**
7.	**Won gilaban Rromane gilya**
8.	**Amári grasni nai melali**
9.	**(Wo) marel le chorre grastês**
10.	**(Won) xan le thule khainya**

Lesson four

Word list

azhukerel	he waits, waits for
blúdka	saucer
cháyo	tea (also **chai**)
fúrka	fork
káfa	coffee
kai	where (interrogative and relative)
kidel	he gathers, collects, saves (money)
kuchi	cup
love (m.pl.)	money
mas (m.)	meat
pai (m.)	water (also heard in the alternative form of **páni**)
phagav	I break, snap
pharravav	I smash, shatter, break to pieces
phiravel	he wears
porrárro	stein, pitcher
rroiyi	spoon
rroiyorri	small spoon, teaspoon
shkafedi	coffee table, end table
síniya	table
skamin (m.)	chair
taxdai (m.)	glass (as in **taxdái pai** 'glass of water'. Plural **taxda***)
thud (m.)	milk
tyára	plate
wuzharel	he cleans
zaharnítsa	sugar bowl
zaháro	sugar, sugar diabetes

---

*   In expressions like **taxdái pai** 'glass (of) water', the word 'of' as a function word is not translated into Romani. It translates as 'glass water' in English but the 'of' is understood in Romani.

Personal pronouns

A review of nominative pronouns:

me	I
tu	you
wo	he
woi	she
ame	we
tume	you
won	they

When the personal pronouns are inflected in the accusative they change as follows:

man, ma	me
tut, tu	you
lês	him, it
la	her, it
amên	us
tumên	you
lên	them

Reflexive pronouns – long forms:

pês	himself, herself
pên	themselves

Examples

Won róden man	They are looking for me*
Me ródav lên	I am looking for them
Chi ashunel tut	He does not hear you

While the words which appear first in the Romani column for 'me' and 'you' (singular) are correct, the shorter forms are much more commonly used by native speakers, for example, **zhanel ma** 'he knows me' instead of **zhanel man** or **prindjarav tu** 'I recognize you' instead of **prindjarav tut**. Either is correct but the long forms are those which the oblique stems of the case forms are normally attached to (except with **tu** and **la**). You need to be familiar with

---

*   The verb stem **ród-** means 'seek, search for, look for'.

both versions but it is suggested that you use the long form which will be understood by native speakers. Written Romani almost always uses the long form while spoken Romani more often uses the short but there is no consistent rule. The short form will appear in many examples of Romani throughout the lessons.

Short forms

ma	me
tu	you
le	him
la	her
ame	us
tume	you
le	them

Reflexive pronouns – short forms:

pe	himself, herself
pe	themselves

The forms **lês**, **la** and **lên** are also used for things (inanimates) when they are the object of an action. Since there are only two genders in Romani, the English word 'it' must be expressed as 'him' (**lês**) or 'her' (**la**) depending on the gender of the object. Alternatively **lên** 'them' covers both genders. These also have the short forms listed above.

Examples

Dikhes le raklês? Dikhav lês	Do you see the boy? I see him
Dikhes o lil? Dikhav lês	Do you see the letter? I see it
Dikhes le phaba thai ambrola?	Do you see the apples and pears?
Dikhav lên	I see them

Spoken exercises

Read through the table once carefully, then cover over the right-hand column and read the whole table aloud:

Wo	chi avel	me azhukerav*	**lês**
Wu	chi aves	me azhukerav	**tut**

*   **azhukerav** 'wait for'.

Woi	chi avel	me ...	la
Tume	chi aven	...	tumên
Won	chi aven	... ...	lên
Me	chi zhav	wo azhukerel	man
Ame	chi zhas	... ...	amen

Possession

How to express 'I have', 'you have' etc.

There is no verb 'to have' in Romani so there is no equivalent of 'I have a book' using a verb. In Kalderash-Romani, possession is expressed in the present tense by using the verb combined with the accusative personal pronoun. For example, 'I have an apple' is expressed as **Si man phabai** (the rough translation into English is 'It is me an apple') and 'I have apples' would be translated into Romani as **Si man phaba** 'There are me apples'.

Study the following examples:

Si man kníshka/búkfa	I have a book
Si tut shey	You have a daughter
Si lês dui phenya	He has two sisters
Si la dui sheya	She has two daughters
Si amên grasni	We have a mare
Si tumên grast	You have a horse
Si lên baro kher	They have a big house
Nai man kher	I do not have a house
Nai lês kher	He hasn't (got) a house

Note that **shey, phenya** and other words for persons and animals are not in the accusative form and that the English word 'a' or 'an' has no Romani equivalent other than **yêkh** or **êkh** which has more of a definitive meaning of 'one'.

Test whether you have understood

Translate these sentences into Romani by following the pattern of the above examples:

1.   We have a black caravan
2.   We have a big dog
3.   We haven't (got) a house

Reflexive pronouns

Reflexive pronouns **pês** and **pên** (himself, herself and themselves) have a special form based on the possessive pronouns outlined below. These two reflexive pronouns refer to the subject of the sentence:

	Masculine	Feminine	Plural
his	**lêsko balo**	**lêski stagi**	**lêske phrala**
her	**láko balo**	**láki stagi**	**láke phrala**
their	**lêngo kher**	**lêngi grasni**	**lênge shurya**

When they become reflexive pronouns ('his own', 'her own', 'their own') they change as shown below:

pêsko	**pêski**	**pêske***	his own, her own
pêngo	**pêngi**	**pênge**	their own

Examples of the reflexive pronoun

Farbov lêsko kher	I am painting his house
Farbol pêsko kher	He is painting his own house
Farbol lêsko kher	He is painting his (somebody else's) house
Farbol avrêsko kher	He is painting the house of another person (see Lesson fourteen for **avrêsko**)

Further examples

Dikhel pêski stagi	He sees his (own) hat
Phiravel láki stagi	She is wearing her (somebody else's) hat
Phiravel pêski stagi	She is wearing her (own) hat
Dikhel pêsko kher	She sees her (own) house

Notice that the word 'own' is often left out in English: 'I saw him painting his house'. If you are not sure which form to use, try to put in the word 'own'. If this can be put in the Romani sentence, and it makes sense, then use the reflexive pronoun. For example, 'She hit her with her broom' could either be with the broom of the assailant or the broom of the victim. In English the word 'own' would be used here but 'He wrecked his car' could either mean his own car or somebody else's car.

---

*   The feminine form below is used in North America and can be ignored unless the student is learning Romani from native speakers in North America:

páko	**páki**	**páke**	her own

Test

Try to put 'own' in the blank space in the English sentences and then choose the right form. Do not translate the whole sentence, just the missing word:

4.   I am looking for his ... hat
5.   She is looking for her ... hat
6.   Are you looking for Mary's hat? No, John is looking for her ... hat

Oblique possessive personal pronouns

The endings are similar to those given for the nominative in the last lesson but they are not exactly the same as the following table shows. Try to memorize them since this form is used with the accusative and all the other inflected cases:

	Masculine	Feminine	Plural
my	**múrre**	**múrra**	**múrre**
your	**tíre**	**tíra**	**tíre**
his	**lêske**	**lêska**	**lêske**
her	**láke**	**láka**	**láke**
his/her own	**pêske**	**pêska**	**pêske**
our	**amáre**	**amára**	**amáre**
your	**tumáre**	**tumára**	**tumáre**
their	**lênge**	**lênga**	**lênge**
their own	**pênge**	**pênga**	**pênge**

Examples

Dikhav múrra sheya/sha	I see my daughter
Marel tíre shavês	He is hitting your son
Woi azhukerel pêska phenya	She is waiting for her (own) sister
Dikhav tumáre phralên	I see your brothers
Dikhav lêske phralês	I see his brother
Marel múrre pralês	He is hitting my brother
Marel pêske pralês	He is hitting his own brother
Marel lêske pralês	He is hitting his (somebody else's) brother

but

Dikhav lêsko kher	I see his house (a house is not a person or animal)

Spoken exercises

Make up sentences choosing words from each column in turn. Say them aloud and think of the meaning:

Me pharravav	**lêsko**	**porrárro**
Wuzharav	**lêski**	**tyára**
Wo phagel	**múrro**	**skamin**
	pêsko	
	múrri	**kuchi**
	pêski	

Written exercises

Translate into English:

1.   **Piyel pêsko cháyo**
2.   **Nai lên mas**
3.   **Lav láki rrôiyorrí**
4.   **Chi kamav láka phenya**
5.   **Si tumên skamina?**

Translate into Romani:

6.   Have you (got) a fork?
7.   Yes, I have two
8.   I know their daughter
9.   He eats his meat
10.   Where is the cup? I want it

Reading exercise

A Romani poem by M. Germano (adapted)*

Nárto phuranipe
Ryat kali.
E balval phúrdel

---

*   M. Germano (1893-1955) wrote novels, short stories and plays for the Moscow Romani
     Theatre. I have changed some of the Romani words in the original poem to bring the lan-
     guage in line with this course. I have left **nárto** 'bitter' even though it is not standard
     Kalderash which is **kêrko** and so the expression **nárto phuranipe** 'bitter old age' would
     be **kérko phuranimos** in Kalderash. **Fêldítko** is not in Kalderash because the root is
     'field' as a loan word from OHG (Old High German) *feld*, thus 'man of the field, nomad'.

Peréla iv po drôm.
Ándo vôrdòn
Morrozil-pês yêkh Fêldítko Rrôm.
Akana le Rrôm beshen ánde tate khera
O nárto Rrôm inkya trádel
Phirel sa le drômá.

Translation

Bitter old age
Black night.
The wind blows
Snow falls on the road,
In the wagon
Freezes a Russian nomad Rom.
Now the Roma live in warm houses.
The bitter Rom still wanders
He walks all the roads.

A Romani song from Macedonia

Le tampánya máren, dáyo,
Le Rroma kíden-pe.
O Agúshi bashalel.
Múrro yílo del.
Mek man, dáyo, me te zhav
Le Agúshi te dikhav.
Sôrro ryáto píyen
Diminyátsa sóven.*

Translation

They are beating the drums, mother,
The Roma collect together [collect themselves]

---

*   The words in the song are compatible with this course except for the following: **tampánya** 'drums' (**tóbi** in Kalderash) and **dáyo** 'oh Mother' which is a vocative form of Yerli-
Romani **dai** 'mother' used in direct address but not used in Kalderash where the word is
dey and the vocative form is **dále**. **Kíden-pe** 'they are collecting themselves, gathering' – a reflexive verb (see Lesson five for more details).

Agushi is playing
My heart beats.
Mother, let me go,
To see Agushi.
All night they drink,
In the morning they sleep.

Answers to questions in this lesson

1.   **Si amên kalo vôrdòn**
2.   **Si amên baro zhukel**
3.   **Nai amên kher**
4.   **lêski**
5.   **pêski**
6.   **láki**

Answers to the written exercises

1.   He drinks his tea
2.   They have no meat
3.   I take her teaspoon
4.   I do not love her sister
5.   Have you got any chairs?
6.   **Si tut fúrka?**
7.   **Ya. Si man dui**
8.   **Zhanav lênga sheya**
9.   **(Wo) xal pêsko mas**
10.   **Kai si e kuchi? Mangav la**

Lesson five

Word list

asal	he laughs, smiles
avel	1) he, she becomes, is becoming; 2) he, she comes, is coming
bibi	aunt
bírto	bar, tavern, saloon, pub
but	much, many, very
chachimos (m.)	truth
dey	mother
Del (m.)	God
del	he gives
del-dúma*	he speaks (**del-dúma Rromanes** 'he speaks Romani')
doryávo	river
filástra	window
fóro	city, large town
gad (m.)	shirt, blouse
gav (m.)	town, village
kak	uncle
kamel	1) he loves, wants; 2) he owes (money etc.)
kerel buki	he works, is doing work
lazhal	he is ashamed
lipil	he sticks, pastes
maren-pên	they fight, they are hitting one another/each other
naiyarel-pês	he bathes himself
phabol	he burns
pushel	he asks
Rromanes[†]	like a Rom

---

*   **del-dúma Rromanes** literally means 'he gives speech like a Rom'. **Del-dúma** is what is called a compound verb, a verb combined with a noun, like the English 'give ground' or 'make way'. (For Romani compound verbs, see Lesson twelve.)

†   **Rromanes** is an adverb meaning 'like a Rom, in a Romani manner'. It is not a noun meaning Romani as a language, although it is often used this way by non-Roma and even

tover (m.)	axe, cleaver
xabe (m.)	food
xalavel	he washes
xalavel-pês	he washes himself

Possessive pronouns

Short forms

Múrro and **tíro** have alternative short forms which can be used before a noun:

Long form	Short form			
múrro	mo	mo dad	**Mo dad avel**	My father is coming
múrri	mi	mi stagi	**Dikhav mi stagi**	I see my hat
múrre	me	me phrala	**Me phrala aven**	My brothers are coming
tíro	tyo	tyo dad	**Tyo dad avel**	Your father is coming
tíri	tyi	tyi stagi	**Kai tyi stagi?**	Where is your hat?
tíre	tye	tye phrala	**Tye phrala aven**	Your brothers are coming

When used with objects in the oblique, in this case the accusative, the above forms behave as follows:

Dikhav me phralês	I see my brother
Dikhav ma phenya	I see my sister
Dikhav me phralên thai phenyan	I see my brothers and sisters
Dikhes tye dadês	You see your father
Dikhes tya phenya	You see your sister
Dikhes tye phralês	You see your brother
Dikhes tya phenya	You see your sister
Dikhes tye phralên thai phenyan	You see your brothers and sisters

Throughout Canada, the US and in some European dialects, especially in France, there are also the following long and short forms which usually replace the **tíro** and the **tyo** forms given above in North American-Kalderash. Those

Footnote **†** cont.

many young Roma sometimes say **Phen mánge ánde Rromanes** 'Tell me in Romani' instead of **Phen mánge Rromanes**. Some of the worst offenders in this misuse of **Rromanes** are non-Roma who work in Romani agencies and educated Roma who do not speak Romani. 'The language' in Romani is **Rromani shib** 'Romani speech, language'. Likewise **Gazhikanes** means 'like a non-Rom' so **Del-dúma Gazhikanes** means 'He is speaking like a non-Rom (in a non-Romani language)'.

learning from this course do not need to learn these forms unless they are planning to learn Kalderash in North America or in France where the speakers substitute **chiro, cho, chíri, chi, chíre** and **che**:

kíro	kyo	kyo dad	your father
kíri	kyi	kyi dey	your mother
kíre	kye	kye phrala	your brothers

Examples of North American-Kalderash short forms

Mo dad avel	My father is coming
Mi dey sovel	My mother is sleeping
Kai si kyi phey?	Where is your sister?
Aven kye phrala?	Are your brothers coming?
Mo phral kerel buki	My brother is working
Dikhav kye grastês	I see your horse
Mi grasni merel	My mare is dying
Me zhukla xan	My dogs are eating

Note that these short forms can only be used before the word they describe. In the sentence **kako tover si murro** 'this axe is mine', the short form cannot be used.

Test whether you have understood

In four of the sentences below the short forms can be used. Give these forms and say also in which sentence the short form cannot be used:

1.   **Múrre tsáliya si kathe**
     My clothes are here (**tsáliya** is a plural word like **love** 'money')
2.   **Chi kamel múrra sheya**
     He does not love (want) my daughter
3.   **Kako zhukel nai tiro**
     This dog is not yours
4.   **Kai kerel buki tíri dey?**
     Where does your mother work?
5.   **Lel múrri kníshka**
     He takes my book

Imperative of the thematic verb

Giving commands

Dropping the < el > ending from the 'he' form in thematic verbs makes a command (imperative) to one person:

dikhel	he sees, looks
dikh!	look! see!
avel	he comes
av!	come!

However, there are exceptions:

de!	give!
le!	take!

Verbs ending in **< al >** in the third person singular drop the **< l >** only:

xal	he eats
xa!	eat!
zha!	go!
asa!	laugh!

There are also a few more exceptions such as **daral** 'he fears', **shpídel** 'he pushes', **suvel** 'he sews', **tsírdel** 'he pulls' and **wushtyal** 'he gets up, rises'. For example:

dara!	fear!
shpíde!	push!
súva!	sew!
tsírde!	pull!
wúshte!	get up!

Furthermore, there are the following exceptions ending with **< ol >**:

phabo!	burn! (the verb is **phabol** 'it burns')
tho!	put! (the verb is **thol** 'he puts')
motho!	tell! (the verb is **mothol** 'he tells')

Athematic verbs

Verbs ending in **< il >** and **< ol >** drop the **< l >** and add **< sar >**:

volil	he loves	**volisar!**	love!
farbol	he paints	**farbosar!**	paint!

Some common commands are not formed from verbs, however, and these must be learned as idioms:

ále!	take it! (to one person)
Éta!	behold! (to one or more than one person)
gáta!	end this! cease! (command to stop arguing at a meeting, for example)
háide!	come! come on! (to one person)
háiden!	come! come on! (to more than one person)
yásha!	come on! let's go! (to one or more than one person)

Plural imperative

To give a command to more than one person the **tume** form of the verb is used (but with **tume** left out):

daran!	fear!
dikhen!	look! see!
farbon!	paint!
shpíden!	push!
suven!	sew!
tsírden!	pull!

There are no exceptions to this rule.

The negative imperative

For 'don't do something' use **na** before the command:

na dara!	don't fear (don't be afraid)!
na dikh!	don't look!
na aven!	don't come! (to more than one person)

Note that the third person of the present tense can also be used as a form of imperative as in English, 'let's go' or 'let's play (music)'.

Zhas, Rromále!	Let's go, Romani men!
Bashavas, shavále!	Let's play (music), boys!

Spoken exercises

Tell the person mentioned to stop doing the action:

Example: **O Stévo phagel e filástra**   **Stévane na phag e filástra**

E Mára zhal ka o bírto   ... ...

Tyo phral lel tye love	… … …
O Yórgalo farbol pêsko vôrdòn	**Yórgale** … … …
O Matey marel le grastês	**Matey** (no change) … … …
Katerína thai Róza xan	… … …

(The names **Katerína** and **Róza** follow the rules given above in this lesson for the vocative case.)

Give the command form (to one person):

6.   cut!
7.   paste! stick!*
8.   don't be ashamed!†

The vocative case

The vocative case is used to call or address a person. It is also used to address God and other spiritual and supernatural entities such as Saints, demons and astral bodies and is often used in folk tales and songs. The vocative case ending is not formed from the accusative which is the oblique stem, but instead there are special forms which are used for calling someone's attention as in 'Listen, John!' and in direct address, 'Mary, bring (some) tea!'. At this point it is suggested that the student simply learn the most commonly used vocatives and refer to the tables because to try and learn everything at this stage of the course would be too difficult and the basic grammatical structure will be more important. Vocatives are used when talking to native speakers and many students will not have this opportunity until fluent in the basic language structure.

Male names ending in **< o >** usually change to **< ane >**:

Stévo	becomes **Stévane**
Yánko	becomes **Yánkone**

Male names ending in a consonant usually add **< e >**:

Bab	becomes **Bábe**
Shándor	becomes **Shándore**

Thematic singular masculine nouns ending in a consonant add **< a >**:

---

*   **lipil** 'he pastes, sticks'.
†   **lazhal** 'he is ashamed'.

Rrôm 'husband'   becomes **Rróma**   plural **Rromále**
phral 'brother'   becomes **phrála**   plural **phralále**
bêng 'devil'   becomes **bênga**   plural **bêngále**

Athematic singular masculine nouns ending in **< a >** change as follows:

gázda 'boss, owner'   becomes **gazdéya**   plural **gazdále**
katána 'soldier'   becomes **katanéya**   plural **katanále**

Thematic singular masculine nouns ending in a diphthong:

rai 'gentleman'   becomes **ráiya**   plural **raiyále**
rashai 'priest, clergyman' becomes **rasháiya**   plural **rashaiyále**
shoshoi 'male rabbit'   becomes **shoshóiya**   plural **shoshoiyále**

Thematic singular masculine nouns ending in a stressed **< o >**:

shávo 'Romani boy'   becomes **shavéya**   plural **shavále**
Gazho 'non-Romani man'   becomes **Gazhéya**   plural **Gazhále**

Athematic singular masculine nouns ending in an unstressed **< o >** generally behave as follows:

xarápo 'cannibal ogre'   becomes **xarapóna**   plural **xarápi**

But athematic singular masculine nouns ending in an unstressed **< o >** preceded by **< k >**, **< g >** or **< t >** (note the patterns of inflection) become:

wortáko 'partner'   becomes **wortakóna**   plural **wortáchi**
kolégo 'colleague'   becomes **kolegóna**   plural **kolédji**
emperáto 'king, emperor'   becomes **emperátona**   plural **emperátsi**

Athematic singular masculine nouns ending in **< áno >**:

murtáno 'tomcat'   becomes **murtanóna**   plural **murtayále**

Athematic singular masculine nouns ending in **< ásh >**:

birtash 'bartender'   becomes **birtashóna**   plural **birtásha**

Athematic singular masculine nouns ending in **< ách >**:

tolmach 'translator'   becomes **tolmachína**   plural **tolmácha**

Athematic singular masculine nouns ending in **< áchi >**:

kopáchi 'giant tree'   becomes **kopachína**   plural **kopácha**

Athematic singular masculine nouns ending in **< ári >**:

krichimári 'innkeeper'   becomes **krichimarína**   plural **krichimáreya**

Singular male nouns ending in **< óri >**:

mudaritóri 'murderer'   becomes **mudaritorína**   plural **mudaritóreya**

Female names ending in **< a >** change the ending to **< o >**:

Mára 'Mary'   becomes **Máro**

Singular female names and feminine nouns ending in a stressed **< i >** add **< yo >**:

Buzni (name)   becomes **Buzníyo** (this also means female goat)
Rrômní 'wife'   becomes **Rrômníyo**   plural **Rrômnyále**
lulugi 'flower'   becomes **lulugíyo**   plural **lulugyále**

Thematic singular feminine nouns ending in a consonant change as follows:

phen 'sister'   becomes **phéno**   plural **phenyále**

There are many exceptions to the above rules and some of these will be given in the following lessons, both in the text and in examples of recorded Romani. Different groups of speakers often use different forms in people's names and in commonly used nouns. If in doubt, use the basic form of the name or the word in the nominative; a native speaker will not fault somebody for not using the vocative as even native speakers do not always use it, for example, **Ashun, Yánko!** 'Listen, Yanko!' instead of **Ashun, Yánkone!** in the vocative.

Note also the following commonly used vocatives:

báxto	luck
bênga	devil
báchi	sir, uncle (Lovára dialect)
bibíyo	auntie (to a female elder as well as a relative)
boríyo	sister-in-law, daughter-in-law
brey!	you there! hey! (to a young male person)
dadorréya	dear daddy
dále	mother, mom
Dévla	God
dóyka	madame (to an elderly lady)
doykítso	dear old lady
fína	godson
fíno	goddaughter
káko	uncle (to a male elder. Also used as a noun as in **Káko Zóli** Uncle Zoltan')

kirivéya	godfather
kirivíyo	godmother
manúsha	sir, elder
mo	elderly man, elder
ráiya	sir (in respect, to a peer or an elder)
Rromále	Roma, adult Romani men (married men)
shavále	Romani youths, young Romani men (unmarried youths)
shavorrále	youngsters, kids
shéyo	girl (to a young Romani girl or young woman)
sokríyo	mother-in-law
sokróna	father-in-law
xanamíka	co-father-in-law (father of the spouse of a son or daughter)
xanamíko	co-mother-in-law (mother of the spouse of a son or daughter)
zhamutréya	son-in-law

Examples

So keres? Djanéto?	What are you doing, Jeanette?
Brey! So keres?	Hey! What are you doing, young man?
Dále, mangav phabai	Mum, I want an apple!
Yoi, Dévla	Oh, God

Some vocative forms found in songs, poems and folk tales are not used in normal conversation. You would hardly address a tree or the sun in normal speech but the vocative forms of these often appear in creative forms. Sometimes in anger, however, a person will yell at an inanimate object in frustration or address an animal in the vocative:

Wudaréya, pharravav tut	Oh door, I will smash you
Grastéya, tsírde o vôrdòn!	Horse, pull the wagon!

Vocatives used with adjectives

When the vocative inflection is used with an adjective, the adjective must be inflected to the oblique, just as it is used with the accusative. For example:

Drágonya Máro!	Dear Mary!	(from **drágo** 'dear')
Drágone Yánkone!	Dear Yanko!	
Bare emperatóna!	Great king!	(from **baro** 'great')
Swúntone Dévla!	Holy God!	(from **swúnto** 'holy, saintly')
Swúntonya Máro!	Saint Mary!	
Pakivale raiyále!	Honoured gentlemen!	(from **pakivalo** 'honoured')
Dile zhukléya!	Stupid dog!	(from **dilo** 'stupid')

Reflexive verbs

In English we can say 'I am shaving', and it is understood that this also means 'I am shaving myself'. In Romani, the accusative personal pronoun must be used when this applies to the person speaking, and these pronouns must be used with transitive verbs which require an object. For example:

Xalavav le grastês	I am washing the horse (transitive verb used with a noun in the accusative)
Xalavav-man	I am washing myself (transitive verb used with accusative personal pronoun)

Look carefully at the following table:

me xalavav-man	I wash myself
tu xalaves-tut	you wash yourself
wo xalavel-pês	he washes himself
woi xalavel-pês	she washes herself
ame xalavas-amên	we wash ourselves
tume xalaven-tumên	you wash yourselves
won xalaven-pên	they wash themselves

For 'himself', 'herself' and 'themselves' there are special forms of the accusative pronouns, but there are no special forms for 'myself' and the others. The regular accusative pronouns are used:

me xalavav-man	I wash myself
o Rrôm xalavel-pês	the Rom washes himself

In common speech in North America and in some European dialects of Kalderash, the above forms are not pronounced as they are written. The following short forms are usually used:

xalava-ma	I wash myself, I am washing myself
xalaves-tu	you wash yourself, you are washing yourself
xalavel-pe	he washes himself, he is washing himself
xalavel-pe	she washes herself, she is washing herself
xalavas-ame	we wash ourselves, we are washing ourselves
xalaven-tume	you wash yourselves, you are washing yourselves
xalaven-pe	they wash themselves, they are washing themselves

The pronouns are usually shown as hyphenated to the verb because otherwise this could create confusion between **xalavel-pe** 'he is washing himself' and **sovel pe ponyáva** 'he is lying on the carpet' (**pe** 'on').

The word **kórkorro/kólkorro** 'alone' is also used in common expressions. It serves both as an adjective and an adverb. This word does not change for gender:

Kerav lês kólkoro	I'll do it alone, by myself
Woi beshel kólkorro	She is sitting alone, by herself
Me sim kólkorro	I am alone, all by myself

Test whether you have understood
Complete the following sentences using the pattern of the first example and read them aloud using the long form of the pronouns:

me shinav-man	I cut myself
tu shin ...	you cut yourself
wo shin ...	
woi shin ...	
tume shin ...	
ame shin ...	
won shin ...	
le Gazhe shin ...	

Written exercises
Translate into English:

1.   **O raklo avel thulo**
2.   **Tyi dey xalavel le gada**
3.   **O Gazho del-dúma Rromanes**
4.   **Na shinen tumên!**
5.   **Andréas, naiyares-tut ándo doryávo?***

Translate into Romani:

6.   Your uncle is undressing himself (**nangyarel** 'he undresses, disrobes')
7.   Eat your food, Peter! (**Péte,** vocative of **Pétro,** an exception to the general rule)
8.   He is hitting his brother
9.   Your brother is not working
10.   Burn his old caravan! (speaking to one person)

---

*   **Andréas** is a man's name.

Answers to questions in this lesson

1.   **me**
2.   **ma**
3.   short form cannot be used
4.   **tyi**
5.   **mi**

Answers to the spoken exercises

Máro na zha ka o bírto!

(Mára) Mary, don't go to the tavern!

Phrála, na le múrre (me) love!

Brother, don't take my money!

Yórgane, na farbosar tíro vôrdòn!

(Yórgo) Yórgo, don't paint your wagon!

Matéya, na mar le grastês!

(Matéyo) Matéyo, don't beat the horse!

Kateríno thai Rozíyo, na xan!

(Katarína and **Rózi)** Catherine and Roza, don't eat!

6.   **shin**
7.   **lipisar**
8.   **na lazha**

Tu shines-tut	You cut yourself
Wo shinel-pês	He cuts himself
Woi shinel-pês	She cuts herself
Ame shinas-amên	We cut ourselves
Tume shinen-tumên	You cut yourselves
Won shinen-pên	They cut themselves
Le Gazhe shinen-pên	The non-Roma cut themselves

The given names of the subjects of the sentences are given in parentheses.

Answers to the written exercises

1.   The boy becomes (gets) fat
2.   Your mother washes the shirts
3.   The non-Rom speaks like a Rom
4.   Don't cut yourselves!
5.   Andreas, are you bathing (yourself) in the river?

6.   **Tyo (Tíro) kak nangyarel pes**
7.   **Xa tyo (tíro) xabe, Pêtre!**
8.   **Wo marel pêske phralês**
9.   **Tyo (Tíro) phral chi kerel buki**
10.   **Phabo lêsko phuro vôrdòn!**

Lesson six

Word list

akana	now
akanash	presently, in the near future
ánda	about, because of
ánde	in, inside, into (before feminine nouns)
ánde l'	in, inside, into (before plural nouns of both genders)
ándo	in, inside, into (before masculine nouns)
ánde vúrma	in the end, finally, eventually (**vurma** (f.) 'end')
ándo mizméri	in the afternoon (**mizméri** (m.) 'afternoon')
anel	he brings
araki	yesterday, last night
atwéto	answer (plural **atwéturya**)
avér-tehára	day after tomorrow
baxt (f.)	luck
bêrsh (m.)	year
buki	work, business, thing, object
but*	much, many; also very
cháso	hour (also means 'time' and 'clock' plus 'o'clock' if 'one o'clock')
chásurya	hours (plural of **cháso**) and o'clock after one o'clock
chokáno	hammer
chorro	poor
dar (f.)	fear
do mult	a long time ago
doryávo	river (in folk tale in this lesson)
fistáno	traditional ankle-length Kalderash skirt (plural **fistáya**)
ges (m.)	day

---

* The word **but** means 'much' and 'many'. When used with adjectives it is used to express diminution as in **tsino** where **but tsino** means 'very small/really small'. Another common way of expressing both diminution and augmentation is to repeat the adjective twice, for example, **tsino, tsino** 'very small' or **baro, baro** 'very big'. **O Rrôm dihkel le harapos, baro, baro si** 'The Rom sees the cannibal ogre, he is really big (enormous)'.

kai	where (interrogative and relative)
kamav	I want, I love
khánchi (m.)	nothing, anything
khangri	church
koshtil	it costs
kothe	there, yonder
kurko	week
mai*	more (used idiomatically)
mai drobroi tut	greetings, hello
manush (m.)	older man, elder, male human being (feminine is **manushni**)
mashári (m.)	fisherman, fishmonger
meázol	he, she, it looks like, resembles
mekel	he lets, allows, leaves
minúto	minute
minútsi (m.pl.)	minutes
mishto	all right, well, OK
mishtomos (m.)	favour (plural **mishtomáta**)
mizméri (m.)	noon
mobíli (m.)	car, automobile
mothol	he tells, says
mudarel	he kills, murders, extinguishes
mursh (m.)	guy, male, man (in general but usually applied to a non-Romani man)
nevo	new
owêrish (m.)	day before yesterday
pála mizmêri	after noon
pálpale	back, back again
pansh chásurya	five o'clock
phaleya (f.pl.)	floor (literally 'planks' from **pal** (f.) 'plank')
phenel	he says, tells
pushimos (m.)	question (plural **pushimáta**)
shon (m.)	month; moon

---

* **mai** has the basic meaning of 'more' but appears in many Kalderash idioms. **Mai drobroi tu** means 'More good to you' ('I hope things are good for you'). In idioms, it can be used as follows: **Mai dikhav tut** 'I'll see you *again*', **Na mai ker!** 'Don't do (that) *any more!*', **Mai dikhes Rromên ánda l' thema?** 'Do you *ever* see Roma from the (European) countries?' It also means 'ever' as in **Mai dikhlan tu kodya?** 'Did you ever see anything like that?'

sikavel	he shows, teaches
so	what (relative and interrogative)
sórro ges	all day
sórro ryáto	all night
súmnakai (m.)	gold
sumnakásko	gold, made of gold
sumnakuno	golden, colour of gold
tehára ánde diminyátsa	tomorrow (in the) morning
tehára ánde ryat	tomorrow (in the) evening
tehára	tomorrow
tolmachimos (m.)	translation
tsálya (f.pl.)	clothes, clothing
tsêra	tent (also extended family)
tsino	little, small, tiny
tsóxa	skirt (also **rrókya** in North American-Kalderash)
zhávo	sorrow

Possession: 'has' and 'have'

In Romani, the sentence 'the man has a hammer' is **o mursh si lês chokáno** and word for word this is 'the man, it is him hammer'. In the same way **e rakli si la shukar tsóxa** is literally translated as 'the girl it is her nice skirt' which means 'the girl has a nice skirt'.

Test whether you have understood

How would you say in Romani:

1.   The Roma have a big tent*
2.   My mother has a new hat

The preposition and

The preposition **and** combined with the definite articles **< o >** and **< e >** means 'inside', 'in' and 'at'. If used with a masculine singular noun, it becomes **ándo** and if used with a feminine singular noun, it becomes **ánde**. When used with plural masculine or feminine nouns it becomes **ánde** followed by **le** which is usually elided (shortened) to **< l' >** and then appears as **ánde l'**.

---

*   **tsêra** 'tent'.

Examples

ándo kher	in the house, at home (masculine singular noun)
ánde ófisa	in the office, at the office (feminine singular noun)
ánde l' gava	in the towns (masculine plural noun **gav** 'town')
ánde l' tsêri	in the tents (feminine plural noun **tsêra** 'tent')
ánde le báre tsêri	in the big tents (**le** is not usually elided (shortened to **< l' >**) when used with nouns that are not stressed on the final vowel)
ánde l' bare wêrshá	in the great forests (when the final vowel is stressed, **le** usually becomes **< l' >**)

The future prefix kam

For actions taking place some time in the future, place **< kam >** before the present tense verb forms you have already studied in previous lessons. For example:

Present indicative	Future
(Me) dikhav	**(Me) kam-dikhav** I shall see!
(Won) chi aven	**(Won) chi kam-aven** They will not come!
Zhas ka o fóro tehára	We are going to the town tomorrow
Kam-zhas ka o fóro tehára	We shall go to the town tomorrow

Do not forget that the present tense in its short and long forms also serves as the simple future tense:

Dikhav lês tehára	I'll see him tomorrow (short form of present tense)
Dikháva lês tehára	I'll see him tomorrow (long form of present tense)
Kam-dikhav les tehára	I shall see him tomorrow (short form with prefix **kam**)
Kam-dikháva lês tehára	I shall see him tomorrow (long form with prefix **kam**)
Ame zhas tehára	We'll go tomorrow (indefinite, may or may not)
Ame kam-zhas tehára!	We shall go tomorrow! (definite, we shall)
Avav pálpale tehára	I'll return tomorrow
Me kam-avav pálpale tehára!	I shall return tomorrow!

Future tense of the verb 'to be'

The verb 'to be' is formed from the root **< av >** and takes the regular conjugation of verbs in **< av >** except in the present and past tenses. In the future tense, it has the following forms:

(me) avav	I will be
(tu) aves	you will be
(wo) avel	he will be
(woi) avel	she will be
(ame) avas	we will be
(tume) aven	you will be
(won) aven	they will be

The prefix **< kam >** can be added to make the emphatic future tense:

(me) kam-avav!*	I shall be!
(tu) kam-aves!	you shall be!

The rest follow, as with the **avav** table above, with the prefix **< kam >**.

Examples

Kam-avel tehára	He will come tomorrow
Wo kam-avel láko Rrôm	He will become her husband
Me kam-avav o baro	I shall become the leader
Tehára, me kam-avav ánde ôfisa	Tomorrow, I shall be in the office
Wo avel ánde ófisa tehára	He will be in the office tomorrow
Kai kam-aves tehára?	Where will you be tomorrow?

Future tense: 'has', 'have'

To form the future tense of **si man** 'I have':

Avel man baxt tehára	I'll have luck tomorrow

Here the present tense of the verb 'to be' is used to express the indefinite future:

Kam-avel man baxt tehára	I shall have luck tomorrow

---

*   **kam-avav** means 'I will become' and 'I will come', but the meaning will be clear from the other words in the sentence.

For the emphatic future, use the future tense of the verb 'to be' as shown below:

kam-avel man	I will have (it will be to me)
kam-avel tut	you will have
kam-avel lês	he will have
kam-avel la	she will have
kam-aven amên	we will have
kam-avel tumên	you will have
kam-avel lên	they will have

If the item possessed is plural, like **love** 'money', then the plural verb conjugation must be used:

Kam-aven man love tehára	I shall have money tomorrow
Kam-aven la shukar tsáliya	She shall have nice clothes (**tsálya** (f. pl.))

Examples

Kam-avel man nevo mobíli akanash	I shall have a new car presently
Kam-aven tut love tehára?	Will you have money tomorrow?
O raklo kam-aven lês love tehára	The boy will have money tomorrow
Le rakle chi kam-avel lên baxt	The boys will not have (any) luck
Kam-aven lêski Rrômní but shave	His wife will have many children

Numbers 1–10

1.	**yêkh** and **êkh**	6.	**shov**
2.	**dui**	7.	**hifta**
3.	**trin**	8.	**ôxtó**
4.	**shtar**	9.	**inya**
5.	**pansh**	10.	**desh** and **dêsh**

Zero is **núla** (in Europe) and **zêro** (in North America). Their respective plurals are **núli** and **zêrya**.

The numbers from two onwards are followed by the plural noun:

yêkh raklo	one boy
dui rakle	two boys
pansh raklya	five girls

The dative case

The English words 'for' and 'to' (as the indirect object) are usually expressed in Romani by the dative case endings of nouns. There are seven case endings in Kalderash-Romani including the vocative. The accusative has already been covered in Lesson three. The accusative is the oblique stem from which the other five case endings, not yet explained in the course, are formed. It would be advisable at this point to review the accusative case and learn the accusative inflections (forms) for masculine and feminine nouns by heart which will be very useful when learning the other case endings. The accusative case endings for inanimates, some of whose accusative forms differ from those of animates, will be introduced in following lessons. The vocative, already explained in Lesson five, is not formed from the accusative (oblique stem) and must be learned separately.

Dative case endings

To form the dative singular add **< ke >** (singular) or **< ge >** (plural) to the accusative case of nouns. Inanimates do not usually have an accusative but their oblique stems (accusatives) are given in singular and plural forms by families in Lesson seven. These tables or paradigms will enable you to find the oblique stems of thematic and athematic animate and inanimate nouns.

Examples

Thematic nouns ending in a stressed vowel:

raklo	boy	**raklêske**	for the boy	oblique stem **raklês-**
rakli	girl	**raklyáke**	for the girl	oblique stem **raklya-**
rakle	boys	**raklênge**	for the boys	oblique stem **raklên-**
raklya	girls	**raklyánge**	for the girls	oblique stem **raklyan-**

Thematic nouns ending in a consonant:

phral	brother	**phralêske**	for the brother	oblique stem **phralês-**
phen	sister	**phenyáke**	for the sister	oblique stem **phenya-**
phrala	brothers	**phralênge**	for the brothers	oblique stem **phralên-**
phenya	sisters	**phenyánge**	for the sisters	oblique stem **phenyan-**

Athematic nouns

Watch for noun families that are athematic. The dative case of athematic animates can be formed from their accusative cases (oblique stems), outlined in Lesson three. One example is given below:

wortáko	male partner	wortakóske	for the partner	oblique stem wortakos-
wortácha	male partners	wortachênge	for the partners	oblique stem wortachen-
wortáika	female partner	wortaikáke	for the female partner	oblique stem wortaika-
wortáiki	female partners	wortaikánge	for the female partners	oblique stem wortaikan-

Examples of the dative case with animate nouns

Mothol le Rrômèske o nevimos	He tells the Rom the news (**Rrôm** is the indirect object and **nevimos** 'news')
Anav le grastênge xabe	I bring food for the horses (I bring the horses food)
Dav le Stevóske o lil	I give Steve the letter
Anav xabe múrra phenyáke	I bring food for my sister
Mothov le bare raklêske	I say it for the sake of the big boy
Kerel lês le Rromênge	He is doing it for (the sake of) the Roma
Dav le raklêske le love	I give the boy the money

Beware of English translations of sentences like the above. The last example could be translated in English as 'I give the money to the boy' but this would be **Dav le love le raklêste** in Romani which is the prepositional case, not the dative case. Remember, the dative is the indirect object and the prepositional is the direct object. The prepositional case follows this section.

Note also that the definite article ('the') plus the adjectives and the possessive personal pronouns ('my', 'your', etc.) also take the same forms as the accusative for all inflected case endings.

Dative personal pronouns

mánge	me, for me
túke	you, for you
lêske	him, for him
láke	her, for her
amênge	us, for us
tumênge	you, for you
lênge	them, for them
pêske	himself/herself, for himself/herself

| **pênge** | themselves, for themselves |
| **káske** | whom, for whom |

The dative case endings are also used in some expressions where 'for' is not used in English:

Koshtil túke but	It costs you a lot
Nayis túke	Thank you
Nayis Devlêske	Thank God
Meázol le Babêske	He looks like Bob

Test whether you have understood

Translate the words in italics into Romani:

3.   I give the book *to the Romani girl*
4.   It costs *me* ten pounds
5.   We show *the men* the way

In some eastern European dialects of Kalderash and among Vlax-Romani-speaking newcomers to Canada and the US, the preposition **vash**, meaning 'for', is becoming widely used as a preposition to replace the dative case endings given above in some cases. This word is also appearing more and more in printed material from Europe, for example, **Kerav buki vash le Rróma** 'I work for the Roma' or **Kinav káfa vash o djulêshi** 'I am buying coffee for the business meeting'. Do not rely on this use of **vash,** as the dative case is vital in Romani.

The endings **< ke >** and **< ge >** are also used with inanimate nouns. Notice that they then take the same endings as living persons and animals in the dative and other inflected case endings:

| **Kakala tsáliya si bukyáke** | These clothes are for work |
| **O lond si le xabenêske** | The salt is for the food |

The dative case cannot be used to translate 'to' when motion from one place to another occurs:

| **Me zhav kai khangri** | I am going to the church |
| **Wo avel ka o Târánto** | He is coming to Toronto |

For this meaning of 'to' use **kai** before a feminine noun and **ka** before a masculine noun.

Examples

ka e sláva	'to the feast' is shortened to **kai sláva** but **ka o dukyáno** 'to the store' is not shortened. You can also use the prepositional case (explanation follows shortly) to translate motion from one place to another
Me zhav le Târantóste	I am going to Toronto (prepositional case)

Idiomatic use of the dative case

The dative case is often used in idioms to replace the verb 'to be':

Chi zhav, dar mánge	I am not going, I am afraid (fear for me)
Zhávo mánge	I am sorry (sorrow for me)
Lazhav mánge te phenav	I am ashamed to say (sorrow for me that I say so)
Nashti lêske	He can't (is not able to)
Dar lêske te kerel	He is afraid to do it (fear for him that he does (it))

It is also used as follows:

Nai mánge khánchi	I couldn't care less (it is not for me anything)
Mánge, chi darav khánchi	As for me, I don't fear anything
Nai lêske khánchi ánda so keras	He doesn't give a damn about what we do
Zhav mánge te sováv-man	I am going to fall asleep
Trobul te lel pêske Rrômní	He needs to take himself a wife (to get married)
Zhas te kinas amênge pimos	Let's go buy ourselves some liquor
Chi kerav, ke dar mánge	I won't do (it), I am afraid

The prepositional case

The prepositional case in Romani, often called the locative or illative case, can easily be confused with the dative case and it is introduced here so that the two can be studied together. As with the dative, the prepositional case endings are formed from the oblique stem.

The thematic accusative case endings are **< te >** (singular) and **< de >** (plural), attached to the oblique stem which is also the accusative case ending for animates.

Nouns ending in a stressed vowel:

	Singular	Plural
raklo 'boy'	**raklêste**	**raklênde**
rakli 'girl'	**raklyáte**	**raklyánde**

Nouns ending in a consonant:

phral 'brother'	**phralêste**	**phralênde**
phen 'sister'	**phenyáte**	**phenyánde**

Athematic nouns:

wortáko ' male partner'	**wortakóste**	**wortachênde**
wortáika 'female partner'	**wortaikáte**	**wortaikánde**

Personal pronouns:

mánde	to me
túte	to you
lêste	to him
láte	to her
pêste	to himself/herself
amênde	to us
lênde	to them
pênde	to themselves
káste	to whom

The prepositional case is used as follows:

a) In commands with the meaning of 'to' or 'at' and as a locative:

De lês lêste!	Give it to him!
Shúde les le zhuklênde!	Throw it to the dogs!
Ashun mánde!	Listen to me!
Dikh pe lêste!	Look at him!

but watch out for

Dav lêske le love	I give him the money (dative case)
Dav le love lêste	I give the money to him (prepositional case)

and

Dav le Rrômèske le love	I give the Rom the money (Rom is the indirect object)

Dav le love le Rrômèste   I give the money to the man (Rom is the locative of the direct object)

You cannot say **Dav le love lêske**, **Dav lêste le love** or **Dav le love le Rrômèske**. The rule depends on where the inflected pronoun or noun is placed in the sentence. Not all Vlax-Romani dialects follow this rule but it applies in North American-Kalderash. Other dialects may follow forms calqued (copied) from a second language other than English in Europe or elsewhere, so this is what makes the use of the dative and the prepositional confusing to students learning Romani.

b) To indicate a direction or location:

Wo phirel ángla mánde	He walks in front of me (**ángla** 'in front of, before')
Zhal ánde l' wêrshèste	He is going into the forest
Háide pála mánde!	Come along with me (**pála** 'along with, after')
Wo si ánde Kanadáte	He is in Canada
Zhas ka láte	We are going to her (place)
Háide aworde amênde	Come over here to us (**aworde** 'over here, this way')
Woi si la Maráte	She is over at Mary's place
O Yánko si le grastênde	Yanko is over by the horses
Beshel ándo Târantóste	He resides in Toronto

While the examples above are used in formal speech and are very common in European-Kalderash dialects, North American speakers and many younger European speakers do not always adhere to this for inanimates. Expressions like **Wo si ánde Kanáda** 'He is in Canada' are commonly heard.

Common prepositions used with the prepositional case

pa amênde	about us (**pa** 'about')
pála lêste	after, behind him (**pála** 'after, behind' also for him, for his sake)
ánda láte	because of her (**ánda** 'because of')
mashkar tumênde	between you (**mashkar** 'between, in the middle')
ángla mánde	in front of me (**ángla** 'before, in front of')
nêg lêste	instead of him (**nêg** and **négo** 'instead of')
pásha pêste	next to himself (**pásha** 'close to, nearby')
pe túte	on you (**pe** 'on, upon')
aworde amênde	over here to us (**aworde** 'over here, this way')
tela lênde	under them (**tela** 'under')

More dative and prepositional case examples

The first example introduces a dependent clause which here takes the dative case, while the second example refers to whom the information was given and requires the prepositional:

Motho le *Rromênge* te aven kai sláva	Tell the *Roma* to come to the feast (dative)
Mothodem le *Rromênde*	I told the *Roma* (prepositional)

Here, the 'dog' is in the dative position in the sentence:

Dav le *zhuklêske* kokalo	I give the *dog* a bone (dative)

Here, the prepositional 'to the dog', as a locative, requires the prepositional case:

Dav kokalo le *zhuklêste*	I give a bone to the *dog* (prepositional)

Examples using pronouns

Dav *lêske* le love	I give *him* the money (dative)
Dav le love *lêste*	I give the money *to him* (prepositional)
Woi kerel *mánge* xabe	She is making *me* (some) food (dative)
Woi del o xabe *mánde*	She gives the food *to me* (prepositional)

The prepositional case should be studied carefully with the rules for the dative case so as to avoid confusion. The dative case cannot be the last word in a sentence such as 'I give the money to him'. In this type of sentence, the last word must be the prepositional case. On the other hand, 'I give him the money' requires the dative case.

Further prepositional case examples

Dav le love le raklêste	I give the money to the boy
Zhav pála le raklêste	I am going after (following) the boy
Merel ánda la raklyáte	He is dying because of the girl (he is madly in love with her)
Wo si pêske wortakóste	He is at his partner's (house)
Zhav múrre wortakóste	I am going to my partner's place
Dav lês múrre wortachênde	I am giving it to my partners
Zhav le Târantóste	I am going to Toronto (athematic in **< óste >**)
Zhav la Italiyáte	I am going to Italy

'Who' and 'whom' with dative and prepositional cases

Kon avel?	Who is coming? (nominative)
Kas ródes?	Whom are you looking for? ('Whom' is the object of the action (the accusative case))
Tu des káske le love?	To whom are you giving the money? (dative)
Káste des le love?	Who are you giving the money to? (prepositional)

Days of the week

Adverb		Noun	
Kurkone	on Sunday	**Kurko**	Sunday
Luwine	on Monday	**Lúya**	Monday
Martsune	on Tuesday	**Mártsi**	Tuesday
Tatradjine	on Wednesday	**Tatrádji**	Wednesday
Zhowine	on Thursday	**Zhóya**	Thursday
Parashtune	on Friday	**Paráshtuvi**	Friday
Savatone	on Saturday	**Sávato**	Saturday

These words vary among different groups of speakers in different countries. Those listed here are from North American-Kalderash and are generally understood by European speakers.

The expressions for time are given for reference and for use in conversation.

Spoken exercise

Compose suitable answers to the questions in the left-hand column, using phrases from the right-hand column.

Example: **Káske kines e kníshka?**	For whom are you buying the book?
Answer: **Le raklêske**	For the boy

Káske anes le grastes?	**Le chorre manushêske**
Káske kam-kines o xabe?	**Le chorre Gazhênge**
Káske gilabas tu?	**Múrra Rrômnyáke**
Káske keres o mishtomos?	**Múrra phenyáke**

Do the same thing as above with the examples of time in Romani given below:

Aves akana?	**Na, chi avav akana. Kam-avav Tatradjine**
Bikines le grastês ages?	**Na, Savatone**
Zhas tu ka o fóro aryat?	**Na, tehára ánde ryat**
Kam-des mánge le love Luwine?	**Na, tehára ánde diminyátsa**

Written exercise

Read the following, which is part of a folk tale. Note that Romani folk tales are often recited in the present tense where English would use the past tense. Then translate it, and answer the questions below in Romani. The words in italics have been added to bring this in line with the course and should simply be read as words in the text.

Si yêkh chorro Rrôm, **thai** si lês phuri Rrômní. Yêkh ges e Rrômní phenel **lêste**: 'Chi zhanav so kam-xas aryat. Nai xabe ándo kher.'

O Rrôm phenel pêske **Rrômnyáte**: 'Me kam-zhav ka o doryávo te astar-av mashên.'

Zhal ka o doryávo* hai ródel mashên. Shtar chásurya beshel kothe numa chi astarel **khánchi**.

Ánde vúrma astarel tsine mashês. O masho si but tsino hai sum-nakuno. Del-dúma Rromanes, o masho. Mothol le Rrômèske (**phenel**): 'Mishto, Rróma. Na mudar man. Mek man ándo doryávo pálpale. Me kam-dav túke so manges.'

(The rest of this tale is in *The Language of the Coppersmith Gypsy*, *Taikoni*, p.149, Gjerdman, Olof and Ljungberg, Erik, Uppsala: Lundequist, 1963.)

Pushimáta *'Questions'*

1.   **Kako Rrôm si barvalo?**
2.   **Lêski Rrômní si terni?**
3.   **So chi zhanel e Rrômní?**
4.   **Kai zhal o Rrôm?**
5.   **Sóstar** (why) **zhal kothe?**
6.   **Astarel but mashên?**
7.   **Save mashês astarel ánde vúrma?**
8.   **So kam-kerel o masho?**

Author's note

While the dialect recorded by Gjerdman and Ljungberg is generally regarded by many authorities to be a Kalderash dialect, it shows more of a Churarítska vocabulary and pronunciation according to my mentor, Waso Russel Demitro,

---

*   **doryávo** 'river'. This word is used in European dialects but is not used in North American-Kalderash as 'river', which is the athematic masculine noun **rivêri**. It seems to appear in a Canadian-Romani folk tale as **Daryévo** 'Danube' (see folk tale, Lessons fourteen and fifteen).

to whom I read this and other excerpts from Gjerdman and Ljungberg's book. This is probably as a result of intermarriage between Kalderash and Churára in the clan and extended family of Johan Dimitri Taikoni, the main informant and source of the vocabulary and the examples of the dialect in folk tales. My Kalderash partner at the time, Vanya Kwiek, also confirmed the Churarítska influence. Some changes, in italics in the text, have been made to bring this Churarítska-influenced dialect in line with standard Kalderash. The word **phenel** in the original would not be used here in Kalderash. Kalderashítska and Churarítska are mutually intelligible to native speakers, along with Lovarítska and Machwanítska. Only minor dialectical differences occur, along with a few differing loan words.

The **< ítska >** endings are used to indicate languages and dialects of languages, for example, **Inglézo** 'Englishman' and **Inglezítska** 'English' or **Franzúzo** 'Frenchman' and **Franzuzítska** 'French'. Kalderashítska, Churarítska, Lovarítska and Machwanítska are dialects of Vlax-Romani spoken by the Kalderash and Churára; Lovára and Machwáya are subdivisions of the Vlax-Roma. Again, these dialects are mutually intelligible to native speakers. Machwanítska is the other main Vlax-Romani dialect spoken in the US and Canada which was brought to California around 1900 by immigrant Vlax-Roma from Serbia who reached the US from Greece via Australia.

Reading exercises

Two Hungarian Lovari songs
La Rozáke kale yakha,
phabol **pe man sar e lámpa.**
Ále, **Rozíka, kam-malav tyi** *trombíta,*
Ke nai man tsóxa, nai man gad
kinel mánge múrro dad, o phuro.
Sharga **papúchi thai gálbeno papúchi**
pe múrro pûnrró.*

---

*   Notes on the italics: phabol should be **phabon** since 'eyes' are plural. The plural **yakha** (f.pl) 'eyes' is often used in songs but not in daily speech where instead the singular serves as the plural but is inflected as a plural in the case endings, **ále!** 'hey!' when used in this sense, **trombíta** 'backside' is not used in Kalderash nor is **shárga** 'yellow' which is **gálbeno** in Kalderash, the use of **pûnnró** (foot) for feet probably reflects calquing from Hungarian.

Tolmachimos 'Translation'

Rosa's black eyes,
She burns me like a lamp.
Hey, little Rosa, I will hit your bottom [trumpet]
Because I have no skirt, I have no shirt,
my father buys [them] for me, the old man.
Yellow slippers and golden slippers
on my feet. [foot used as plural]

Márku, múrro shávo
Le pe túte sáma
Mánge si te zháv-*tar vádi kámav vádi níchi*
ke nasvali si te mámo thai búki si te kérav.
Ke but si le shavórra
ke mánrro si te ródav.*

Translation

Marku, my son.
Look after yourself.
I must go off, whether I wish to or not,
for mother is ill and there is work for me to do
for the small children are many
for there is food to be looked for.

(Collected by G. Meszaros from Hermina Csiki)

Canadian Kalderash-Romani song

Based on the melody of the theme song from the film *Samson and Delilah* (released in 1949).

Diláila, ánda lako *kúchi státo*
Ka meázol *ikonáko*

---

*   **Notes on the italics: Márku (Márko)** should be **Márkone** in the vocative in Kalderash, **< tar >**, a suffix attached to a verb of motion in Kalderash and Lovari, is an ablative particle as in **zháv-tar** 'I depart, go away', **vad níchi** 'whether or not' in Kalderash so **vádi kamav vádi nichi** would be **vad kamav vad níchi** in Kalderash. **Mami** means 'grandmother' in Kalderash. If **mámo** (apparently a vocative here) is meant to mean 'mother' in this song it should be **tye dey**. Note also the stress accents in Lovari which are influenced by Hungarian pronunciation where final vowels are seldom stressed.

Yoi Diláila
Kátar woi phirel, lulugya *bai* baryon
Kátar woi chi phirel, lulugya *bai* kernyon
Deláila, me *gêlem* te sovav-man (twice)
Pe láke *chúnga*
Zurales woi *xoxádyas* man
Zurales woi xoxádyas man
Woi shinyas múrre bal
Díláila.*

Translation

Delilah, because of her sexy figure
That resembles a Holy Icon
Oh, Delilah
From where she walks, flowers will surely bloom,
From where she walks not, flowers will surely wither

---

*   **Notes on the italics: kúchi** 'sexually attractive', **ikonáko** 'icon, religious statue', **yoi**
'oh', **kátar** 'from where', **bai** 'surely, are sure to' (used mainly in songs, poems and folk
tales), **gêlem** 'I went' in the past tense which will be explained in Lesson seven, **pe** 'on'
and 'for' when used before singular feminine nouns or masculine and feminine plurals,
po 'on', **chúnga** 'knees', **zurales** 'quickly', **xoxádyas** 'she deceived' (past tense of **xoxavel**). In songs like this, the singers ad-lib extra verses and repeat verses when presented as table songs at group gatherings.

I recorded this version in my early teens at group gatherings in Montreal in the l950s
and recently heard almost the same version from Canadian Roma in 2001 at a Romani
Baldo 'ball' in Toronto at a table of refugee Romani speakers and Canadian Kalderash-
Romani speakers, along with Pentecostal hymns by Canadian Roma and Romanian and
Hungarian Romani folk songs by Romani newcomers to Canada.

The use of the word '**kúchi**' to mean 'sexually attractive' or 'sexy', seems to have
developed in the US. In European dialects there is **kuch** meaning 'dear' or 'expensive'
and **kuchi** (f.) 'cup' which also has a slang meaning of '*pudendum muliebre*' or 'female
pudenda'. These all appear in North American-Kalderash.

The adjective **kúchi** seems to have evolved from the carnivals, in the term 'hootchy-
kootchy dancer' which originated with the dancer "Little Egypt" (Farida Mazar Spyropou-
los) who introduced this so-called "shake dance" to the US in 1893 at the World
Columbian Exposition in Chicago. Later, another "Little Egypt" (Ashea Wabe) became
famous when she danced at a lavish party for Herbert Seeley in New York in 1896. After
this, many dancers adopted the name "Little Egypt" and popularised an Americanised

Delilah, I went to sleep
On her knees
Swiftly she deceived me
Swiftly she deceived me
She cut off my hair
Delilah.

Atwéturya 'Answers' to questions in this lesson

1.   **Le Rrom si lên bári tsêra**
2.   **Mi (múrri) de si la nevi stagi**
3.   **la sheyáke**
4.   **mánge**
5.   **le murshênge**

Questions from the written exercise translated

1.   Is this husband rich?
2.   Is his wife young?
3.   What does the wife not know?
4.   Where is the husband going?
5.   Why is he going there?
6.   Does he catch many fish?

*Footnote * cont.*

form of the Middle East Dance through the carnivals in the 20th century when these carnivals were a major source of income for both Kalderash-Roma and *Romanichels* (English Romanies) in the US and Canada.

From this, the Roma derived an intransitive/reflexive loan verb in **kuchiyil-pe** 'to shake dance, shake, shimmy'. More oddly, a transitive verb then appeared with thematic conjugations in **kuchyar-** meaning 'to cause to shake dance, shimmy, wiggle, move rapidly' as in the very common expression **Love kuchyaren e bul** 'Money makes the ass shake (greasing the pot brings results)'. As a matter of interest, did the Romani term **kúchi** come from the carnival term 'kootchy' or did the carnival term come from Romani **kúchi-khelitórka** 'shake dancer'? Dictionaries give 'unknown origin' for 'hootchy-kootchy'.

There may also be another carnival term in English derived from Romani: lollipop from **loli phabai** 'red apple', originally an apple on the end of a stick dipped in liquified toffee and sold by Romanies in Britain at fairs and markets and much later at the carnivals and circuses by *Romanichels* and Kalderash immigrants.

7.   Which fish does he finally catch?
8.   What will the fish do (for the husband)?

Model answers

1.   **Na, wo si chorro**
2.   **Na, nai terni, phuri si**
3.   **Chi zhanel so kam-xan**
4.   **Zhal ka o doryávo**
5.   **Zhal kothe te astarel mashên**
6.   **Chi astarel but mashên**
7.   **Ánde vúrma astarel tsine mashês**
8.   **O masho kam-del lêske so mangel**

Lesson seven

Word list (with some common expressions)

ánde wúrma	late (opposite of **rano** 'early'), also finally, in the end, eventually
araki	yesterday, last night
bánka	bank
barruno	stone, made of stone
baxtalo	lucky, fortunate
bírto	bar, tavern
bokhalo	hungry
bori	bride
Devlésa	'Go with God' (said when somebody leaves: man or woman, singular or plural)
fátsa	face
filástra	window
gogi	brain, mind, intelligence
harzópo	lift, elevator
ilêktriko	electricity, electric power
khere	at home, home (adverb. **Zhav khere** 'I am going home')
kólkorro	alone
kui (f.)	elbow
lámpa	lamp
mai drobroi tu	an old formal idiomatic greeting said to a newly arriving Rom. Literally 'more good to you' (may more good come to you). This is a Romanian idiom and used only in very formal speech. It has survived in folk tales.
mashkar	among, amongst, midway, in the middle
mol (f.)	wine
mui (m.)	mouth
nai (m.)	finger, toe
nakh (m.)	nose
nêg	instead of

pe*	for, at, on
pûnrró	leg, foot
pûrr (m.)	stomach, entrails, guts
ratyáko	at night (also **ánde ryat**)
Sar bushos?	What is your name? (How are you called?)
Sar mai san?	How are you? (singular and plural address) This is the standard formal greeting in North American-Kalderash. It appears to be based on Romanian *'Ce mai faci?'* and *'Ce mai faceţi?'* In Europe, the usual form is **Sar san?** The North American-Kalderash form must have been brought to the Americas in the late nineteenth century by the ancestors of the current generation of Roma.
shib (f.)	tongue, language
shoro	head
So mai keres tu?	How are you doing? This is an even more exact translation of Romanian *'Ce mai faci?* The plural form of address is **So mai keren tume?** *'Ce mai faceţi?'*
Sóde?	How much?
Sodya?	How many?
Te aven baxtale	May you be lucky (said to two or more people of either sex or a mixed gender group). This expression is now used internationally by Kalderash and other Roma as a formal greeting.
Te aves baxtali	May you be lucky (said to one woman)
Te aves baxtalo	May you be lucky (said to one man)
televízhono	television
tréla	trailer, travel trailer (North American-Kalderash)
wárekon	somebody
wast (m.)	hand
wórka	or
zéya	back (anatomical)

---

* **pe** and how it is used:

Beshen pe sófta	They are sitting on the sofa
Marel po wudar	He is knocking on the door (with a masculine singular noun)
Beshel pe l' paleya	He is sitting on the floor (with a plural feminine noun)
Bikinel lês pe l' lovênde	He is selling it for money (masculine plural noun in the prepositional case)

Noun plurals and oblique inflections

The following tables are introduced here to serve as a reference source. Do not attempt to learn all of these by heart at this point. Try to become familiar with the noun plurals and oblique stems gradually over time and as you start to understand the language.

Some of the plurals and oblique inflections in these tables will differ from other books on Romani dialects and Dr Ian Hancock's *A Handbook of Vlax Romani*. This is because I am listing mainly the forms used in the US and Canada by the North American-Kalderash for a specific dialect, which I speak, with a few additions used in our NGO in Toronto and introduced by European Vlax-Romani-speaking Romani refugees. European dialects of Kalderash can have variant forms of the words in this list. Hancock's excellent grammatical study is not for a specific dialect but is an overview of Vlax-Romani dialects in general. It should be referred to by students interested in morphology, grammatical rules and variations between related dialects and in pronunciation. For an in-depth analysis of Vlax-Romani and non-Vlax-Romani dialects see: *Romani: A Linguistic Introduction*, Matras, Y, Cambridge University Press, 2002.

Thematic nouns

Thematic inanimate nouns almost always follow the plural and accusative case inflections already shown. The following tables are a review of animate nouns already introduced plus new thematic animates and thematic and athematic inanimates. They should be referred to in order to find the plural and oblique stems of the various families of nouns.

Masculine nouns ending in a stressed < o > (including insects, which have only one gender):

Singular	Plural	Oblique (also accusative case for animates)	
choxãnó	**choxãné**	**choxãnès- / choxãnèn-**	ghost
djoro	**djore**	**djorês- / djorên-**	mule
gono	**gone**	**gonês- / gonên-**	sack, bag
goro	**gore**	**gorês- / gorên-**	poor fellow*
kermo	**kerme**	**kermês- / kermên-**	maggot
shelo	**shele**	**shelês- / shelên-**	rope

---

*   This has no exact one-word translation. It means 'poor fellow, unfortunate fellow' similar to the French *pauvre* as in *Il est malade, le pauvre* 'He is sick, the poor wretch'. The feminine of this word is **gêrí**.

A few inanimate masculine nouns ending in a stressed **< o >** which are themat-ic items from Byzantine Greek take a stressed **< á >** in the plural:

kokalo	**kokala**	**kokalês- / kokalên-**	bone
petalo	**petala**	**petalês- / petalên-**	horseshoe

Masculine inanimates ending in diphthongs:

musai	**musaiya**	**musaiyês- / musaiyên-**	arm
pai	**paiya**	**paiyês- / paiyên-**	water, sweat
xeroi	**xeroiya**	**xeroiyês- / xeroiyên-**	leg

but

súmnakai	**(none)**	**sumnakas-**	gold

Note also this exception:

mui	**muiya**	**mos- / mon-**	mouth

Thematic masculine animates and inanimates ending in a consonant take a stressed **< a >**:

chakal	**chakala**	**chakalês- / chakalên-**	jackal
nav/anav*	**nava/anava**	**(a)navês- / (a)navên-**	name
rin	**rina**	**rinês- / rinên-**	file (tool)
ruv	**ruva**	**ruvês- / ruvên-**	wolf
than	**thana**	**thanês- / thanên-**	place
vôrdòn	**vôrdôná**	**vôrdônès- / vôrdônèn-**	caravan

When exceptions to this rule appear in this course they will be indicated and plurals given.

Feminine nouns which end in a stressed **< í >** drop the **< í >** and add   **< ya >**:

chakalni	**chakalnya**	**chakalnya- / chakalnyan-**	jackal
choxãní	**choxãnyá**	**choxãnyá- / choxãnyán-**	female ghost
chuchi	**chuchya**	**chuchya- / chuchyan-**	breast, teat
djorni	**djornya**	**djornya- / djornyan-**	hinney

---

*   Both **nav** and **anav** are correct.

frangoshti	**frangoshtya**	**frangoshtya- / frangoshtyan-**	cactus, prickly pear
kakhli	**kakhlya**	**kakhlya- / kakhlyan-**	spinning wheel
kakyavi	**kakyavya**	**kakyava- / kakyavan-**	kettle
morki	**morkya**	**morkya- / morkyan-**	skin
rroiyi	**rroiya**	**rroiya- / rroiyan-**	spoon
shuri	**shurya**	**shurya- / shuryan-**	knife
wushandi	**wushandya**	**wushandya- / wushandyan-**	strainer

A few rare masculine nouns also end in a stressed **< í >** like 'lead' (which has no plural):

molivi	**(none)**	**molives-**	lead

The majority of feminine nouns ending in consonants take a stressed **< a >**. Some also have masculine plural case endings in the oblique stem which are not used by all native speakers:

ambrolin	**ambrolina**	**ambrolina- / ambrolinan-**	pear tree
balval	**balvala**	**balvala- balvalên-**	wind
baxt	**baxta**	**baxta- / baxtan-**	luck, fortune
bokh	**bokha**	**bokha- / bokhan-**	hunger
bul	**bula**	**bula- / bulan-**	posterior
chingar	**chingara**	**chingara- / chingarên-**	squabble, fight
dab	**daba**	**daba- / dabên-**	blow (as struck)
dosh	**dosha**	**dosha- / doshan-**	fault, blame
dukh	**dukha**	**dukha- / dukhan-**	pain
minzh/mizh	**minzha**	**minzha- / minzhan-**	vulva
rêg	**rêgá**	**rêgá- / rêgèn-**	side, edge
sung	**sunga**	**sunga- / sungan-**	foul odour, stink
zor	**zora**	**zora- / zoran-**	power, strength
zûn	**zûná**	**zûná - / zûnán-**	saddle

A very few thematic feminine nouns ending in a consonant add **< ya >**:

makh	**makhya**	**makhya- / makhyan-**	fly
phuv	**phuvya**	**phuvya- / phuvyan-**	soil, earth, ground
suv	**suvya**	**suvya- / suvyan-**	needle

When in doubt, use a stressed **< a >** for plurals and form the oblique stems like feminine nouns with plurals in stressed **< a >**. Many Roma do use this plural for the above words.

Some feminine inanimates in this family are subject to noun root inflection and others take the masculine thematic plural case ending **< en >** instead of the feminine plural thematic case ending **< an >**. This use of the masculine plural case ending in the oblique stem (and accusative of animates, is common throughout almost all the families of feminine animates and inanimates, including both thematic and athematic examples. This will become obvious in the tables given here:

aswin	**aswina/aswaiya**	**aswa- / aswên-**	teardrop
patrin	**patrya**	**patrya- / pateryan-**	leaf
ryát	**rakya**	**rakya- / rakyan-**	night

Feminine nouns ending in a diphthong behave as follows (some have masculine plural oblique stems):

bai	**baiya**	**baiya- / baiyan-**	sleeve
goi	**goiya**	**goiya- / goiyan-**	sausage
phabai	**phaba**	**phaba / -phabên-**	apple
rrai	**rraiya**	**rraiya- / rraiyan-**	switch, cane

Thematic plural nouns which have the same form in the singular and plural nominative

Some thematic nouns (animates and inanimates) do not change in the plural (as in English 'one sheep, two sheep' etc.). Their oblique forms are the same as those of the accusatives of animates. They are all masculine except **yakh** 'eye' and are inflected to the oblique like **bal**:

bal	**bales- / balên-**	hair (of head)
bêrsh	**bêrshès- / bêrshèn-**	year
char		grass
chor		thief

dand	tooth
ges	day
grast	horse
kak	uncle
kan	ear
kasht	tree
khar	penis
Rrôm*	Romani man, husband, if Romani
them	Romani person
wast	hand (some dialects also have a plural in **wása**)
yakh (f.)[†]	eye (oblique **yakha- / yakhên-**)

Examples

Si lês dui párne grast   He has two white horses
Le chor lên le love   The thieves are taking the money

When these words are the object of an action they take the accusative singular and plural endings:

Kinav le grastên   I buy the horses

---

*   The nominative plural **Rroma** is hardly ever heard in North American-Kalderash. The usual nominative plural is **Rrom** which then takes the regular thematic accusative (oblique stem) of **Rromên**, for example, **Le Rrom aven** 'The Roma are coming' and **Dikhav le Rromên** 'I see the Roma'.

†   The plural **yakha** appears in songs and poems. In normal speech the plural is usually **yakh** in the nominative singular and plural and accusative singular and plural. Note that the plural oblique stem is masculine. It is quite common for feminine inanimates to have masculine plural forms in the oblique stem of the case endings other than the vocative, especially in songs and poems to rhyme with masculine case endings, for example, one line will end with **lungone balênsa** 'with long hair' and the following with **kale yakhênsa** 'with black eyes'. The ending **< ênsa >** is the plural instrumental case ending (which will be introduced in Lesson nine). On the other hand, masculine nouns never take a feminine case form in the oblique, except in rare cases in songs where two or more feminine case forms are followed by a masculine case form. This may then be switched to the feminine form in order to rhyme.

Phandade le chorên   They arrested the thieves

When used with other case endings they are inflected:

Thodyas zûn pe l' grastêste   He placed a saddle on the horse
(prepositional case)

Anel le grastênge xabe   He brings food for the horses (dative case)

Thematic nouns whose plurals are not obvious from the regular thematic rules:

rrûl (f.)	**rra**	**rrûlá- / rran-**	fart
shav	**shave**	**shavês- / shavên-**	Romani boy, son
xabe (m.)	**xabena**	**xabenes- / xabenen-**	food

Athematic nouns

There are many groups (families) of athematic nouns that have their own plural and oblique forms. Some are to be found in this course among the lessons, in songs and reading exercises. All the examples listed in the following tables illustrate the family the examples belong to. Remember that the oblique inflections (endings) also serve as the accusative singulars and plurals for animate nouns. Example: **wortáko** 'partner'. In the singular this forms its oblique stem in < **wortakos-** > but since its plural is **wortácha** it forms its plural oblique stem in < **wortachên-** >.

Athematic masculine nouns ending in unstressed < o >

This is the largest masculine group and new loan words are constantly being added. For singular athematic nouns ending in an unstressed < **o** >, change this to < **úrya** > (or < **úri** > in some Vlax-Romani dialects) in the plural. This course uses the form < **úrya** > which is the most common Kalderash form and that mainly used in North American-Kalderash.

Singular	Plural	Oblique	
azilánto	**azilánturya**	**azilantós- / azilantonên-**	refugee
bizêrrùwo	**bizêrrùwurya**	**bizêrrûwós- / bizêrrûwonên-**	embroidery
cháso	**chásurya**	**chasos- / chasonên-**	hour
chêrbo	**chêrburya**	**chêrbós- / chêrbonên-**	moose
harzópo	**harzópurya**	**harzopos- / harzoponên-**	lift (elevator)
iméylo	**iméylurya**	**imeylos- / imeylonên-**	email
késo	**késurya**	**kesos- / kesonên-**	case (in court)
gláso	**glásurya**	**glasos- / glasonên-**	voice
harnûvo	**harnûvurya**	**harnûvós- / harnûvonên-**	tarpaulin
magarêsto	**magarêsturya**	**magarêstós- / magarêstón-**	stud donkey

swáto*	swáturya	swatos- / swatonên-	word
tonomáto	tonomáturya	tonomatos- / tonomatonên-	jukebox
trôko	trôkurya	trôkós- / trôkonèn-	truck
valóvo	valóvurya	valoves- / valovonên-	horse trough

Masculine athematic nouns ending in an unstressed **< i >** change to **< ya >** in the plural:

basmáli	basmálya	basmaliyês- / basmaliyên-	large kerchief
chilimóli†	chilimólya	chilimolyês- / chilimolyên-	Chile Mole
mobíli	mobíliya	mobilês- / mobilên-	car
samovári	samovárya	samovariyês- / samovariyên-	samovar
solavári	solavárya	solavariyês- / solavariyên-	bridle
tinzhíri	tinzhírya	tinzhiriyês- / tinzhiriyên-	cooking pot

Some nouns in this group have no plural form:

astáchi	(none)	astachiyês-	cast iron
archíchi	(none)	archichiyês-	tin

Athematic feminine nouns ending in **< a >** change to **< i >**. This group is also large and is constantly adopting new loan words:

bêlzùna	bêlzùni	bêlzûná- / bêlzûnán-	blowtorch, gas torch
hárkoma	(none)	harkoma-	copper
kolumpíra	kolumpíri	kolumpira- / kolumpiran-	potato
kyáiya	kyáiyi	kyaiya- / kyaiyan-	key
lámpa	lámpi	lampa- / lampan-	lamp
motúra	motúri	motura- / moturan-	broom
síniya	síniyi	siniya- / siniyan-	table
stampíla	stampíli	stampila-/ stampilan-	corporate stamp
shantíra	shantíri	shantira- / shantiran-	construction site

---

*   Some European-Kalderash dialects and more formal speakers in North America use a variant masculine plural oblique stem for words in this group. Romanian-Kalderash speakers also often employ this alternative form. Either is correct:

swáto	swáturya	swatós-/swaton-	word

†   Chile Mole is a Tex-Mex meal very popular among Roma who have devised their own variant recipes both in North America and in eastern Europe.

shwártsa	shwártsi	shwartsa- / shwartsan-	apron
tigáiya	tigáiyi	tigaiya- / tigaiyan-	skillet
vídra	vídri	vidra- / vidran-	beaver
xírpa	xírpi	xirpa- / xirpan-	rectum

Masculine athematic nouns ending in **< áno >**, **< óno >** and **< úno >** change to **< áiya >**, **< óiya >** and **< úya >** in the plural:

Amerikáno	Amerikáiya	Amerikanês- / Amerikanên-	American
dushmáno	dushmáiya	dushmanês- / dushmayên-	enemy
murtáno	murtáiya	murtanês- / murtayên-	tomcat
plapóno	plapóiya	plaponês- / plapoiyên-	quilt
maimúno	maimúya	maimunês- / maimuyên-	monkey
pavúno	pavúiya	pavunês- / pavuyên-	peacock
zabúno	zabúya	zabunês- / zabuyên-	leather jacket

There are a few exceptions to this rule:

aropláno	aroplánurya	aroplanos- / aroplanonên-	aeroplane
diwáno	diwánurya	diwanos- / diwanonên-	meeting
yalakráno	yalakránurya	yalakranos- / yalakranonên-	scorpion

Athematic feminine nouns ending in **< ánka >**, **< ínka >**, **< onka >** and **< únka >** change the final unstressed **< a >** to an unstressed **< i >** in the plural:

dushmánka	dushmánki	dushmanka- / dushmankan-	enemy
kustománka	kustománki	kustomanka- / kustomankan-	customer, client
gazdínka	gazdínki	gazdinka- / gazdinkan-	boss, owner
kleyônka	kleyônki	kleyônká- / kleyônkán-	oilcloth, linoleum
mashûnka	mashûnki	mashûnká- / mashûnkán-	machine
púshka	púshki	pushka- / pushkan-	rifle, gun

Feminine nouns ending in **< êrka >** and **< êlka >** usually change to **< erchi >** and **< êlchi >** in the plural:

nupêrka	nupêrchi	nupêrká- / nupêrchán-	newt
shupêrka	shupêrchi	shupêrká- / shupêchán-	lizard
skatêrka	skatêrchi	skatêrká- / skatêrchán-	tablecloth

and

butêlka	butêlchi	butêlká- / butêlchèn-	bottle

wuchitêlka   wuchitêlchi   wuchitêlká- / wuchitêlchán-   school teacher

But feminine nouns in **< êrka >** formed from masculine nouns in **< êri >** change to **< êrki >** in the plural:

pômpèrka   pômpèrki   pômpêrká- / pômpêrkán-   firewoman

Some athematic feminine nouns ending in **< íka >** change to **< ichi >** in the plural:

fábrika	**fábrichi**	**fabrika- / fabrichan-**	factory
rradíka	**rradíchi**	**rradika- / rradichan-**	radish

A large number of athematic feminine nouns with the terminal **< ára >** change to **< èri >** in the plural. All this group takes feminine oblique singular endings and masculine plural oblique endings:

bíra/byárya	**byèri**	**bira- / byêrèn-**	beer, bottle/can of beer
kukashtára	**kukashtêri**	**kukashtara- / kukashtêrèn-**	toilet, men's room
skára	**skêri**	**skara- / skêrèn-**	step, stairs (in the plural)
tilára	**tilêri**	**tilara- / tilêrèn-**	dollar
tsigára	**tsigêri**	**tsigara- / tsigêrèn-**	cigarette
tsimptsára	**tsimptsêri**	**tsimptsara- / tsimptsêrèn-**	mosquito, helicopter
vára	**vêri**	**vara- / vêryán-**	cousin
zgyárra	**zgyêrri**	**zgyarra- / zgyêrrèn-**	claw, talon

Masculine athematic nouns ending in the diphthong **< ói >** change to **< oiya >** in the plural:

brashkoi	**brashkoiya**	**brashkês- / brashkoiyên-**	bullfrog
pitsagoi	**pitsagoiya**	**pitsagoiyês- / pitsagoiyên-**	swallow

Athematic feminine nouns ending in a stressed **< i >** change to **< ya >** in the plural:

bragi*	**bragya**	**bragya- / bragyan-**	milking can
shkafêdí	**shkafêdyá**	**shkafêdyá- / shkafêdyán-**	coffee table

---

*   This type of small milking can is also used as a hand drum by Vlax-Roma musicians in Hungary and Transylvania.

kharavdi   **kharavdya**   **kharavdya- / kharavdyán-**   lobster

A small athematic feminine group is subject to root inflection:

firánga   **firênzhi**   **firanga- / firênzhèn-**   curtain
kriyánga   **kriyênzhi**   **kriyanga- / kriyênzhèn-**   branch

Athematic feminine nouns ending in **< íya >** and **< iya >** change to **< íyi >** or **< iyi >** in the plural. This includes a large number of Romanian loan nouns which are similar to English because of their Latin origin and which have retained a Romanian plural in Kalderash, along with words from other languages which are similarly formed. A few of the nouns in this group are thematic and have taken the suffix **< íya >**.

With **< íya >**:

dushmaníya **dushmaníyi**   **dushmaniya-/ dushmaniyan-**   emnity
Gazhikaníya* **(none)**   **Gazhikaniya-**   (see note)
Rromaníya† **(none)**   **Rromaniya-**   (see note)
vorrûtsíya   **vorrûtsíyi**   **vorrûtsiyá- / vorrûtsiyán-**   disgust

With **< iya >**:
These members are athematic nouns:

diligátsiya   **diligátsiyi**   **diligatsya- / diligatsyan-**   delegation
ginerátsiya   **ginerátsiyi**   **gineratsiya- / gineratsiyan-**   generation
hârtíya   **hârtíyi**   **hârtiyá- / hârtiyán-**   paper,
newspaper
kumpaníya††kumpaníyi   **kumpaniya- / kumpaniyan-**   (see note)
matánsiya   **matánsiyi**   **matansiya- / matansiyan-**   place of
execution
nátsiya   **nátsiyi**   **natsiya- / natsiyan-**   nation,
nationality

*   **Gazhikaníya** non-Romani society as compared to Romani society.

†   **Rromaníya** is difficult to translate in one word. It means adherence to Romani culture and values, including the rules of purity and defilement, respect, honour and all the things that make somebody an acceptable member of the group.

††   **Kumpaníya** means all the Roma living in a town or city (territory) who follow the **Rromaníya** and who claim this territory collectively. It can also mean all the members of a travelling group of Roma. The **kumpaníya** also has **naihíya** 'jurisdiction' over the members in it through the council of elders (**Kris-Rromani**) and the **Rrôm Baro** (Big Man). In its other meanings, it is used for a commercial company or a company of soldiers.

naihíya	naihíyi	naihiya- / naihiyan-	jurisdiction
ôbligátsiya	ôbligátsiyi	ôbligatsiyá- / ôbligatsiyán-	obligation
stántsiya	stántsiyi	stantsiya- / stantsiyan-	station

There are some very large groups of nouns whose roots are sometimes thematic but whose endings are athematic suffixes denoting trades or association with a specific function, state or condition.

Masculine nouns ending in **< ári >**:

ardjentári	ardjentáriya	ardjentariyês- / ardjentariyên-	silversmith
gunoiyári	gunoiyáriya	gunoiyariyês- / gunoiyariyên-	garbage collector
masári	masáriya	masariyês- / masariyên-	butcher

There are also some masculine exceptions to this rule which are nouns in themselves and are not root elements which have been given the **< ári >** suffix:

amnári	amnáriya	amnariyês- / amnariyên-	cigarette lighter
depanári*	depanárya	depanariyês- / depanariyên-	convenience store
kuntári	kuntáriya	kuntariyês- / kuntariyên-	scale, balance
kutári	kutáriya	kutarês- / kutarên-	so-and-so (m.)
magári	magáriya	magarês- / magarên-	donkey (m.)
zhandári	zhandáriya	zhandarês- / zhandarên-	policeman, gendarme

Feminine athematic nouns derived from male forms in **< ári >** or which stand alone without masculine equivalents which end in **< árka >** change this to **< árki >**:

| gunoiyárka | gunoiyárki | gunoiyarka- / gunoiyarkan- | bag lady |
| masárka | masárki | masarka- / masarkan- | female butcher |

Also:

kutárka	kutárki	kutarka- / kutarkan-	so-and-so (f.)
magárka	magárki	magarka- / magarkan-	donkey (f.)
zhandárka	zhandárki	zhandarka- / zhandarkan-	policewoman

---

*   Canadian-Kalderash from French *dépaneur*.

Masculine nouns ending with the suffix **< itóri >**:

khelitóri	**khelitóriya**	**khelitorês- / khelitoriyên-**	dancer (m.)
mudaritóri	**mudaritóriya**	**mudaritorês- / mudaritoriyên-**	murderer

Some masculine athematic nouns ending in **< óri >** are loan words in themselves:

adaptóri	**adaptóriya**	**adaptoriyês- / adaptoriyên-**	adapter
amplifikatóri	**amplifikatóriya**	**amplifikatoriyês- / amplifikatoriyên-**	amplifier

Feminine equivalents of masculine nouns in **< óri >** end in **< otórka >** and change to **< itórki >** in the plural:

khêlitórka	**khêlitórki**	**khêlitorká- / khêlitorkán-**	dancer (f.)
mudaritórka	**mudaritórki**	**mudaritorka- / mudaritorkan-**	murderess

Masculine nouns ending in **< èri >** and **< êli >** change to **< èrya >** and **< êlya >** in the plural:

pishtolèri	**pishtolêriya**	**pishtolêriyès- / pishtolêriyèn-**	gunman
plômbèri	**plômbèriya**	**plômbêriyès- / plômbêriyèn-**	plumber
pômpèri	**pômpèriya**	**pômpêriyès- / pômpêriyèn-**	fireman
rivêri	**rivêriya**	**rivêriyès- / rivêriyèn-**	river
wuchitêli	**wuchitêliya**	**wuchitêlès- / wuchitêlèn-**	teacher

Masculine nouns ending in an unstressed **< o >** following **< r >**, **< l >** or **< ly >**, like the following, change to **< ya >** in the plural:

báiyêro	**báiyêrya**	**baiyêrès- / baiyêrèn-**	amulet
kavalêro	**kavalêrya**	**kavalêrès- / kavalêrèn-**	gentleman
krályo	**králya**	**kralês- / kralên-**	king
pishtólo	**pishtólya**	**pishtolês- / pishtolên-**	spray gun (for paint), revolver
porrárro	**porrárrya**	**porrarrès- / porrarrèn-**	stein, goblet
sênzèro	**sênzèrya**	**sênzerès- / sênzeryèn-**	ashtray
swiyádêro	**swiyádyêrya**	**swiyadêrès- / swiyadyêriyèn-**	(electric) drill
vêro	**vêrya**	**vêrès- / vêrèn-**	cousin

Masculine athematic nouns ending in the suffixes **< ásh >** and **< ách >** add **< a >** in the plural:

birtash	**birtásha**	**birtashês- / birtashên-**	bartender
Kalderash	**Kalderásha**	**Kalderashês- / Kalderashên-**	Coppersmith Rom
swatash	**swatásha**	**swatashês- / swatashên-**	spokesman
trokash	**trokásha**	**trokashês- / trokashên-**	truck driver (m.)
tolmach	**tolmácha**	**tolmachês- / tolmachên-**	translator

Feminine athematic nouns ending in the suffix **< áshka >** drop the final **< a >** and add **< i >**:

birtáshka	**birtáshki**	**birtashka- / birtashkan-**	barmaid
bráshka	**bráshki**	**brashka- / brashkan-**	frog
swatáshka	**swatáshki**	**swatashka- / swatashkan-**	spokes woman
trokáshka	**trokáshki**	**trokashka- / trokashkan-**	truck driver (f.)

Masculine nouns ending in **< áko >** (some are formed from thematic nouns):

gansáko	**gansácha**	**gansakos- / gansachên-**	gander
khuláko	**khulácha**	**khulakos- / khulachên-**	squalid man, 'sleazo'
wortáko	**wortácha**	**wortakos- / wortachên-**	partner

Feminine nouns ending in the suffix **< áika >** (some are formed from thematic nouns):

wortáika	**wortáiki**	**wortaika- / wortaikan-**	partner, copine
khuláika	**khuláiki**	**khulaika- / khulaikan-**	squalid woman
klêpováika	**klêpováiki**	**klêpovaiká- / klêpovaikán-**	clumsy woman, klutz

Masculine athematic nouns ending in **< ko >** as in **< iko >** and **< urko >** usually change to **< íchi >** and **< urchi >** in the plural:

cháiniko	**cháinichi**	**chainikós- / chainichên-**	teapot
prázniko	**práznichi**	**praznikos- / praznichên-**	holiday
sobôdniko	**sobôdnichi**	**sobôdnikós- / sobôdnichên-**	lodger, roomer
kokostúrko	**kokostúrchi**	**kokosturkos- / kokosturchên-**	stork

Feminine athematic nouns ending in **< ítsa >** and **< útsa >** change to **< ítsi >** and **< útsi >** in the plural:

Kalderashútsa	**Kalderashútsi**	**Kalderashutsa- / Kaldarashutsan-**	
			a woman member of the Kalderash Roma
kôtunítsa	**kôtunítsi**	**kôtunitsá-/ kôtunitsán-**	gopher
králitsa	**králitsi**	**kralitsa- / kralitsan-**	queen
mútsa	**mútsi**	**mutsa- / mutsan-**	cat
vítsa	**vítsi**	**vitsa- / vitsan-**	clan
xêvítsa	**xêvítsi**	**xêvitsá- / xêvitsán-**	porridge

A few masculine athematic nouns also end in **< ítsa >** (these are indicated in the word lists and the dictionary) and they too take a plural in **< ítsi >**:

izêlítsa	**izêlítsi**	**izêlitsès- / izêlitsèn-**	traitor, sell-out
pampurítsa	**pampurítsi**	**pampuritsês- / pampuritsên-**	homosexual

The masculine athematic nouns ending in **< ítsa >** are following the general rule for masculine nouns ending in an unstressed **< a >** which always take their plurals in **< i >**, like those following:

artísta	**artísti**	**artistês- / artistên-**	artist
bulabásha	**bulabáshi**	**bulabashês- / bulabashên-**	clan leader, chieftain
dêntísta	**dêntísti**	**dêntistès- / dêntistèn-**	dentist

but

soldáta	**soldátsi**	**soldatês- / soldatsên-**	soldier

or

kâtána	**kâtáiya**	**kâtanès- / kâtanèn-**	soldier

A very large group of nouns are formed from both thematic and athematic verbs and adjectives to form the abstract noun with the nominalizing suffix **< imos >**. These are all masculine in gender.

a) Masculine nouns ending in the suffix **< imos >**:

chachimos	**chachimáta**	**chachimas- / chachimatan-**	truth, justice
marimos	**marimáta**	**marimas- / marimatan-**	fighting, war
mudarimos	**mudarimáta**	**mudarimas- / mudarimatan-**	murder
múndrimos	**mundrimáta**	**mundrimatas- / mundrimatan-**	wonderment

ansurimos	**ansurimáta**	**ansurimatas- / ansurimatan-**	marriage (of a man)
moritimos	**moritimáta**	**moritimas- / moritiman-**	marriage (of a woman)

There is also one irregular noun in the nominative:

sastimus	**sastimáta**	**sastimas- / sastimatan-**	health

Some nouns of this group take an ending of **< omos >** in the masculine singular:

mishtomos	**mishtomáta**	**mishtomatas- / mishtomatan-**	favour
tristomos	**tristomáta**	**tristomatas- / tristomatan-**	sadness

b) Masculine nouns ending in **< ipe >**. These are few in North American-Kalderash but there is a large group in European Kalderash and other related dialects where this suffix often replaces the **< imos >** ending:

maxripe	**maxrimáta**	**maxrimatas- / maxrimatan-**	defilement
shinipe	**shinimáta***	**shinimas- / shinimatan-**	cutting

Irregular noun plurals

In some Romani dialects, abstract substantives (nouns) ending in the suffix **< pe >** have the following forms:

chachipe	**chachipéya**	**chachipas- /chachipan-**	truth, justice

Given here is a table of nouns whose plurals and oblique forms are difficult to determine from the rules given for thematic and athematic nouns. Most of these stand alone or have two or three like them at most:

---

*   When the abstract noun in **< ipe >** is used in a compound noun the plural nominative given above **< imáta >** becomes **< ipéya >**, for example **Kashtêngo-shinimos** 'wood shaving' (singular) becomes **kashtênge-shinipéya** 'wood shavings, sawdust' in the plural. There is a tendency for this to occur in North American-Kalderash when the nominalizing suffix in **< ipe >** is used to denote something that has a physical reality and can be touched as opposed to an abstract concept like 'truth' which would be **chachimos**, or **shukarimos** 'beauty'.

Singular	Plural	Oblique stems	
ángêlo	ánzhêlyá	angêlès- anzhêlèn-	angel
aríche (m.)	aricheyi	arichês- / aricheyên-	hedgehog
arman (f.)	armaiya	armana- / armaiyên-	curse, damnation
chirash (m.)	chirêsh	chirashès-/ chirêshèn-	cherry
darro	dárrya	darrês- / darronên-	bridal offering
dáta	dêtsi	data- / dêtsèn-	time, occasion
djámena	djámeni	djamina- / djameyan-	female twin
djámeno	djámeya	djamenês- / djamenên-	male twin
djédjêsh (m.)	djedjêshi	djedjêshès- / djedjêshèn-	train
djulêshi (m.)	djulêsha	djulêshyès- / djulêshyèn-	business meeting
êmpêratyása*	êmpêratyási	êmperatyá- / êmpêratyán-	queen, empress
fóro[†]	fóri	forês- / forên-	city
gálbeno	gálbi	galbenês- / galbên-	gold coin
gáta[††]	gêtsi	gata- / gêtsèn-	finish, conclusion
grápa	grópi	grapa- / gropên-	hole, pit, wall plug
hamishágo	hamishégurya	hamishagês- / hamishegurên-	jealousy
Harángêlo[¶]	Haránzhêlya	Harangêlès- / Haranzhêlèn-	Black Angel
hatázheno	hatázheni	hatazhenês- / hatazhenên-	floor, storey
kalts (f.pl.)	káltsi / kaltsa-	/ kaltsan-	pair of trousers
katya (m.pl.)	katyi	katya- / katyan-	scissors, shears
klépovo	klepováiya	klepovês- / klepovên-	clumsy man, clod

---

*   Limited to North American-Kalderash. The European variant is **êmperatáika**.

†   **Fóro** also has a plural in **fórurya** (see athematic nouns in unstressed **< o >** in the table).

††   **Gáta** is also used as an adjective and an idiomatic imperative command.

¶   The **Harángêlo**, or Black Angel, comes from Kalderash folklore, a sinful man cursed by God and condemned to see all the misery in the world and to be able to do nothing to change it except to do service to others until he receives grace from God and his curse is then lifted.

kokósho*	kokósha	kokoshês- / kokoshên-	male breeding cock
kriyánga	kriyênzhi	krianga- / kriyênzhèn-	bough, branch
mamalíga	(none)	mamaliga-	polenta
máriya	mêri	mariya- / mêriyán-	sea, ocean
motsyúne (m.)	motsyúni	motsyunês- / motsyunên-	motion (at a meeting)
mustáka	mustêtsi	mustaka- / mustatsên-	moustache
papúka	papúchi	papukês- / papuchên-	woman's slipper
pecháta	pechêtsi	pechata- / pechêtsèn-	spot, patch
ponyáva	ponyévi	ponyava- / ponyevên-	carpet
prekáza	prekézhi	prekaza- / prekezhên-	jinx
rráka	rráchi	rraka- / rrachyan-	crab
rráta	rróti	rrata- / rrotên-	wheel
rrátsa	rrêtsi	rratsa- / rrêtsan-	female duck
rrûmo	rrêmi	rrûmès- / rrêmèn-	worm
skála	skéli	skala- / skelên-	scale (in music)
skêri (f.pl)	skêrya	skêrèn- / skêryèn-	steps, ladder
skîní	skîní	skîniyès- / skîniyèn-	skinhead
telázo	telúzhi	telazos- / teluzhên-	wave
telúzhi (m.pl.)	telúzhiya	teluzhya- / teluzhyan-	tide
tsokóla	tsokóliya	tsokola- / tsokolen-	shoe
vryámya	vrêmi	vramya- / vrêmèn-	time
vyástya	vêsti	vyastya- / vêstèn-	news, news report
Zhúdovo	Zhudováya	Zhudovês- / Zhudovên-	Jew

The past tense of thematic verbs

Many verbs form the past by removing the < e > from the 'he' form of the present tense < astar-el > and adding the endings shown in the table below. The pronouns **me**, **tu**, etc., are used only for emphasis:

me astardem	I caught (verb stem < astar- > with < dem >)
tu astardyan	you caught
wo/woi astardyas	he/she caught

* The thematic noun **bashno** is a rooster. Most other domesticated fowl have both male and female nouns. **Kokósho** is the breeding cock or stud cock of any species of fowl, especially fighting cocks.

ame astardyam   we caught
tume astardyan   you caught
won astarde   they caught

Other verbs (from Lessons one to three) following this pattern are **gindem** 'I counted', **gilabadem** 'I sang', **kerdem** 'I did, made', **lashardem** 'I repaired', **mardem** 'I hit', **prindjardem** 'I recognized', **phuterdem** 'I opened' and **shindem** 'I cut'.

Rules

The following rules are given to help form the past tenses of all thematic verbs. If the verb stem ends in **< r >**, **< l >**, **< n >** or **< v >** the past tense is usually formed with the **< dem >** endings as given for **astardem**. Examples:

astardem   I caught
kheldem   I danced
bikhindem   I sold
shindem   I have cut
xala(v)dem   I washed

With verbs where the stem ends in **< v >** in the present tense, the **< v >** (as in **xalav**) is usually dropped to form the past tense which becomes **xaladem**.

In most other verbs, the past tense ending is **< lem >** as in **< mang- >** 'to want' or **< dikh- >** 'to see', but there are exceptions.

manglem   I wanted
manglan   you wanted
manglas   he/she wanted
manglam   we wanted
manglan   you wanted
mangle   they wanted

dikhlem   I saw
dikhlan   you saw
dikhlas   he/she saw
dikhlam   we saw
dikhlan   you saw
dikhle   they saw

Learn these commonly used exceptions (including three irregular third person plural endings in the past tense):

1) **phan-dav** 'I tie' **phan-glem** 'I tied' **-glem**
   zhanav-zhanglem 'know'

2) **piyav** 'I drink' **pilem** 'I drank' **-ilem** (the < y > in **piyav** is
   dropped here)

3) **phutrav** 'I open' **phuterdem** 'I opened' **-erdem** (root inflection of verb stem)
   bishtrav-bishterdem 'forget'
   mutrav-muterdem 'urinate'

4) **asav** 'I laugh' **asaiyem** 'I laughed' **asanile** 'they laughed'
   -áiyem (root inflection of verb)

5) **rovav** 'I cry' **ruyem** 'I cried' **runile** 'they cried'
   -uyem (root inflection of verb)

6) **sovav** 'I sleep' **sutem** 'I slept' **sutile** 'they slept'
   -utem (root inflection of verb)

There are also a number of commonly used thematic verbs whose endings in the past tense third person singular and plural are not the same as the verbs listed above:

Avav 'I come' has a past tense in **avilem** like **piyav** 'I drink' but the past tense is different in the third person singular and plural:

avilem	I came
avilan/avilyan	you came (either form is correct)
avilo	he came (alternative form in **avilyas**)
avili	she came (alternative form in **avilyas**)
avilam	we came
avilan/ avilyan	you came
avile	they came

Verbs like **avel** include **ashel-ashilo** 'stay, remain' and **sikel-sikilo** 'learn, show'. Other verbs resembling the above in their third person singular and plural past tenses are **aresel-areslo** 'arrive', **bashel-bashlo*** 'crow, bark', **nakhel-nakhlo** 'pass' and **nashel-nashlo** 'run', which has an alternative third

---

*   This verb is used to indicate most animal noises and the sounds of some musical instruments:

O zhukel bashel	The dog is barking
O bashno bashel	The rooster is crowing
O grast bashlo	The horse whinnied
O liondári bashlo	The lion roared
Le tóbi bashen	The drums are playing/sounding

person singular past tense in **nashlas**. A similar verb is **perel-pelo** 'fall' (note verb root inflection in the past tense).

The following verbs should also be noted:

1) **langal** 'he limps'

langáilem	I limped
langáilan	you limped
langáilo	he limped
langáili	she limped
langáilam	we limped
langáilan	you limped
langáile	they limped

Also following this pattern are **daral-daráilo** 'fear', **bilal-biláilo** 'melt, vanish', **istral-istráilo** 'slip', **izdral-izdráilo** 'tremble', **pakyál-pakyáilo** 'believe', **rrongyal** 'thunder peals' and **shtrafyal** 'lightning flashes'.

2) **anklel** 'he ascends'

anklistem	I ascended
anklistan	you ascended
anklisto	he ascended
anklisti	she ascended
anklistam	we ascended
anklistan	you ascended
ankliste	they ascended

Another verb like this is **xulel-xulisto** 'descend'.

3) **merel** 'he dies' has a past tense in **mulo** 'he died'

mulem	I died
mulan	you died
mulo	he died (alternative form in **mulas**)
muli	she died (alternative form in **mulas**)
mulam	we died
mulan	you died
mule	they died

---

* An alternative form, widely heard among Kalderash speakers, has a past tense in **djêlèm** instead of **gêlèm**.

4) **zhal** 'he goes' has a past tense in **gêlo**

gêlèm*	I went
gêlán	you went
gêló	he went (alternative form in **gêlás**)
gêlí	he went (alternative form in **gêlás**)
gêlám	we went
gêlèn	you went (note **< en >**)
gêlé	they went

The verbs **wushtyal** 'he rises, gets up' and **xutel** 'he jumps' have irregular conjugations in the present and past tenses:

wusht-	'rise'		
wushtyav	I rise	**wushtilem**	I rose, have risen
wushyas	you rise	**wushtilan**	you rose
wushtyal	he rises	**wushtilo**	he rose
wushtyal	she rises	**wushtili**	she rose
wushtyas	we rise	**wushtilam**	we rose
wushten	you rise	**wushtilan**	you rose
wushten	they rise	**wushtile**	they rose

xut-	'jump' (note verb root inflection in the past tense)		
xutyav	I jump	**xuklem**	I jumped
xutes	you jump	**xuklan**	you jumped
xutel	he jumps	**xuklo**	he jumped (alternative form in **xuklas**)
xutel	she jumps	**xukli**	she jumped (alternative form in **xuklas**)
xutas	we jump	**xuklam**	we jumped
xuten	you jump	**xuklan**	you jumped
xuten	they jump	**xukle**	they jumped

Some of the verbs listed here which have masculine and feminine past tense endings in **< o >** and **< i >** also have alternative forms with regular endings. The only rule that can be given is that when the subject is a person or live entity, the endings are **< o >** and **< i >**:

Avilo o Yánko araki	Yanko came yesterday
O zhukel xuklo pe mánde	The dog sprang at me

The alternative past tense form is sometimes, but not always, used in reference to the distant past and in folk tales or for inanimates:

Múrro dad avilyas ánda e Sêrbiya do mult	My father came from Serbia a long time ago
O xarápo nashlas pála lêste	The cannibal ogre ran after him (folk tale)
O milái avilyas but ánde wúrma ándo kuko bêrsh	Spring came very late that year

For students using this course the forms given in the tables can be safely used. They may, however, hear the alternative forms from native speakers depending on which country they are living in or visiting. Kalderash and Vlax-Romani speakers in certain geographical regions use the alternative forms more than others.

Examples of past tense

Prindjardem lês kána dikhlem lês	I recognized him when I saw him
Woi shindyas o manrro	She sliced (cut) the bread
Gilabade gilya sórro ryáto	They sang songs all night
Xaladem múrre wast	I washed my hands
Lashardyan amári ófisa?	Did you straighten out our office?
Kindem nevo mobíli thai vôrdòn	I bought a new car and trailer
So dikhlan tume po têlevízhono?	What did you (plural) see on television?
Mudarde o ilêktriko	They shut down the electricity (hydro power)
Mulo o ilêktriko	The power has gone out (died)
Mardem lês ánde fátsa	I punched (hit) him in the face
Sóde pokindyan pe l' grastês?	How much did you pay for the horse?
Sodya mashen astardyan?	How many fish did you catch?
Dukhadem múrri zéya	I hurt my back
Wárekon pharradyas e filástra	Somebody broke (shattered) the window
Phendem lêske, "Devlésa!"	I said to him, "Go with God"
"Te aves baxtalo!" phendyas mánge	"Greetings!" he said to me

Mulo ándo Târánto	He died in Toronto
O harzópo anklisto	The lift (elevator) ascended
Aresli ánde diminyátsa	She arrived in the morning
Ashundem thai asaiyem	I heard and laughed
Pelo ánde wúlitsa	He fell in the street
Kai gêló o Yánko?	Where has Yanko gone?

Past tense idiom

There is a special idiomatic form of the past tense of **phenel** 'he tells, says' which is used when relating a story where narration back and forth between two or more people is the topic. It is also used in telling folk tales and relating past events where conversations between characters in the story take place. It is not necessary to use this idiomatic form and it is simply pointed out here since it will be encountered from native speakers.

Phênga is used as follows:

"So keres?" phendyas o Yánko?	"What are you doing?" said Yanko
"Chi kerav but", phênga me	"I am not doing much", said I
"Sóstar?" phênga wo	"Why?" he said
"Nasvalo sim", phênga me	"I am sick", I said

Past tense of the verb 'to be'

(me) símas	I was, I used to be, I have been
(tu) sánas	you were, you used to be, you have been
(wo) sas	he was, he used to be, he has been
(woi) sas	she was, she used to be, she has been
(ame) sámas	we were, we used to be, we have been
(tume) sánas	you were, you used to be, you have been
(won) sas	they were, they used to be, they have been
sas	it was, there was, there used to be, there has been

Examples

Kai sánas?	Where were you?
Símas le Stevóste	I was at Steve's
Bokhalo símas sórro ges	I was (have been) hungry all day (man speaking)
Bokhali símas	I was hungry (woman speaking)
Baxtale sámas	We were fortunate

The negative particle **chi** expresses 'not', as with other verbs. Note that **sas** becomes **nas** 'he was not' and 'they were not' and **manas** 'there were not, there were no':

(me) chi símas	I was not
(tu) chi sánas	you were not
(wo) nas	he was not
(woi) nas	she was not
(ame) chi sámas	we were not
(tume) chi sánas	you were not
(won) nas	they were not

Examples

Chi símas bokhalo	I was not hungry
Chi sánas khere	You were not home
Wo nas baxtalo	He was not lucky
Nas múrri buki	It was not my business
Manas kónik ándo kher	There was nobody in the house
Manas love ánde bánka	There was no money in the bank

Spoken exercises

Form plurals from the words in the left-hand column following the first example in the list:

yêkh kher	**dui khera**
êkh chirikli	**dui ...**
mo wortáko	**me ...**
o baro kasht	**le...**

Make up more examples for yourself.

Answer the questions (changing the present tense to the past) following the given example:

Lashares o skamin?	**Lashardem lês araki**
Shines tye bal?	
Tyo kak del túke love?	
Tume róden neve lámpi?	

Written exercise

Translate into Romani:

1. Who sang instead of him?
2. I paid him for the wood ('him' is the **< ke >** of the dative case. The word 'for' in 'for the wood' is not translated)
3. She cut her finger when (**kána**) she was working in the factory (**e fábrika**)
4. We did not recognize their language
5. Our friends hit the thieves

Common sayings

Tu kerdyan man wórka me kerdem tut?	Did you give birth to me (make me) or did I give birth to you? (said by a father to a disrespectful son)
Si man love pe moláte, núma nai man love pe boryáte	I have money for wine, but I have no money for a bride
Rrôm mashkar le Rromênde, thai Gazho mashkar le Gazhênde	(Be) a Rom among the Roma, and a non-Rom among the non-Roma

The stone bar (a Canadian-Romani song)

Ói, ándo bírto barruno
Bírto, bírto, barruno
Si yêkh síniya marmuróski
Ándo bírto barruno.
Thai kon beshéla pála láte?
Kon beshéla pála láte?
Óthe beshéla, o Yováno,
Ándo bírto barruno.
Thai pêske wása têlé pe síniya
Thai pêske múiya ánde l' wása
Pêske múiya ánde l' wása
Ándo bírto barruno
Hai so gindos tu, So gindos tu?
So gindos tu, Yovanéya?

Si tu êkh gûndo ansurimásko?
Si tu êkh gûndo nashimásko?
Ói nai ma gûndo ansurimásko
Nai ma gûndo nashimásko
Si ma êkh gûndo piyimásko
Ándo bírto barruno.
Bírto, bírto barruno
Bírto, bírto barruno
Si yêkh síniya marmuróski
Ándo bírto barruno.

Translation

Oh, in the stone bar
The stone bar
There is a marble table
In the stone bar
And who is sitting at it?
Who is sitting at it?
Yovano is sitting there
In the stone bar
And his hands (are) down on the table
And his face in his hands
His face in his hands
In the stone bar.
And what are you thinking?
What are you thinking, Yovano?
Have you a thought of marriage?
Have you a thought of eloping?
Oh, I have no thought of marriage
I have no thought of eloping
I have a thought of drinking
In the stone bar,
Bar, bar of stone
Bar of stone
There is a marble table
In the bar of stone.

(Composed by Jimmie Mitchel, c.1962, in Montreal, and heard from Canadian-Kalderash at a group gathering in 2001.)

The broken home (a Canadian-Kalderash song using the past tense)

This was composed to the melody of the Aria from *Madame Butterfly* after this film (released 1932) became popular. It was still going strong in the 1960s and is still sung by many older Canadian-Kalderash.

Sóstar, brey, tu man dilyardyan
Múrre sháven chorrárdyan
Múrro kher pharrádyan
Óide me merav,
Te na pharruvav*
Óide me merav
Te na pharruvav.
Xúli, Dévla, hai dikh so si míla
Hai dikh so si zhávo
Hai so si kíno
Óide me merav
Te na pharruvav
Óide me merav
Te na pharruvav.
Tu gêlyantar
La kurvása nashlántar
Múrro yílo pharrádyan
Múrre sháven chorrárdyan
Óide me merav
Te na pharruvav
Óide me merav
Te na pharruvav.

Translation

Why, man, did you make a fool of me?
Pauperize my children?
Destroy my home?
Oh, I will die
May I not disintegrate. [twice]
Descend, God, and see what is pity
What is sorrow

---

*   **parruv** 'blow up, explode, disintegrate, burst apart' (intransitive verb).

What is torment
Oh I will die
May I not disintegrate. [twice]
You took off
You eloped with the bitch
You broke my heart
You pauperized my children
Oh, I will die
May I not disintegrate. [twice]

The song is about a man whose wife was stolen by another man and he is left with his children and a broken home. There were many versions of this song and this one was popular in the early 1960s in Montreal when I and other young Roma would gather to play music. Note the stress accents which are typical in Romani songs.

Answers to the written exercise in this lesson

1. **Kon gilabadyas nêg lêste?**
2. **Pokindem lêske o kasht**
3. **Shindyas pêsko nai kána kerdyas buki ánde fábrika**
4. **Chi prindjardyam lêngi shib**
5. **Amáre wortácha marde le choren**

Lesson eight

Word list*

anrro	egg (plural **anrre**)
bishtrel	he forgets (past **bishterdyas** 'he forgot')
buzno	goat (plural **buzne**)
chirikli	female bird (plural **chiriklya**)
gáta	ready, finished, completed (**o chai si gáta** 'the tea is ready')
hakyarel	he understands (past **hakyardyas** 'he understood')
khil (m.)	butter (in the US butter is **báda**)
kiral (m.)	cheese
kodo	that (thing, object if masculine)
kodya	that (thing, object if feminine)
lônd (m.)	salt
mai yêkh dáta	one more time, once more
mai	more
mato	drunk, intoxicated
nashavel	he makes to run, stampedes (past **nashadyas** 'he stampeded')
nasvalo	ill
sábiya	sword, sabre (plural **sábiyi**)
shon (m.)	month, moon
xasarel	he loses (past **xasardyas** 'he lost')
yêkh mai	one more

A review of the past tense

Study the following past tense forms:

asal	he laughs	**asaiyas**	he laughed
zhanel	he knows	**zhanglas**	he knew
lazhal	he is ashamed	**lazháilo**	he was ashamed (note stress here)

*   About twenty common words and verb forms are listed in each lesson but it is recommended that the serious student of Romani should buy one of the dictionaries listed in the Bibliography.

merel	he dies	**mulo**	he died
phandel	he shuts	**phanglo**	he shut, has shut
rovel	he cries	**ruyas**	he cried
sovel	he sleeps	**sutyas**	he slept

There are also a few verbs where the 'they' form of the past tense takes an unexpected turn:

lel	he takes	**lem**	I took	**line**	they took
del	he gives	**dem**	I gave	**dine**	they gave

These two follow the model given below:

lem	I took
lyan	you took
lyas	he took
lyam	we took
lyan	you took
line	they took

Survey of verb types with paradigms

Do not attempt to memorize all these paradigms (models) as part of this lesson. They should simply be referred to when necessary.

Thematic verbs

For the purpose of this course, without going into detailed grammatical explanations, Romani verbs can be divided into the following categories. The verb stems are listed here without conjugations as **av-** 'come' or **darav-** 'frighten'. The conjugated tenses in the present and past are in the third person singular.

(1) Primary verbs

These can be transitive or intransitive depending on whether they take an object. Examples:

Beshel pashal e filástra	He is sitting close to the window (intransitive)
Daral	He fears, he is afraid (intransitive)
Daral o rrongyáto	He fears the thunder (transitive)

Primary verbs have, as a rule, only one syllable and no suffix. A few have only an initial consonant like **d-** 'give' or **zh-** 'go'. Typical are the following:

Verb stem	Present tense	Past tense
av- come	**avel** he/she comes	**avilo/avili** he/she came
besh- sit	**beshel** he/she sits	**beshlas** he/she sat
dar- fear	**daral** he/she fears	**daráilo/daráili** he/she feared
kin- buy	**kinel** he/she buys	**kindyas** he/she bought
sov- sleep	**sovel** he/she sleeps	**sutilo/sutili** he/she slept
zh- go	**zhal** he/she goes	**gêló/gêlí** he/she went

A few have two syllables but no suffix:

bikin- sell	**bikinel** he/she sells	**bikindyas**	he/she sold
gilab- sing	**gilabal** he/she sings	**gilabadyas**	he/she sang

These are the most difficult verbs to deal with because their past tenses cannot be predicted. (They were explained in detail in Lesson seven.)

(2) Causative verbs

Causative verbs are formed from primary verbs by the addition of the suffix **< av >**. Some are formed from primary verbs which have now been lost. They are called causative verbs because they cause something to take place, *to cause* to be afraid by frightening or *to cause* to learn by teaching etc.

The causative verb **darav-** 'frighten' is formed from the primary verb **dar-** 'fear' plus the suffix **< av >** and many other causative verbs are formed like this. Causative verbs are usually transitive but some can be used absolutely (without an object).

Typical formation of causative verbs:

Primary verb	Causative verb
bash- sound	**bashav-** cause to sound, play music
bil- melt	**bilav-** smelter
per- fall	**perav-** cause to fall, knock down
phag- break	**pharrav-** smash into pieces
phand- close	**phandav-** enclose, arrest
shin- cut	**shinav-** cut up, divide into pieces
sik- learn	**sikav-** teach

Causative verbs can also be formed from nouns. Examples:

drab (m.) 'drug, herb' gives a causative verb in **drabar-** which originally meant to practise herbal medicine but now means to do readings for clients
araki 'last night, yesterday' gives a causative verb in **arakyar-** 'stay overnight'

Causative paradigms

Verb stem	Present tense	Past tense
darav- frighten, scare	**daravel** he/she frightened	**daradyas** he/she frightened
garav- conceal	**garavel** he/she conceals	**garadyas** he/she concealed
sikav- teach, show	**sikavel** he/she teaches, shows	**sikadyas** he/she taught, showed
drabar- read	**drabarel** he/she reads	**drabardyas** he/she read
arakyar- stay overnight	**arakyarel** he/she stays overnight	**arakyardyas** he/she stayed overnight

As can be seen here, the past tense is regularly formed with **< dyas >** and the conjugation is as follows:

pharrav- 'smash, destroy'

I	**pharravav**	**pharradem**
you	**pharraves**	**pharradyan**
he/she	**pharravel**	**pharradyas**
we	**pharravas**	**pharradyam**
you	**pharraven**	**pharradyan**
they	**pharraven**	**pharrade**

(3) Denominative verbs

These are simply causative verbs that are formed from adjectives with the suffix **< yar >**. They are all transitive but some can be used absolutely.

Taking the adjective **parno** 'white', this can become a denominative verb in **parnyar-** 'whiten, whitewash':

parnyar- whiten	**parnyarel** he/she whitens	**parnyardyas** he/she whitened
lolyar- redden, to make blush	**loyarel** he/she reddens	**lolyardyas** he/she reddened

Again, the past tense conjugations are regular and predictable. The conjugation paradigm is as follows:

dilyar- 'make crazy'

I	**dilyarav**	**dilyardem**
you	**dilyares**	**dilyardyan**
he/she	**dilyarel**	**dilyardyas**
we	**dilyaras**	**dilyardyam**
you	**dilyaren**	**dilyardyan**
they	**dilyaren**	**dilyarde**

(4) Inchoative and passive verbs

Inchoative and passive verbs are intransitive and are formed from nouns, the past participles of verbs and from adjectives. There are two third person past tense conjugations for these verbs. See Lesson nine for a fuller explanation and paradigms of the inchoative and passive verbs .

From adjectives:

a) **bar-** 'grow' from the adjective **baro** 'big'

bar-   **baryol** he/she grows   **barilo/barili** he/she grew

b) **dil-** 'become senile' from the adjective **dilo** 'foolish, silly'

dil-   **dilyol** he/she becomes senile   **diláilo/deláili** he/she became senile

From past participles:

mudard- 'to be killed' from **mudardo**, the past participle of **mudar-** denominative verb 'kill'

mudard-   **mudárdyol** he/she is killed   **mudárdyilo/mudárdyili** he/she is killed

From nouns:

bêng 'devil' gives **bêngávol** 'he goes into a fit, becomes possessed by devils'
xoli 'anger' gives **xolyávol** 'he becomes angry'

Many of these verbs formed from adjectives have a denominative equivalent:

kalyol 'he becomes black'   **kalyarel** 'he makes black'
dilyol 'he becomes silly'   **dilyarel** 'he makes crazy'
baryol 'he becomes bigger'   **baryarel** 'he makes bigger, increases'

Here are a few couplets of inchoative and transitive verb equivalents in the third person singular of the present and past tenses:

Inchoative/passive (intransitive)	Causative/denominative (transitive)	
bangyol/bangilo become bent	**bangyarel/bangyardyas**	bend, make bent
bêngávol/bêngáilo have a fit	**bêngyarél/bêngyardyás**	induce a fit
dilyol/diláilo go senile, silly	**dilyarel/dilyardyas**	make crazy
lolyol/lolilo blush, go red	**lolyarel/lolyardyas**	embarrass, make red
xasáwol/xasáilo become lost	**xasarel/xasardyas**	lose, waste

(5) Athematic verbs

These have been defined in Lesson three and paradigms are given for transitive and reflexive forms in Lesson twelve. Their conjugations are regular and predictable.

Included here is a list of the most commonly used athematic verbs since few appear in the lessons and in the reading material. Those which are reflexive only are indicated by the reflexive pronoun **< -pe >** in the third person singular. Those without this are transitive but many of these can become reflexive when used intransitively (without a direct object) by using the reflexive personal pronouns.

The past participles of these verbs, which also serve as adjectives, are formed regularly in **< me >**: **ansuril** gives **ansurime**, **ansuchil** gives **ansuchime** and **volil** gives **volime**. Their abstract nouns are regularly formed in **< mos >**: **ansurimos** 'marriage' (for a man), **ansuchimos** 'confusion' and **volimos** 'love'.

Athematic verbs ending in **< il >**:

âmpôchíl-pe	he reconciles
ankolil	he is surrounding, encircling
ansuchil	he is confusing
ansuchil-pe	he is becoming confused
ansuril	he marries (a son)
ansuril-pe	he gets married (a man)
badil	he annoys, bothers
barrudil	he blows up, detonates
branil-pe	he objects
buntayil-pe	he is agitating, rioting, making trouble
chôgníl	he whips
chokanil	he hammers (as in hammered brass)
chuplil	he pinches, pecks
dashtil-pe	he is able to

divizil	he divides
drunchêníl	he shakes, rattles
dubil-pe	he wins
duchil-pe	he is taking a shower
dushil	he milks (a cow etc.)
farmakuyil	he enchants, bewitches
feril	he protects
frumentil	he kneads
frumentil-pe	it is fermenting
galbonil-pe	he is turning yellow, jaundiced
gêtíl-pe	he is getting ready
gichil-pe	he is guessing
gindil	he thinks
gindil-pe	he is thinking
gonil	he chases away, ostracises
gulayil-pe	he is having a good time, enjoying himself
gustil	he tastes
hamil	he is confusing, mixing up
hamil-pe	he meddles
hodêníl-pe	he rests, relaxes
kamfuzil	he slanders
kinowil	he tortures, torments
konchayil	he concludes
koshtil	it costs
krisil	he judges
kuchiyil-pe	she sways, shimmies, shakes
kununil	he marries
kununil-pe	he gets married
kurtilil	he sets free, liberates, gets rid of
kurtilil-pe	he escapes, sets himself free, gets rid of
lewudil	he praises, lauds
lichil	he cures
limbutsil-pe	he lisps
lipil	he sticks, pastes
logodil	he proposes
lopuntsil	he hobbles (a horse)
maril	she defiles
marmuril	he amazes, astonishes
mêritíl	he deserves

mirishil	he sniffs, smells
mishkil-pe	he moves, jiggles, wiggles
mituvil	he bribes
mômíl	he baits, lays bait
môritíl	he marries (a daughter)
môritíl-pe	she gets married (a woman)
mukil-pe	he moves, relocates
musaiyil	he compels
nashtil-pe	he cannot do it, it cannot be done
nayisil	he thanks
notil-pe	he swims
otêshíl	he lulls
pakil	he respects, pays respect, honours
parruwil	he compares
pelsuyil	he vaccinates, injects
peril-pe	he gets scalded
plevil	he launches
plevil-pe	it floats, drifts
plugil	he ploughs
pochitayil	he pays respect, honours
pomenil	he arouses, wakens
pomenil-pe	he wakes up, rouses himself
porril	he tattles
prekazhil	he jinxes
prêpêdíl	he destroys, ruins
prishkil	he sprays, hoses down
probil	he proves
pûkêlíl	he pollutes, disgraces
pûkêlíl-pe	he becomes polluted, disgraces himself
pushkil	he shoots
pustil	he abandons
rranil	he wounds
rranil-pe	he becomes wounded
rimol	he spoils, makes a mess of
rimol-pe	it is going bad, spoiling
rinil	he files (in metalwork)
rrêspundíl-pe	he acts like a cry-baby (whining tot)
rrugil-pe	he prays, beseeches
rrûspíl	he litters, scatters

ruzhenil-pe	it rusts, gets rusty
shpiwonil-pe	he spies (as in espionage)
shuril	he stabs
silowil	he rapes, plunders, loots
siyil	he plants, sows
skopil	he castrates
slavil	he feasts (a Saint)
slavil-pe	he is feasting
sluchayil-pe	it happens
sokotil	he calculates
sokotil-pe	he reckons, reasons
tavalil-pe	he rolls, tumbles
tolmachil	he translates, interprets
trayil	he lives
trayil-pe	it comes into existence
tsêgêtsíl-pe	he has the hiccups
tsipil-pe	he yells, shouts
tumnil	he betrothes
tumnil-pe	he becomes engaged
vakil-pe	he complains
vesolil	he makes happy
vorbil	he speaks, talks, converses
vôrrûtsíl	he hates
vuzheyil-pe	it wails, whistles, moans
wodil	he leads
wotrayil	he poisons
wurtsil	he brushes
wuzdil-pe	he trusts, has trust in
xashtil-pe	he yawns
xayil-pe	he is perishing, it is wilting
yêrtíl	he pardons, forgives
yêrtíl-pe	he is being forgiven
zabayil-pe	he lags behind, delays
zhalowil	he mourns
zhalowil-pe	he is in mourning
zumbil-pe	it is buzzing (as a bee)

Athematic verbs ending in **< ol >**:

The past participles of **< ol >** verbs regularly end in **< me >**: **angropol** gives

angropome, **hanol** gives **hanome** and **kegol** gives **kegome**. Their abstract nouns are formed ending in **< mos >**: **angropomos, hanomos** and **kegomos**.

There are fewer of these athematic verbs ending in **< ol >** and no new ones seem to be appearing. The following are the most useful:

angropol	he buries, inters
burchol-pe	it wrinkles, shrinks
bushol-pe	he is called
chitol	he reads
farbol	he paints
farbol-pe	she applies make-up
gindol-pe	he thinks
griyatsol	it disgusts
grizhol	he cleans up, tidies up
hanol	he plates, does wipe tinning*
kegol	it clots
kleyol	he glues, sticks
kretsol	she curls
lantsol	he chains
mârzól	it freezes
mârzól-pe	he is freezing
naiyol-pe	he swims
pavol-pe	it is icing up
ramol	he writes
skutsol	he sharpens
swatol	he swears, promises
swintol	he is sanctifying
swintol-pe	she is going through the menopause
têmnól-pe	it is getting dark, gloomy
tergol-pe	he deals, is a dealer in
tristol	he saddens
tristol-pe	he becomes sad

---

*   Wipe tinning is an American expression meaning to plate the interior of a copper mixing bowl (as used in bakeries) with tin. The copper bowl is heated with a propane gas torch and tin, in long pre-prepared strips, is melted onto the copper then smeared by the right hand, protected by an asbestos glove, all over the interior of the basin with a rag that has been daubed in sal ammoniac. This is a special Kalderash technique that is described in my autobiographical novel *Goddam Gypsy*, Tundra Books, 1971, pp.21–2.

tserkol	she weans
tumpol	he blunts, dulls the edge of
wortol	he straightens out
wortol-pe	it is being straightened out

The ablative case

The ablative case takes the endings **< tar >** (singular) and **< dar >** (plural) which are suffixed to the oblique stem of nouns. It is used to express 'from' and 'away from':

raklêstar	from the boy	**raklêndar**	from the boys
raklyátar	from the girl	**raklyándar**	from the girls
le kherêstar	from the house	**le kherêndar**	from the houses
molátar	from the wine	**molándar**	from the wines

Personal pronouns in the ablative case

mándar	from me	**So manges mándar?**	What do you want from me?
tútar	from you	**Lem lês tútar**	I took it from you
lêstar	from him	**Ashundem lêstar**	I heard from him
látar	from her	**Le lês látar!**	Take it away from her!
pêstar	from himself/ herself		
amêndar	from us	**Zha amêndar**	Get (go) away from us
tumêndar	from you	**Lem lil tumêndar**	I got a letter from you (plural)
lêndar	from them	**Manglas love lêndar**	He asked for money from them
pêndar	from themselves		
kástar	from whom	**Kástar lyan kodya?**	From whom did you get that?

Examples with personal pronouns

Lyas lês mándar	He took it from me

Chi ashundem tútar do mult	I haven't heard from you for a while
So mangel látar?	What does he want from her?
Chi lel khánchi mándar	He'll get nothing from me

Examples with nouns

Gêló le kherêstar	He went from the house
Ashundem Le Rromêndar	I heard from the Roma
Lyas lês la raklyátar	He took it from the girl

It is also used with a small number of verbs as shown below:

Izdral darátar	He is trembling from fear
Mulo darátar	He died from fear
Pushel mándar	He asks me (he asked from me)
Rrugiv Devlêstar	I beseech from God
Te yertil lês le Devlêstar	May God forgive him (may he be forgiven by God)

It is used in certain expressions:

Wo si Rrôm amarêndar	He is one of ours (our Roma)
Wo sas dinó-Devlêstar*	He was smitten by God (born mentally-challenged)
Chorromos si. E gêrí sas diní-Devlêstar	It's a pity. The poor girl was smitten by God

It is also used to form comparisons:

Me sim mai barvalo lêstar	I am richer than him
Si lês mai but love mándar	He has more money than I do

The preposition **katar** can also be used instead of the ablative case in the following examples:

katar o kher	from the house
Avilyas katar e Ivrópa	He came from Europe
Katar aves?	Where do you come from (from where do you come)?
Lem lês katar múrro dad	I got it from my father

---

*   This is a compound adjective, not a verbal construction.

Verbs of motion

The use of the suffix < **tar** > with verbs of motion is not the ablative case. It is included here to make this clear. For example, **zhav** 'I go' and **zhávtar** 'I go away, depart' or **nashav** 'I run' and **nasHávtar** 'I flee, run away'.

Examples

Akushlas man thai gêlèmtar	He insulted me and I went away (departed)
Nashêntar katar e pêrsekútsiya	They are fleeing (running away from) persecution
Nashlótar múrra shása	He eloped with my daughter
Zháltar o djédjêsh	The train is departing
Zhátar!	Depart, remove yourself!
Zhávtar ánde vakántsiya	I am going away for a holiday

When this suffix is used with verbs of motion the third person plural of the past tense is sometimes different from the regular conjugation in stressed < **é** >:

nashle	they ran	**nashlêntar**	they ran away, fled
gêlé	they went	**gêlèntar**	they departed

The masculine and feminine singular endings in < **ó** > and < **í** > of the past tense do not change:

gêló	he went	**gêlótar**	he departed
gêlí	she went	**gêlítar**	she departed

Other verbs which behave like this are:

avilêntar	they came out from, emerged from
nakhlêntar	they passed through, got through
pelêntar	they fell from
phirdêntar	they walked away
têlyardèntar	they departed
tradinêntar	they drove off

Examples

Avilêntar kátar o wêrsh	They came out from the forest
Nakhlêntar pa e gránitsa	They got (passed) through the border
Pelêntar dur-tele* ánde grápa	They fell deep into the pit

*   **dur-tele** 'far down, deep'.

Têlyardèntar rano ánde diminyátsa   They departed early in the morning
Tradinêntar ándo mobíli   They drove off in the car

More numbers (continued from Lesson six)

11. **desh-u-yêkh**
12. **desh-u-dui** (and so on to 16)
17. **desh-ifta**
18. **desh-uxto**
19. **desh-inya**
20. **bish**
21. **bish-tha-yêkh** (and so on to 29)
30. **triyánda**
31. **triyánda-tha-yêkh** (and so on 39)
40. **shtar-war-desh**
50. **pínda** and **pansh-war-desh**
51. **pínda-tha-yêkh** and **pansh-war-desh tha yêkh** (and so on to 59)
60. **shó-war-desh**
70. **hífta-war-desh**
80. **oxtó-war-desh**
90. **inyá-war-desh**
99. **inyá-var-desh-tha-inya**
100. **shêl**
200. **dui shêlá**
1,000. **mil** and **miya**
2,000. **dui mil** and **dui míyi**
1,000,000. **miliyóno**
2,000,000. **dui miliyónurya** or **dui milivóya**
A trillion. **yêkh triliyóno** (plural **triliyónurya**)

Notice that **< u >** is used to join the numbers 11 to 19 and **< tha >** those from 21 upwards, however, some speakers do say **desh-tha-yêkh** instead of **desh-u-yêkh**.

Written exercises

I.   Write out the numbers 18, 65 and 400.
2.   Translate the following into English. It is the 23rd Psalm in Mateo Maximoff's version. This text is written in the Kalderash dialect spoken in Montreuil and in France in general so the spelling is somewhat influenced by

French spelling. I have edited the notes on the text in bold typeface to bring the spelling and meanings in line with the Romani in this course and some notes are given to cover forms not yet met in the lessons as well as new words.

E bish-tha-trito sálma

O Báro Del si múrro Pastúxo,
chi trubul man khántchi.
Thol man te beshav ánde le zéleya char
Ningerel man ka l' paiya kai chi buntuyin-pe
Lel sáma katar múrro dúxo.
Ningerel man ánde le vúrmi chachimáske pála lêsko anav.
Kána phirav ánde e usalin le merimáski,
nai mánge dar katar chi yêkh nasulimos, ke tu san mánsa.
Tyiri rovli (h)ai tyíri rrai len sáma mándar.
Thos ángla mánde yêkh skafidi ángla múrre dushmáya,
tu makhes vuloiyésa múrro shoro
(h)ai múrro taxtáno del opral,
(h)ai beshava ándo kher le Báre Devlêsko
jikin avéna man diésa.*

Translation

The Great God is my herdsman (cowboy)
I don't need anything
He places me that I sit on the green grass

*   **Notes: Del** 'God', **o pastúxo** 'shepherd' (**pastúxo** 'herdsman, cowboy' and **bakrári** or **chobáno** 'shepherd' would be better), **trubul man** 'I need (it lacks me)', **thol** 'he puts', **zéleno** 'green' (**zéleya** is strange here because it should be **zélene char** 'green grasses, pastures', **char** 'grass'), **ningerel** 'he leads', **dar** 'fear', **nasulimos** 'evil, badness', **mánsa** 'with me', **rovli** 'stick' (**ruvli**), **rai** 'rod' (**rrai**), **sáma** 'attention, care', **dushmáya** 'enemies' (**dushmáno** 'enemy'), **paiya** 'waters', **buntuyin pe** 'are troubled' (**buntuyin-pe** 'they riot, create a disturbance'), **vúrma** 'end', (**vúlma** 'pathway, path', **wúrma** means 'end', **ánde wúrma** 'in the end'), **chachimáske** 'of truth', **anav** 'name', **phirel** 'he walks', **usalin le merimáski** 'valley of death' (**e wushalin le merimáski** 'shadow of death'), **makhel** 'he spreads' (**makhel** 'he stains, smears'), **vuloiyésa** 'with kerosene' (**zêtinósa** 'with oil' would be better here, **wuloi** 'stove oil, kerosene'), **taxtáno** 'glass' (**taxdai** 'glass'), **del opral** 'overflows', **Devlêsko** 'of God', **jikin** 'until' (**zhêkùn** and **zhi-ka** 'till, until'), **diésa** 'days' (**gesa**).

He leads me to the waters that do not agitate
He takes care of my soul
He leads me in the paths of truth for the sake of his name
When I walk in the shadow of death
I have no fear from any evil, because you are with me
Your staff and your switch (cane) take care of me
You place before me a coffee table in front of my enemies
You smear my head with kerosene
And my glass overflows
And I will remain in the house of the Great God
Until all my days have come to me.

Reading exercises

A poem recorded from Waso Russel Demitro in Montreal, 1963, in Canadian-Kalderash:

Kána ánde kríchma zháva
Triné-rupêske mol kináva
Ternya Gazhya pásha mánde tháva
Triné-shêlé Gazhêndar chi daráva
Shtrángo ánde mol kingyaráva
Pe lêngo kálo mas maráva.*

Translation

When I go into the inn
I buy three silver coins' worth of wine
I take a young non-Romani woman next to me
I do not fear three hundred [non-Romani] men
I will soak a rope in the wine
and thrash their evil hides.

---

*   The long form of the present tense is used here which is usual in songs and poems. In the last line '**Pe lêngo kálo mas maráva** 'On their black (evil) flesh I will strike' there is a singular object in **lêngo kálo mas** instead of **lênge kále mas**. In Kalderash-Romani, this type of idiom is very common, for example, **Chungardav ándo lêngo mui** 'I spit in their face' (not faces), **Xav lêngo shoro** 'I will eat their head' (destroy them) or **Xan pêngo shoro** 'They are eating their own head' (destroying themselves).

Palechíno 'Song'

A Kalderash song from Canada and the US (also called "Gypsy Samba" by Roma):

Palechíno, me kamav tu	Palechino, I love you
Palechíno, me mangav tu	Palechino, I want you
Palechíno, nai ma love te dav	Palechino, I have no money to give you
Shey, shorríyo de mui kalíyo	Girl, dear girl, black-faced one
Sikav mánde de kolkorro	Show it to me alone
Shey, shorríyo de mui kalíyo	Girl, dear girl, black-faced one
Na shudav tut, Na phagav tut	I won't throw you down, I won't beat you
Nai ma love, thai mangav tut	I have no money, and I want you
Na sim Gázho, na pachyav tut	I am not a Gazho, I don't believe you
Shey	Girl
Palechíno, muiyangátar	Palechino, from your face
Kai si kále firangátar	That is a black curtain
Palechíno, dui kale yakha	Palechino, only two black eyes
Ándo sádo me dikhlem tu	I met you in the garden
Gádya míshto, nashadem tu	That was great, I made you elope
Che galbênsa, shey pherdem tu	I loaded you with your gold coins
Yo!	Oh!
Palechíno desh-uxto	Palechino, all of eighteen,
Kai le love kai chi lem yo?	Where's the money I never got?
Palechíno, me sim kolkorro	Palechino, I am all alone
Palechíno, shúkar státo	Palechino, your beautiful figure
Kai chordyan, shey, baro soldáto	That stole, girl, a big soldier
Palechíno, shúkar státo, shey.	Palechino, beautiful figure, girl.*

This was originally a Machwáya song made popular in Canada and the US by Singing Sam, aka Sammy Stevens. Some minor dialect differences from Machwanítska have been retained. The song now exists in many versions.

Proverbs

Na mukh o drôm o baro pála o tsíno
Don't leave the big road for (the) little (one)

* **Notes: Palechíno** is the vocative of the name **Palechína**, **shorríyo** is a contraction of **sheyorríyo** (vocative of **sheyorri** 'dear girl'), **na** negative particle replacing **chi** in Kalderash, **pachyav** for **pakyav** 'I believe'.

Na push tehára so te keres ages
Don't ask tomorrow what to do today

Nashti beshes pe mule grastêste
You can't ride on a dead horse

Mai mishto te aves o angluno mashkar le Rromênde nêg o paluno mashkar le Gazhênde
Better to be the first among the Roma than the last among the non-Roma

Chi pérel e phabai dur katar o kasht
The apple doesn't fall far from the tree (meaning 'like father to son or mother to daughter')

O grast kai xinel súmnakai chi kam-kines ándo vashári
You won't buy the horse that voids gold at a horse fair (meaning 'there are no miracles for sale')

Answers to questions in this lesson

18.	**deshu-uxto**
65.	**sho-war-desh-tha-pansh**
400.	**shtar shêlá**

Lesson nine

Word list

baxtalo	lucky
bokhalo	hungry
but	a lot, much, many
dilo	silly, foolish, mad
djédjêsh (m.)	train
gi (m.)	soul (also 'stomach' in some Vlax-Romani dialects)
ka l' pansh	at 5 o'clock (here **le** ('the' in the plural) has been contracted to **< l' >**. This is quite common in Kalderash-Romani, for exam ple, **Zhav ka l' Rromênde** 'I'm going to (visit) the Roma')
khántchi	nothing
kêrkó	bitter
khatênde	nowhere
kónik	no one, nobody
kuch	dear, expensive
maxrime	ritually unclean, defiled (pronounced **marime** in North America)
shilo	cold (in temperament, aloof; **shilo-yilêsko** 'cold hearted')
shudro	cold (temperature, opposite of hot)
shudrol	it grows cold (past **shudrilo)**
Sode?	How much?
Sodya?	How many?
sórro ges	all day
sórro ryáto	all night
stántsiya	station
tato	warm, hot
te	that, a conjunction used to join two verbs (**Mangav te zhav** 'I want to go (I want that I go)')'
than (m.)	place (also means 'bed' in North American-Kalderash)
them (m.)	country, land, kingdom, people*

* **them** also means people, especially Romani people in the local community, for example, **Motho l' themêske te aven kai sláva** 'Tell the people (all the Roma in town) to come to the feast'. Here **them** means 'people' as a singular collective noun. Note also there is no word in Romani for 'anybody' and this must be expressed by 'somebody' or 'nobody':

trushalo	thirsty
tsirra	a little
vésolo	happy
wárekai	somewhere
wárekon	somebody
wáreso	something
yába, ába	already, yet

The instrumental case

The instrumental case translates 'with' and 'by' in English. The ending **< sa >** is added to the oblique stem or **< a >** is added if the oblique stem already ends in **< s >**.

Personal pronouns in the instrumental case

mánsa	with me	**Háide mánsa**	Come with me
túsa	with you	**Zhav túsa**	I'll go with you
lêsa	with him	**Dem-dúma lêsa**	I spoke with him
pêsa	with himself/herself		
lása	with her	**Kheldem man lása**	I danced with her
amênsa	with us	**Beshel amênsa**	He is staying with us
tumênsa	with you	**So si tumênsa?**	What's wrong with you? (plural. Literally, 'What is there with you?')
lênsa	with them	**Gêlótar lênsa**	He went away with them
pêsa	with himself	**Del-dúma pêsa**	He is talking to (with) himself

Footnote * cont.

Chi dikhav kónik	I don't see anybody (nobody)
Zhanel wárekon?	Does anybody know? (somebody)

This is also true of 'anywhere' and so you must say 'somewhere' or 'nowhere':

Chi dikhlem lês khatênde	I didn't see him anywhere (nowhere)
Chi zhav khatênde	I am not going anywhere (nowhere)
Dikhlan lês wárekai?	Did you see him anywhere? (somewhere)
Warekai kai zhal, kerel béda	Anywhere he goes, he makes trouble

pênsa	with themselves	**Slavin-pe pênsa**	They celebrate among (with) themselves
sósa	with what?	**Sósa keres?**	With what will you do it?
kãsa	with whom?	**Kãsa zhas?**	With whom are you going?

The instrumental case endings are also added to the oblique stems of nouns, for example, **grastês** in the accusative (oblique stem) becomes **grastêsa** in the instrumental case and **grastên** becomes **grastênsa**:

(masculine singular)	**manushêsa**	with the man	**le manushêsa**
(feminine singular)	**raklyása**	with the girl	**la raklyása**
(masculine plural)	**grastênsa**	with the horses	**le grastênsa**
(feminine plural)	**raklyánsa**	with the girls	**le raklyánsa**

Examples

Róde borya le kanênsa, na le yakhênsa	Look for a bride with the ears, not with the eyes
Kon marel la sabiyása, merel la sabiyátar	He who fights with the sword dies by the sword
Dav-dúma le Rromane shavênsa	I am speaking to (with) the Romani boys

They are also used to indicate 'by' as the instrument of the action:

Avilo mobilêsa	He came by car
O skamin si kerdo wastênsa	The chair is handmade (made by hand)
Avile vôrdonènsa thai pûnrrènsa	They came by caravan and by foot

Athematic masculine nouns which end in an unstressed vowel like < o > and < a > often keep this vowel in the oblique stem. When in doubt, refer to the tables of oblique stems for animates and inanimates.

| **Avilem aroplanósa** | I came by air (oblique stem **aroplanos**) |
| **Dem-dúma le Stevósa** | I spoke to (with) Steve (oblique stem **Stevos**) |

Gêlém le Vanyása   I went with Ványa (oblique
                                        stem **Vanyas**)

Inchoative and passive verbs

(See also Lesson eight for the position of inchoative and passive verbs among verb types.)

(1) Verbs that are formed from adjectives to express 'become', 'get' and 'go' in English such as **dilyávov** 'I become crazy', **phuryávov** 'I get old' and **korryávov** 'I go blind'. The root form of the adjective is used as the stem of the verb to which the following verb endings are attached. There are often two forms for the present tense (shown separated by / below). Watch for stress accents which move around somewhat unpredictably. These verbs are intransitive.

	Present tense	Past tense	
to go crazy, get senile	**dilyávov**	**diláilem**	I went crazy
	dilyávos/dilyos	**diláilan**	you went crazy
	dilyávol/dilyol	**diláilo**	he went crazy
	dilyávol/dilyol	**diláili**	she went crazy
	dilyovas/dilyos	**diláilam**	we went crazy
	dilyávon/dilyon	**diláilan**	you went crazy
	dilyávon/dilyon	**diláile**	they went crazy

The imperative (command form) is **dílyo** (to one person) and **dílyon** (to more than one person).

(2) Another group is formed from the past participles of verbs which are also adjectives in Romani, for example **mudardo** 'killed', from **mudarel** 'he kills', which gives **mudárdyol** 'he gets killed'. Some others are **kingárdyol** 'he gets wet, soaked', **márdyol** 'he gets beaten' and **xasárdyol** 'he gets lost'.

	Present tense	Past tense	
to get (be) killed	**mudárdyovav**	**mudárdyilem**	I got killed
	mudárdyos	**mudárdyilan**	you got killed
	mudárdiol	**mudárdyilo**	he got killed
	mudárdyol	**mudárdyili**	she got killed
	mudárdyovas	**mudárdyilam**	we got killed
	mudárdyon	**mudárdyilan**	you got killed
	mudárdyon	**mudárdyile**	they got killed

The imperatives are **mudárdyo** (to one person) and **mudárdyon** (to more than one person).

(3) A third group is formed from nouns, for example, **xoli** 'anger' gives the following:

to become angry			
	xolyávov	**xolyáilem**	I got angry
	xolyávos/xolyos	**xolyáilan**	you got angry
	xolyávol/xolyol	**xolyáilo**	he got angry
	xolyávol/xolyol	**xolyáili**	she got angry
	xolyávos/xolyos	**xolyáilam**	we got angry
	xolyávon/xolyon	**xolyáilan**	you got angry
	xolyávon/xolyon	**xolyáile**	they got angry

The imperatives are **xolyáwo** (to one person) and **xolyáwon** (to more than one person).

Examples

Phurilo thai diláilo	He got old and senile
Xasárdyilem thai daráilem	I got lost and became afraid
Phandádyilo	He got arrested
Márdyilo	He got beaten up
Chikyáilo	He got covered in mud

Compare:

Sar phutérdyilo o wudar?	How did the door get opened? (passive verb)
Kon phuterdyas o wudar?	Who opened the door? (transitive verb)

In the first example, the door was opened by some unknown cause (by itself) while in the second, somebody deliberately opened it.

Also:

Xasárdyilo múrro grast	My horse got lost (inchoative verb)
Xasardyas pêske grastês	He lost his horse (transitive verb)

In some dialects, the verb **avav-avilem** 'to become' can be combined with adjectives to create expressions such as **Avel thulo** 'He is getting fat'. Often adjectives can be combined with verbs like 'take' or 'give' to express the same thing, for example, **Lem xoli pe múrre dadês** 'I got angry at my father'. This is done by some speakers of Kalderash in eastern Europe but it is not common in North America where the inchoative and passive verbs are used to a much greater extent. In North American-Kalderash, saying **Thulyol-Thulyáilo** 'He is getting fat/He got fat' and **Xolyáilem múrre dadêsa** 'I became angry with my father' would be more correct.

Verbal auxiliaries

Musai meaning 'must'

In Kalderash, the word **musai** is placed before a conjugated verb joined by the particle **te**:

Musai te sovav	I must sleep (I must that I sleep)
Musai te soves	You must sleep
Musai te sovel	He must sleep

Written exercise

Complete the above table with the 'we' and 'they' forms.

In a similar way 'can' and 'might' are translated by **shai:**

Shai dikhav lês	I might see him
Shai aves tu?	Can you come?

Nashti means 'cannot':

Nashti zhav túsa	I cannot go with you

Translate the following sentences into Romani:
1.   We cannot see our brother
2.   He can speak Romani

A modern song from the Balkans in Tsifte-Teli rhythm

La Rrômnyása me te lav
Ándo súno la dikhav
Le rakênsa na* sovav
Phen tu, Dévla, so te kérav?
Ai Rromale, Shavale [twice]
Me sim shávo, têrno shávo

*   In this Vlax-Romani dialect < **na** > again replaces < **chi** > as the negative particle.

Me sim, Dévla, kolkorro
Nai man, Dévla, Rrômniorrí
Kêrko yába múrro gi.
Ai Rromale, Shavale [twice].

Translation

The wife whom I shall marry [take]
I see her in a dream [in repeating dreams]
I don't sleep nights
You tell me, God,
What am I to do?
Oh Romani men, oh Romani boys
I am a youth, a young man
I am, God, alone
I have, God, no wife
My soul* is already bitter.
Oh Romani men, oh Romani boys.

Reading exercise

A horrific tale in the French-Kalderash dialect. The words in parentheses in italics are the variations of the words in the original text and they should be used with this course. I have met the late Mateo Maximoff, the Kalderash Rom who recited this original folk tale, and experienced no difficulty whatsoever communicating with him in Kalderash-Romani as presented in this course. His dialect merely differs somewhat in pronunciation, the use of variant forms of words and in the use of French loan words.

Múrro vórro (*véro*) Vádya ningerdyas pêske trin grastên te bikinel lên ándo fóro baro. E ryat Vádya bikindyas don ánda pêske grast, gêló ándo o obêrzho te xal.
Kána o Vádya anklisto avri ánda o obêrzho, vúzhe ryat. Nashti dikhel mai but de dui metêra ángla pêste.
Kána anklel opre, o oberzhísto pushel lês: (*pushel lêstar* 'He asks from him') "Nakhes o pódo? De yêkh bêrsh sáko (*swáko*) kurko yêkh manush

---

* The word **gi** means both 'soul' and 'stomach' because the older generations of North American-Kalderash believed that the stomach was the seat of the soul.

xasávol wórta ka kudo pódo, o dyes *(ges)* le bazarêsko."
Gêló ándo obêrzho te xal.*

Translation

My cousin Vadya took his three horses to sell them in the big city. By evening, Vadya had sold two of his [own] horses, he went to the inn to eat.

When Vadya arrived outside the inn, it was night. He couldn't see more than two metres in front of himself.

When he comes out, the innkeeper asks him: "Are you crossing the bridge? Every week for a year, one man disappears at that bridge on market day."

He went into the inn to eat. [To be continued in Lesson ten]

Use of de and do

De and **do** are used to express time in Kalderash. Use **de** before numbers and words defining time:

Avilem khate de trin bêrsh	I came here three years ago
Beshlem khate de pansh ges	I have waited here (for) five days
Kerdyas buki de diminyátsa	He has worked since (the) morning

When used before the number 'one' **de** is often contracted to **< d' >**:

Mulo d'êkh kurko	He died a week ago

Do is used in the expression **do mult** 'a long time ago':

Mulas do mult	He died a long time ago

Answers to questions in this lesson

Musai-te sovas	We must sleep
Musai-te soven	They must sleep

1.   **(Ame) nashti dikhas amáre phralês**
2.   **(Wo) shai del-dúma Rromanes**

---

*   Notes: **vórro** 'cousin' (variant form of **véro**), **ningerdyas** 'he took out', **e ryat** 'by the evening', **don** 'two' (accusative and object of an action), **obêrzho** 'inn' (from French *auberge*), **avri** 'outside', **vúzhe** 'already', **mai but de** 'more than', **metêra** 'metres', **opre** 'on (the horse)', **obêrzhísto** 'innkeeper' (from French *aubergiste*), **o pódo** 'bridge', **de yêkh bêrsh** 'since a year ago', **xasávol vórta** 'disappears completely', **o dyes (ges) le bazarêsko** 'the day of the market'.

Lesson ten

Word list

avokáto	lawyer
ambrol (m.)	pear
angushtri (f.)	ring
aparáti (f.pl.)	tools, equipment
arakhel	he protects (past **arakhlas**)
azilánturya (m.pl.)	refugees, asylum seekers
baxt (f.)	luck
béda	trouble
búkfa	book
bukyárnichi (m.pl.)	workmen (singular **bukyárniko**)
dósta	enough
drabarel	she tells fortunes (gives readings), also to read (in Romania). (Past **drabardyas** 'she told fortunes')
djungalimos (m.)	ugliness, ugly conduct
dukhal	it hurts (**dukhal man o shoro** 'my head aches', past **dukháilo** 'it hurt')
fóro	city (plural **fóri** and **fórurya)**
Frantsuzítska	French (language)
ges (m.)	day
hanov	I plate, do wipe tinning, re-tin (past **hanosardem**)
Inglizítska	English (language)
kamfêti (f.pl.)	sweets, candy (also **bambóni**)
khamni	pregnant (**phari** in North America)
kiravel	he boils (past **kiradyas** 'he boiled')
kolompíra	potato
lámpa	lamp
makilem	I got drunk (present **makyovav** 'I get drunk')
morrel	he/she scrubs, rubs (past **morrdyas** 'he rubbed')
nashel	he/she runs (past **nashlo** 'he ran')
pekel	he/she bakes, cooks (past **peklas** 'he/she cooked')
perel	he falls (past **pelo** 'he fell')
phabai (f.)	apple (plural **phaba** 'apples')

pherel	he/she fills (past **pherdyas** 'he filled')
pômeníl	he arouses, wakes up, makes aware (past **pômenis-ardyás** if transitive)
porum (f.)	onion
rrâkíya	whisky
rúzho	red hot, burning
shax (m.)	cabbage
shib (f.)	tongue, language
shîl (f.)	cold, grippe
shîl mánge	I have a cold
shorr (m.)	beard
shudrimos (m.)	cold (opposite of heat)
shtrékya	strike, lucky strike
Shvedítska	Swedish (language)
sikavel	he shows, teaches
sláva	feast, especially a religious feast in honour of a Saint
te	that (as a conjunction), if (as a conjunction and function word)
tyára	plate (plural **tyêri**)
vítsa	clan, extended group of families usually descended from one male ancestor (Kalderash). Lovarítska equivalent is **tsêra** and other Vlax-Romani dialects have **rása** or some other word
vúni/wúni	some, a few
vryámya	time (plural **vrêmi**)

Verbal auxiliaries used with the past tense

In expressions like 'I had to' or 'I could not' the words **musai** and **nashti** must be combined with the verb and pronouns as follows:

Musai sas mánge te zhav	I had to go (I was obliged to go)
Musai sas lêske te pokinel	He had to pay
Musai-sas le Rrômèske te zháltar araki	The Rom had to leave (depart) last night

For expressions such as 'I could' or 'I was able to', use **shai** followed by the past form:

Shai dikhlem lês	I could see him, I was able to see him
Shai avile araki	They could have come yesterday

There is also a verb **dasht-** meaning 'to be able to', which can be used to express certain idioms:

Dashtiv te hakyarav Franzuzítska	I am able to understand French
Chi dashtisardem te hakyarav lês	I was not able to understand him (couldn't understand him)
Chi dashtisáilo	He was not able to (intransitive form)

Shai can be combined with < **-vi** > to mean 'perhaps' or 'maybe':

Shai-vi te mulo	Perhaps he died (he may have died)
Aves ka o djuléshi tehára?	Are you coming to the meeting tomorrow?
Shai-vi. Chi zhanav inkya	Perhaps. I don't know yet

Nashti translates as 'could not' or 'was not able to', which can be used as shown below:

Nashti sas lêske te dikhel man	He could not see me (it was impossible for him that he sees me)
Nashti sas mánge te kerav buki	I could not work (it was impossible for me that I work)

There is also a verb **nasht-** which can be used like **dasht-**:

Nashtiv te avav	I am not able to come (can't come)
Nashtisardem te avav	I was not able to come (couldn't come)
Nashtisardyas te pekel o xabe	She wasn't able to cook the food
Shai hanos avtsûn kai chi mai ruzhenil-pe*?	Can you plate stainless steel?
Nashtil-pe (nashtil-pês)	It can't be done (you can't do it)
Hanov	I plate, I do wipe tinning
Hanov basûni	I re-tin mixing bowls

To translate English expressions like 'I was supposed to go yesterday' the verb 'to be' is used as follows:

Símas te zhav araki	I was supposed to go yesterday

---

*   Idiom: **avtsûn kai chi mai ruzhinil-pe** 'steel that never rusts' i.e. stainless steel.

O Yánko si te avel tehára	Yanko is supposed to come tomorrow
Sam te kinas o xabe	We are supposed to buy the food
Le shave si te bashaven ánde sláva	The boys are supposed to play music at the feast
Won sas te ingaren ma ándo mobíli	They were supposed to drive me in the car

Other meanings of te in Romani

As a conjunction meaning 'if':

Pushlas mándar te shai zhav lêsa	He asked me if I can go with him
Te si lês mobíli, shai ingarel man	If he has a car he can drive me
Te aves mánsa sikavav túke o kher	If you come with me I'll show you the house
Te zhal kothe dikhel pêske	If he goes there he'll see for himself
So keras te na avel?	What do we do if he doesn't come?

As an optative particle to express a wish:

Te del o brêshùn!	May it rain!
Te del o Del!	May God grant it (be so)!
Te del o Del mánge baxt!	May God grant me luck!

The verb **del** 'he gives' is used with nouns to create compound verbs which translate English verbs like 'to rain' and 'to snow'. (For compound verbs see Lesson twelve.)

Del o brêshùn	It gives rain (it is raining)
Del o iv	It gives snow (it is snowing)
Dav paiya ánda mánde	I am sweating (giving water from me)

Demonstrative adjectives

Learn the following words. You are advised to learn them as in the second or third column (together with a noun):

this	(m.)	kako	kako raklo, kako kher
	(f.)	kakya	kakya rakli, kakya lámpa
these	(m.)	kakale	kakale rakle, kakale khera
	(f.)	kakala	kakala raklya, kakala lámpi
that	(m.)	kodo	kodo Rrôm, kodo lil

	(f.)	kodya	kodya Rrômní, kodya shib
those	(m.)	kodole	kodole Rroma, kodole lila
	(f.)	kodola	kodola Rrômnyá, kodola shiba
that	(m.)	kuko	kuko them, kuko fóro
	(f.)	kukya	kukya vryámya
those	(m.)	kukole	kukole gesa
	(f.)	kukola	kukola vrémi (those times)

The difference between **kodo** and **kuko** is that **kodo** means 'that' when the thing is close, as in 'that one there', while **kuko** means 'that one way over there, yonder'. If a person was living in Montreal, Canada, he or she could say **Kodo fóro, o Târánto, si báro fóro numa kuko fóro, o Los Ángêliz, si mai báro fóro** 'That city, Toronto, is a big city, but that city, Los Angeles, is a bigger city' because Los Angeles is much further away from Montreal than Toronto. **Kuko** is also used to describe people, events or time in the past: **Kuko mursh, o Napoleóno, sas o Emperáto le Franzuzôsko** 'That man, Napoleon, was the Emperor of France'.

These demonstrative adjectives can also be used as nouns and given case endings like other nouns:

So si kako?	What is this thing?
Kon si kako?	Who is this man?
Kamav te phiravav tsáliya kodolêndar	I want to wear clothes like those
Ashundem kodya kakalêstar	I heard that from this man
Mai diklan kodya?	Did you ever (**mai**) see anything like that?
Wázdav motsyúne te azhutis kakalêske	I raise a motion that we assist this man
Pála kódo woi mukhlas lês	That's why she left him (because of that she left him)

The demonstrative adjectives can also be used as follows:

Kerav lês kakya	I do it this way, like this
Pála kodya gêlótar	Because of that, he departed
Mai ashundyan kodya?	Did you ever hear anything like that?

Continuous past tense (also called the imperfect tense)

There is a second set of conjugations for actions in the past. They are used when the action was repeated or continued for a long time, like in English 'I used to work in a factory' or 'I was working all day'.

Compare:

Mardyas le zhuklês   He beat the dog (ordinary past)
Marélas le zhuklês swáko ges   He beat the dog every day (continuous past)

To form the continuous past of a word, add **< as >** to the form used in the present tense:

me sovávas   I slept, used to sleep, was sleeping
tu sovésas   you slept, used to sleep, were sleeping
wo sovélas   he/she slept, used to sleep, was sleeping
ame sovásas   we slept, used to sleep, were sleeping
tume sovénas   you slept, used to sleep, were sleeping
won sovénas   they slept, used to sleep, were sleeping

Examples

Kerélas buki ánde fábrika   He used to work in a factory
Woi asálas kána arakhlem la   She was smiling when I met her
Kerávas buki sórro ges   I worked (was working) all day
Kerélas buki sórro ges   He has been working all day
Bashavélas e gitára do mult   He has been playing the guitar (for) a long time
Farbólas o kher de diminyátsa   He has been painting the house since (the) morning
Drabarélas ánde ófisa de desh chásurya She has been telling fortunes in the office (for) ten hours

Possession

Look back at Lesson four and revise how to say 'I have' etc. Now look at these examples of the past:

sas man   I had/used to have
nas man   I had not/I didn't used to have
nas tut   you had not
sas man búkfa   I had a book/used to have a book
sas tut dui lámpi you had two lamps/used to have two lamps
nas lês love   he had no money

Further examples

O Yánko nas lês mobíli te zhal kai sláva	Yanko had no car to go to the feast
O Stévo nas lês vryámya te kerel e buki	Steve had no time to do the work
Le bukyárnichi nas lên dósta aparáti	The workmen didn't have enough tools
Le shavorre nas lên love te kinen kamfêti	The youngsters had no money to buy candy
Le azilánturya nas lên zhutóri te del lênge swáto*	The refugees had no lawyer to represent them

Folk tale (continued from Lesson nine)

O Vádya asayas.
Phendyas, "Ma (na) dara ánda mánde" (h)ai gêló pêsko drôm.
Areslo kai pai.
Vúni minútsi pála kodya, o Vádya dikhlyas o pódo.
Asayas radóstar.
Kána sas mashkaral, e zhigánya xutlyas.
Dikhlyas e diéla (djéla) ángla lêste, yêkh manush, kadya baro, lêsko shero
    xasávol ándo kalipe (kalimos),
phandavel lêsko drôm.
O Vádya amboldyas le grastês.
Pe kodya rêg o baro manush phandavélas vi lêsko drôm.
Pála pêsko baripe (barimos) shai te nashel zurales.
Tsipil pe pêsko zhukel, "Bólo, le lês!"
O lasho zhukel nashlo (h)ai xutlyas (xuklo) po baro manush.
O Vádya dyas ándo pêsko gras(t) (h)ai areslo kai phuv.
Tsirra vryámya pála kodya o Vádya areslo ándo gav.
O grast chi kamélas te zhal mai angle. Musai-sas (lêske) te beshel kothe.
Dikhlyas yêkh kher. Mardyas ándo vudar. Kónik chi dyas anglal. O Vádya
    dyas andre.
Kothe aver daripe (darimos) ángla lêste. Ánde yêkh groposhévo yêkh
    mulo andre.

---

*   Te del lênge swáto 'to present (give) word for them, represent them' (del swáto is a
     compound verb).

Pe swáko rig yêkh bari mômelí. O Vádya lyas tele pêski stadi, (*stagi*) lyas yêkh skamin te beshel.

O wudar putérdyol zurales (*h*)ai o baro mulo si anglal.

O Vádya beshel pe pêsko skamin darátar.

O mulo ándo groposhévo ushtel (*wushtyal*).

"So manges kate?" mothodyas o mulo ándo groposhévo.

"Kako manush si murro," mothodyas o mulo baro.

Antúnchi yêkh maripe (*marimos*) sas mashkar le dui mule, o maripe (*marimos*) nikerélas but, yêkh cháso, dui chásuri.

Kána dur yêkh kokósho gilabadyas, le dui mule avile won dui státuri (*státurya*).

Le dui státuri (*státurya*) phandavénas o wudar.

Kána le peyzánuri zhánas kai pêngi buti, dikhle kodya sodo diéla (*sórro djéla*).

O Vádya phenel sar nakhlyas e ryat. Kónik chi patyal (*pakyal*) lês, kána yêkh peizáno arakhel o státo le chorre Bolósko.

Le dui mule - praxosarde lên ánde mormúntsi. O Vádya beshlo nasvalo trin shon, antúnchi mulo darátar.*

The word **mulo** in the tale has been translated as 'dead man' but it could also mean 'ghost' in Maximoff's original (French *fantôme* 'ghost, spectre, phantom').

---

* **Notes: phenel** 'he/she says', **ma** another way of saying **na** 'don't', **ai** 'and' (usually **hai**), **areslo** 'reached', **vúni minútsi** 'some minutes', **pála kodya** 'after that, later', **radóstar** 'from pleasure (happily)', **mashkaral** 'in the middle', **zhigánya** 'creature, monster', **xutlyas** (**xuklas**) 'jumped up, reared up', **diéla** (another form of **djéla**) 'thing', **kadya** 'so', **kalipe** 'darkness', **phandavel** 'blocks', **amboldyas** 'turned', **rêg** 'side', **vi** 'also', **baripe** 'bigness (size)', **zurales** 'quickly', **tsipil** 'calls (yells)', **Bólo** dog's name, **del ándo** 'spurs on', **phuv** 'ground (at side of river)', **vryámya** 'time', **mai** 'more', **del anglal** 'replies, comes to the door', **del andre** 'goes in', **daripe** 'fearful thing', **groposhévo** 'coffin', **andre** 'inside', **mômêlí** 'candle', **tele** 'off (down)', **stadi** (**stagi**) 'hat', **putérdyol** 'opens', **anglal** 'in front (of the door)', **darátar** 'from fear', **ushtel** (**wushtyal**) 'gets up', **mothol** 'he/she speaks', **antúnchi** 'then'; **maripe** 'fight', **nikerel** 'lasts', **kokósho** 'rooster', **avile won** 'they became', **státuri** 'statues', **peizánuri** 'peasants' (this is from French and not used by Kalderash in other countries. In North American-Kalderash, peasant was xlópo in old folk tales with a plural of xlópurya and xlopáika with a plural of xlopáiki. The word still exists but today it now has more the meaning of 'redneck'.) **Buti** 'work' (**buki**), **sodo diela** (**sórro djéla**) 'the whole thing', **patial** (**pakyal**) 'believes', **Bolósko** Bolo's, **praxosarde** 'they buried', **mormúntsi** 'graves, graveyard'.

'Ghost' in Canadian-Kalderash is **choxãnó** and **mulo** means the corpse of a deceased man or 'dead man'. The physical actions of the **mulo** in this story are typical of those attributed to **choxãné** in North American-Kalderash folk tales. The word **mulo** does mean 'ghost' in many Vlax-Romani and non-Vlax-Romani dialects.

Translation

Vadya smiled.

He said, "Don't worry about me" and he went on his way.

He arrived at the water [river].

A few minutes after that, Vadya saw the bridge.

He smiled from pleasure.

When he was in the middle [of the bridge] the creature sprang.

He saw the monster in front of him, a man, so big, his head was lost is lost in the darkness.

It was blocking his way.

Vadya turned the horse around.

On that side the huge man was also blocking his way.

Because of his size he could run quickly.

He yelled at his dog, "Bolo, get him!"

The good dog ran and jumped on the huge man.

Vadya spurred his horse and arrived on land.

A little after that, Vadya arrived in the village.

The horse didn't want to go any further. He was obliged to remain there.

He saw a house. He knocked on the door. Nobody came forward. Vadya went in.

There, another frightening thing before him. Inside a coffin, a dead man inside.

On each side one large candle. Vadya took off his hat, he took a chair to sit down.

The door opens quickly and the huge man is before him.

Vadya sits on his chair from fear.

The corpse in the coffin stands up.

"What do you want here?" said the dead man in the coffin.

"This guy is mine", said the huge corpse.

Then there was a big fight between the two dead men, the fight carried on a long time, one hour, two hours.

When from afar, a cock crowed, the two dead men became statues.

The two statues were blocking the door.

When the country people were going to their work, they saw the whole thing.
Vadya tells how he passed the night. Nobody believes him. Now a peasant
finds the statue of the unfortunate Bolo.

The two dead men they buried in graves. Vadya remained ill for three months,
then he died from fear.

(Adapted from a tale by Mateo Maximoff which can be found in the *Journal of
the Gypsy Lore Society*.)

Kalderash table song from North America

I have heard this song in differing versions in Canada since the 1950s and on
cassette tapes made by American Rom. In the 1990s I heard it recorded in
Argentina and from Hungarian and Romanian Vlax-Romani refugees in Toronto
from 1999 through to 2003. I recorded it on tape from *Chachi Vorba*, a Hungarian *Lovari* music group, in 1999.

Áven mánde bai Rromále	Come to my place, Roma
Kai bári síniya kai me dáva	To the lavish table I am giving
Áven mánde bai Rromále	Come to my place, Roma
Te xása thai te piyása.	So that we eat and drink.
Óide márdem bári shtrékya	Oh, I made a big strike (run of good luck in business)
Bári shtrékya kai man baxtardyas	A big strike that has made me lucky
Áven mánde bai Rromále	Come to my place, Roma
Kai bári síniya kai me dáva.	To the lavish table I am giving.
Na akushen ma, na mudaren ma	Don't cuss me out, don't put me down
Brey, Rromále	Oh, Romani men
Na akushen ma, na akushen ma	Don't cuss me out, don't cuss me out
Shey, Sheyále	Oh, Romani girls (women)
Kai matílem me pe síniya	Because I got drunk at the table
Thai man daravéla, man daravéla	And it frightens me, frightens me
e rrâkíya.	the whisky.
Ói ánde mánde rúzho kolumpíra	Oh, there is a red-hot potato inside me
Thai phabarel la, phabarel la e rrâkíya	And the whisky is burning it up (repeat both lines)

Áide mêk te pômeníl swakonênge	Oh, let everybody wake up
Le slavorrênge thai le gostonênge	The hosts and the guests
Te arakhel amên, yoi Dévla	Oh, may God protect us
Bedátar thai djungalimástar.	From trouble and ugliness
	(disreputable behaviour).

This song is difficult to translate for readers not familiar with the Kalderash culture. The singer is saying that he has had a run of good luck in work and is celebrating by giving a feast for the community. However, some of the guests are jealous of his luck, get drunk and begin cursing him out of envy. He too has imbibed a fair amount and has a red-hot potato in his stomach which the whisky is revving up and he is trying to control his anger. He then says, "Let the hosts and the guests wake up and try to avoid trouble and strife" because, according to the Kalderash beliefs, profanity and violence at a feast can result in a jinx and a period of bad luck for the person giving the feast.

Table songs (**sinyáke gilya** or **misaláke gilya**) are traditional Romani songs that are sung when Roma get together for a feast, other gathering or when men meet to drink and talk. One man will sing a table song in honour of the others. Both men and women will sing at weddings, feasts and other occasions. The melodies and the themes remain constant but different singers often change the words to fit their own life situations. Usually, before singing a table song, the singer will announce **Pakiv tumênge, Rromále!** 'I honour you, Roma!'

Test paper on Lessons one to ten

(a) Translate into Romani:

1.	I will see you tomorrow in the town
2.	That Romani girl came with her young sister
3.	We were hungry because (ke) we hadn't any money and we couldn't buy food
4.	Are these caravans yours?
5.	Don't break the four plates on the table

(b) Write a letter to a friend describing some things you have done and are going to do and asking a few questions. Start the letter **phrála** or **phéyo** and end it **tíro phral** or **tíri phen**. Hopefully by this time you will know a fluent speaker of Kalderash-Romani who can then check it for you.

Answers to the test paper

1.	**Kam-dikhav tut tehára ándo fóro**
2.	**Kodya shey avili láka ternya phenyása**
3.	**Sámas bokhale kh' nas amên love thai nashti**
	kindyam xabe (or **nashtisardyam te kinas xabe**)
4.	**Kakale vôrdôná si tumáre?**
5.	**Na phag** (or **pharrav**) **le shtar tyêri pe shkafidi**

Phagav and pharravav

Phagav 'I break' means 'to break something in half, snap' while **pharravav** translates as 'I smash/shatter into pieces' which would be more appropriate for a plate. **Phagav** and **pharravav** are easily confused with certain other similar verbs so they are listed here:

phag-
phaghav-phaglem   I break (an arm or leg), snap (a twig)
                                 (transitive)

phagl-
pháglyovav-pháglilem   I get broken, snapped (passive)

pharrav-
pharravav-pharradem   I shatter, smash, demolish (transitive)

pharr-
pharruvav-pharrulem   I fall to pieces, disintegrate, explode
                                 (intransitive)

Present tense:	**pharruvav, pharros, pharrol, pharros,**
	pharron, pharron
Past tense:	**pharrulem, pharrulan, pharrulo, pharruli,**
	pharrulam, pharrulan, pharrule

pharrád-
pharrádyovav-pharrádyilem   I become shattered, broken apart
                                 (passive)

Present tense:	**pharrádyovav, pharrádyos, pharrádyol,**
	pharrádyos, pharrádyon, pharrádyon
Past tense:	**pharrádyilem, pharrádyilan, pharrádyilo,**
	pharrádyili, pharrádyilam, pharrádyilan,
	pharrádyile

parruv-
parruvav-parrudem   I trade, exchange, swap (transitive)

parrúd-
parrúdyovav-parrúdyilem   I become traded, exchanged, changed
                                         (passive)

Present tense: **parrúdyovav, parrúdyos, parrúdyol,**
                                         parrúdyos, parrúdyon, parrúdyon

Past tense: **parrúdyilem, parrúdyilan, parrúdyilo,**
                                         parrúdyili, parrúdyilam. parrúdyilan,
                                         parrúdyile

porrav – (1)
porravav-porradem   I rend asunder, split apart, rip to shreds,
                                         open wide (transitive)

porrav – (2)
porravav-porradem   I sexually excite, arouse, cause an erection
                                         (transitive)

porrád – (1)
porrádyovav-porrádyilem   I become rent, split apart, ripped to shreds,
                                         opened wide (passive)

porrad – (2)
porrádyovav-porrádyilem   I become sexually aroused (passive)

These verbs show the importance of differentiating the aspirated **< ph >** and the **< p >** sounds in Kalderash. With speakers in many countries whose pronunciation is not always clear to those familiar with North American-Kalderash, misunderstanding and confusion can easily occur.

Lesson eleven

Word list

bi-lasho	bad (opposite of **lasho** 'good')
cheran (f.)	star (plural **cheraiya** and **chera**)
chorel	he/she steals (past **chordyas**)
chorro	bad, poor, pitiful, inferior
daral	he/she fears, is afraid (past **daráilo**)
gad (m.)	shirt, blouse
guglo	sweet, fresh (**gúglo pai** 'fresh water')
ke	because (often contracted to **kh**. **Nashti zhav kh nai ma love** 'I can't go because I have no money')
langal	he/she limps (past **langáilo**)
makh (f.)	fly
mal (f.)	field (**níva** is more common in North America)
manush	person, human being, elderly man (formal)
mursh	man, guy, fellow (informal and not usually used to refer to Roma)
nasul (f.)	1) evil, misfortune (noun); 2) evil, bad (adjective)
phuv (f.)	earth, ground, soil
plapóno	quilt (traditionally stuffed with goose feathers, plural **plapóya**)
rovli (f.)	stick, staff (usually **ruvli** in North America)
sano	thin, fine, slender
sherand (m.)	pillow
sóstar	why
than (m.)	place, bed (in European dialects, bed is usually **páto**, plural **páturya**)
thol	he puts, places (past **thodyas**)
trobul	need, needs (this verb exists only in the third person singular of the present tense and the continuous past tense as **trobul** and **trobúlas** in North American-Kalderash)
vêska	because

Examples of trobul and trobúlas

Trobul man love	I need money (it lacks me money)
Trobul te zhav	I need to go
Sóde trobul amên?	How much do we need?
Trobúlas lês love	He needed money
Trobúlas mai but vryámya	More time was needed

Another similar verb:*

mol	it is worth	**mólas**	it was worth
mon	they are worth	**mónas**	they were worth

Sóde mol o mobíli?	How much is the car worth?
Chi móla khánchi	It's not worth anything
Chi móna chi yêkh rrûlyorrí	They aren't worth even a trifling amount (slang use of **rrûlyorrí** 'a miniscule fart')

A more advanced note on pronunciation

At the end of a word < b > is often pronounced as < p > so **shib** is often pronounced **ship**. Also < d >, < g >, < kh > and < v > sometimes change their pronunciation at the end of a word:

d is pronounced **t**:	**thud** becomes **thut**
	dad becomes **dat**
g is pronounced **k**:	**yag** becomes **yak**
kh is pronounced **k**:	**yakh** becomes **yak**
v is pronounced **f** or **w**:	**shov** becomes **shof**
	zhav becomes **zhaw**

It is of course best to write the words in the way they appear in this course, so the word pronounced 'ship' is written **shib** because then it can be recognized easily as the same word in **shiba** and **shibáke**, where < b > has its normal pronunciation.

It is important to note that words ending in < v > are subject to change. The final < v > in the first person singular of verbs (**me dikhav**) is often pronounced as a < w > sound, sometimes as a < f > sound but sometimes it is not pronounced at all. For example:

---

*   Some Kalderesh and other Vlax-Romani dialects have an inchoative verb derived from **mol** (f.) 'price, cost, worth' which means 'to be worth'.
Present tense: **Molyovav, molyos, molyol, molyovas, molyon, molyon**
Past tense: **Molilem, molilan, molilo/molili, molilam, molilan, molile**

Me dikhav is pronounced **Me dikhaw**   I see
Me zhav is pronounced **Me zhaw**   I go
Xalavav man is pronounced **Xalavá-ma**   I wash myself
Zháv-tar is pronounced **Zháf-tar**   I am going away

In many words ending in **< s >** the final **< s >** is not pronounced:

Trobul ma azhutimo   I need help (for **azhutimos**)

Some eastern European speakers replace **< s >** with **< h >** in the instrumental and other case endings:

Zha Devléha   Go with God (for **Devlésa**)

Past tense endings in **< as >** often drop the final **< s >**:

Kon kerdya kakya buki?   Who did this work? (for **kerdyas**)

Sound shifts between mutually intelligible dialects

In some dialects, the **< k >** sound in this course becomes **< ch >**, as shown below:

I am working (doing work)	English
Kerav buki	North American-Kalderash
Cherav buchi	North American-Machwanítska, Gurbeti, (Bosnia) and France

The **< g >** sound becomes **< dj >**:

I am buying flowers	English
Kinav lulugya	North American-Kalderash
Chinav luludja	North American-Machwanítska

In some Hungarian-Romani dialects (also spoken outside of Hungary), the **< l >** sound, when followed by a vowel or when coming between two vowels, can become a **< y >:**

North American-Kalderash	Hungarian-Kalderash	English
lúmiya	**yúma**	world
misáli	**misáyi**	table
Dilyardyas man	**Diyardyas man**	He made me crazy

In some Vlax-Romani dialects, the first person singular of the past tense differs from standard Kalderash. The other past tense endings remain the same.

phendem 'I said'   becomes **phendyom**
dikhlem 'I saw'   becomes **dikhlyom**

Metathesis (the transposition of two phonemes in a word, for instance, the words 'crud' (UK) and 'purty' (USA) are metatheses of 'curd' and 'pretty') can also occur in words in different dialects:

This course	Metathesis in some other dialects	English
manrro	**marrno**	bread
anrro	**arrno**	egg
arman	**amran**	curse
kónik	**níkon**	nobody
gôrmóniya	**grômóniya**	accordion

Other sound shifts also take place and are usually regular and predictable.

French-Kalderash

Since the cassette tape and booklet *Žanés Romanés?* by A. Barthélémy (listed in the Bibliography) may be used by those studying this course, some major differences in pronunciation should be pointed out here.

The **< k >** changes to **< ch >** in French-Kalderash when used before or between vowels:

Kai si kyo dad? becomes **Kai si chyo dad?**   Where is your father?
kerav buki becomes **kerav buchi**   I work
tsáliya bukyáke becomes **tsáliya bucháke**   working clothes
Khino sim becomes **Chino sim**   I am tired

The **< g >** can change to **< dj >** when used before or between vowels:

Bikinav lulugya becomes **Bichinav luludja**   I sell flowers

The **< ñ >** sound is not a consonant in this alphabet but is used here to indicate that a vowel before or after it should be pronounced through the nose like French. It most often occurs with the **< rr >** sound so is described under **< rr >** below. In some Kalderash-Romani words the **< n >** disappears, for example, **rani** 'lady' is pronounced in the US, Canada and France as **rañi**, which then sounds like **< ra-ee >** with the last vowel **< i >** pronounced through the nose. In **shib Rromani** the **< n >** can vanish and the **< i >** again is pronounced through the nose as **shib Rromañi**.

The sound < rr >

One thing to note when the guttural **< rr >** is used before the vowels **< e >** and **< i >** is that it can affect the pronunciation of these vowels so that **múrri** 'my, mine' becomes **múrrû** and **sheyorri** 'young Romani girl' becomes **sheyorrû**. These sounds, commonly heard in the US, Canada and among the French-Kalderash, do not exist in English and must be learned from native speakers or from recordings of Romani sounds.

In the US, Canada, parts of Latin America, France and elsewhere, Kalderash speakers pronounce through the nose some vowels followed by **< ñ >**, such as **pûnrró** 'foot' which becomes **pûñrró**. Others words like this are **anrro** 'egg' which becomes **añrro** and **manrro** 'bread' which becomes **mañrro**. In these last two words the **< añ >** sounds close to French **< en >** as in *Jean* or *enfant*. Those using this course do not have to use this pronunciation. It has simply been pointed out so that if you hear it from native speakers you will understand what is happening. The words can be pronounced as they are written in this course, that is, **pûnrró, anrro, manrro**, etc., since this is how they are pronounced in many Kalderash and other Vlax-Romani dialects in Europe. However, a person learning Romani from North American-Kalderash-Romani speakers or from French-Kalderash might want to use this **< ñ >** to record the pronunciation he or she hears when making notes.

Barthélémy's French-Kalderash is mutually intelligible with the Romani in this course except for these differences which are regular and predictable and, of course, some loan words taken from French which exist only in the French-Kalderash dialect. A good example of French-Kalderash is the folk tale by Mateo Maximoff which has already appeared in this course in Lessons nine and ten.

The ordinal numbers

1st	**pêrvo/angluno**	20th	**bíshto**
2nd	**dúito**	21st	**bish-tha-yêkhto**
3rd	**tríto**	100th	**shêláto**
4th	**shtárto**	1,000th	**miláto**
5th	**pánshto**	1,000,000th	**miliyonáto**
6th	**shófto**		
7th	**hiftáto**		
8th	**oxtóto**		
9th	**inyáto**		
10th	**déshto**		

Most speakers use the above forms unchanged for feminine and plural:

lêski dúito Rrômní	his second wife
o tríto vagóno ándo djédjêsh	the third carriage of (in) the train

Soldui

The word **soldui** 'both' can be used as a plural pronoun:

Soldui avile	They both came
Soldui nashlêntar	They both fled

Plus it can be used as a noun which must be inflected in the oblique. The accusative and oblique stem is **solden** (m.) and **soldan** (f.). Examples:

Dikhlem le soldên	I saw them both
Dem-dúma le soldênsa	I spoke with both of them (if men)
Dem-dúma le soldánsa	I spoke with both of them (if women)

It can also be used as an adjective:

Soldui zhukla xukle pe lêste	Both dogs sprang at him
Soldui grast nashlêntar	Both horses ran off

Declensions of soldui as an adjective

soldui	masculine and feminine nominative singular
soldone	masculine oblique singular
soldonya	feminine oblique singular
soldone	plural oblique for both genders

Adjectives

There are special forms of adjectives used before persons and animals which are the object of an action, for example, **me dikhlem le bare manushês** 'I saw the big man'. Look back at Lessons three and four to review them. They are also used with nouns inflected to any of the case forms.

Examples

Me gêlèm múrre bare phralêsa	I went with my big brother (with instrumental)
Hai múrra barya phenyása	And with my big sister (with instrumental)

Pushlem le bare Rrômèstar	I asked the important Rom (with ablative)
Dem la barya Rrômnyáke o lil	I gave the important Romni the letter (with dative)
Dem xabe le bokhale zhuklênde	I gave food to the hungry dogs (with prepositional)

'This', 'that' (continued from Lesson ten)

When **kako**, **kodo** and **kuko** are used before nouns in the oblique they are inflected as outlined below:

	Nominative	Oblique
(m.)	**kako**	**kakale**
	kodo	**kodole**
	kuko	**kukole**
(f.)	**kakya**	**kakala**
	kodya	**kodola**
	kukya	**kukola**

Examples

Me dikhlem kakale zhuklês araki	I saw this dog yesterday
Na mar kakala raklya	Don't hit (beat) this girl
Avilem kodole manushêsa	I came with that man
Gêlí kodola Gazhyása	She went with that non-Romani woman
Na mar kakale zhuklên	Don't beat these dogs
Nashlótar kodole zhêganèndar*	He fled from those wild animals

Possessive personal pronouns as substantives (nouns)

Like demonstrative pronouns ('this', 'that') when they are used as nouns (substantives), the possessive personal pronouns can take case forms when they are used in this way:

Xalem múrri phabai, so keres tirása?	I ate my apple, what will you do with yours?

---

*   **zhêgáno** 'wild animal' and **zhívina** 'domesticated animal'.

In this type of sentence 'yours' refers to 'your apple' which has now become a substantive (noun) and can be inflected. Used in this way, the possessive pronouns are inflected like nouns and so the inflections must follow the gender and number of the thing possessed. 'Apple' is the feminine gender so **tíro**, which in this sentence means 'your apple', must be inflected to the feminine singular instrumental case ending. Study the following table:

	Masc oblique stems sing/plural	Fem oblique stems sing/plural
múrro	**murrês- / murrên-**	**murra- / murran-**
tíro	**tirês- / tirên-**	**tira- / tiran-**
lêsko	**lêskorrès- / lêskorrèn-**	**lêskorrá- / lêskorrán-**
láko	**lakorrês- / lakorrên-**	**lakorra- / lakorran-**
pêsko	**pêskorrès- / pêskorrèn-**	**pêskorrá- / pêskorrán-**
amáro	**amarês- / amarên-**	**amara- / amaran-**
tumáro	**tumarês- / tumarên-**	**tumara- / tumaran-**
lêngo	**lêngorrès- / lêngorrèn-**	**lêngorrá- / lêngorrán-**
pêngo	**pêngorrès- / pêngorrán-**	**pêngorrá- / pêngorrán-**

Comparison of adjectives

The thematic adjectives behave as follows:

Definitive:

Wo si baro	He is big	**Woi si bari**	She is big

Comparative:

Wo si mai baro	He is bigger	**Woi si mai bari**	She is bigger
Won si mai bare	They are bigger		

Superlative:

Wo si o mai baro	He is the biggest	**Woi si e mai bari**	She is the biggest
Won si le mai bare	They are the biggest		

Athematic adjectives follow this format but most of them have the same form for masculine and feminine in the nominative singular:

Wo/woi si múndro	He/she is wonderful	(definitive)
Wo/woi si mai múndro	He/she is more wonderful	(comparative)
Won si le mai múndri	They are the most wonderful	(superlative)

To form comparisons with adjectives as in the English 'He is bigger than me', the word **mai** is used with the adjective and the pronoun or noun must be in the ablative case:

Wo si mai baro mándar	He is bigger (more big) than me
Wo si mai tsino mándar	He is smaller (more small) than me
Me sim mai baro lêstar	I am bigger than him
Me sim mai vucho le Spiróstar	I am taller than Spiro (**vucho** 'tall', a thematic adjective)
O Spíro si mai vucho mándar	Spiro is taller than me
Woi si mai bari la Marátar	She is bigger than Mary
E Mára si mai bari látar	Mary is bigger than her
Ame sam mai bokhale lêndar	We are hungrier than them
Won si mai baxtale mándar	They are luckier than me

Other examples

Wo si barvalo núma o Stévo si mai barvalo	He is rich but Steve is richer (more rich)
Kako si lasho núma kodo si mai lasho	This one is good but that one is better
Kako si mai baro kodolêstar	This one is bigger than that one (ablative)
Kakya shuri si mai skutsome kodolêstar	This knife is sharper than that one (ablative)
Múrro grast si mai baro kirêstar	My horse is bigger than yours (ablative)
Múrri phabai si mai loli lakorrátar	My apple is redder than hers (ablative)
Múrro kher si mai baro lêskorrèster	My house is bigger than his

Sometimes the word **katar** 'than' can be used to make comparisons of adjectives:

Múrro mobíli si mai zoralo* katar tiro	My car is more powerful than yours

In simple comparatives **katar** can sometimes replace the use of **mai** with the ablative case:

Wo si mai baro katar mánde	He is bigger than me

---

*   **zoralo** 'strong, powerful', **zuralo** 'fast'.

Lêsko kher si mai baro katar múrro kher	His house is bigger than my house

Alternatively:

Lêsko kher si mai baro murrêstar	His house is bigger than mine (ablative of **múrro**)

O mai but means 'the most' as an adjective, and as a noun it is subject to gender and number:

Wo xalyas o mai but xabe	He ate the most food
E Mára xalyas e mai but khaini	Mary ate the most (cooked) chicken
Wo xalyas o mai but mas	He ate the most meat
O Yánko si lês le mai but love	Yanko has the most money (money is plural)

The comparatives 'better' and 'worse'

'Better' and 'worse' are **mai lasho** and **mai chorro** when they are used with adjectives:

Wo si mai lasho pêske phralêstar	He is better than his brother
Tíro zhukel si mai chorro murrêstar	Your dog is worse than mine

Use of de and sar with adjectives

Sar means 'as' in Romani. **De** is a function word used with adjectives, especially when asking a question. In examples such as those shown following, the adjective must be declined for gender and number based on the noun it modifies:

Q. **Sóde si de baro?**	How big is he?
A. **Si sar baro sar o Stévo**	He is as big as Steve
Q. **Sóde si de vuchi?**	How tall is she?
A. **Si sar vuchi sar e Pavléna**	She is as tall as Pauline
Q. **Sóde si de barvale?**	How rich are they?
A. **Won si sar barvale sar thagara**	They are as rich as kings

Note also:

O bíldingo si desh-u-pansh hatázheni de vucho   The building is
                                                      fifteen floors high

E férma si pínda desetíni de lúndji   The farm is fifty
                                            acres long

More about verb stress

Some verbs ending in **< dav >**, **< des >** and so on, do not have the stress on the last vowel of the conjugation. Some have already been listed in past lessons.

Compare:

mangav 'I want' and	**rrándav** 'I shave'
manges	**rrándes**
mangel	**rrándel**

Others following the stress of **rrándel** are **kídel** 'he collects, picks, gathers', **ródel** 'he seeks, searches for', **shúdel** 'he throws' and **xárundel** 'he scratches'. Notice also the command forms and stresses of this group of words: **rránde, kíde, róde, shúde, xarúnde**.

Transitive verbs requiring a personal pronoun

Be aware of transitive verbs like **rrándav** when the action refers to a person because these must have a recipient (object) of the action, for example, **Rrándel-pe** 'He is shaving himself' (the recipient here is himself) but **Rrándel pêske grastês** 'He is shaving his horse' (the recipient here is the horse). **Rrandav-man** means 'I am shaving' not **rrándav**. Transitive verbs like this must take an object in all verb tenses.

Some of the most commonly used reflexive verbs are included in the following list. I have not listed transitive verbs where the reflexive is used in English as most of these will also be reflexive in Romani, for example, **Xoxavel-pe** 'He is lying to himself' or **Hatavel-pe** 'He is deluding himself'.

Present tense	Past tense	
arakhel-pe	**arakhlas-pe**	he is being careful, takes care
del-pe*	**dyas-pe**	he is getting started, starting
huryavel-pe	**huryadyas-pe**	he is dressing
khelel-pe	**kheldas-pe**	1) he is dancing; 2) he is playing
kerel-pe	**kerdyas-pe**	1) he is behaving; 2) he pretends to be
kurrel-pe	**kurrdyas-pe**	he is copulating
lel-pe†	**lyas-pe**	1) he gets going, decides to
del-pe	**dyas-pe**	2) he gets used to
marel-pe	**mardyas-pe**	he is fighting
mudarel-pe	**mudardyas-pe**	he is committing suicide
mutrel-pe	**muterdyas-pe**	he is urinating
naiyarel-pe	**naiyardyas-pe**	he is bathing
nangyarel-pe	**nangyardyas-pe**	he is undressing
phiravel-pe	**phiradyas-pe**	1) he is wandering around
	phiradyas-pe	2) he wears, is wearing
shudel-pe	**shudyas-pe**	he is wrestling
sikavel-pe	**sikadyas-pe**	he is making an appearance
sovel-pe††	**sutyas-pe**	he falls asleep
thol-pe	**thodyas-pe**	he puts on, dons
xalavel-pe	**xaladyas-pe**	he is washing
xinel-pe	**xindyas-pe**	he is defecating

Exercises

No strict exercises are given in Lessons eleven to twenty. If you are not in contact with Roma speaking Kalderash, make up short sentences to practise the new points, and cover the English or the Romani sentences in the examples

---

*   Very idiomatic in use, for example:

Del-pe te gilabal   He is starting to sing

Dem-man thai gêlèmtar   I got ready and departed

Dem-man te piyav   I began drinking

†   Very idiomatic in use, for example:

Lem-man thai gêlèmtar   I decided to go and I departed

Lyas-pe thai kerdyas   He made up his mind and did so (he got his act together and did it)

††   'He is sleeping' is **sovel-sutyas** and is intransitive not reflexive.

and write the English or Romani equivalents. Read the reading pieces aloud to get the feel of the language and preferably read them to a Romani speaker in person.

From a speech made in 1969 on the aspirations of the Roma

Shavále, Rromále! Mangav te mothav tumênge wáreso. Ages le Rrom trayin ándo chorromos. Le Gazhe chi mukhen amên te keras amári buki. Chi den amênge than te beshas. Mangen te xan amáro shoro. Núma so keras, phralále? Musai te merel amári viyátsa? Ages amári viyátsa si zhuklêski viyátsa. Amáre shavorre chi zhan ánde shkóla, tha nai amên than te beshas. Nai amên wóya telal o zakóno le themêsko kai beshas.

Musai te las ame amáro derécho te trayis ándo libêrto sar Rrom. Te chi den amênge kako libêrto músai te pushas lêndar êkh them amênge, êkh them Rromano kai shai zhan sa le Rrom ánde lúmiya te trayin. Rromále, mai-angle le Devlésa zhi-ka amári mai-lashi tehára!*

Translation

Romani youths and men! I wish to tell you something. Today the Roma live in misery. The non-Roma do not let us do our [traditional] work. They don't give us a place to camp. They want to eat our head (destroy us). But what can we do, brothers? Must our way of life die? Today, our life is a dog's life. Our children don't go to school and we have no place to stay. We have no rights under the law of the country where we reside.

We must obtain our rights so that we live in freedom like Roma. If they won't give us this liberty then we must ask them for a country of our own where all the Roma in the world can go to live. Romani men, forward with God towards our better tomorrow!

The ruby and the pearl (a North American-Kalderash song)

Óide parrudyan man pe l'lovênde	Oh you traded me for money
Óide parrudyan man pe l'daimántsi	Oh, you traded me for diamonds

---

*   **Notes: trayin** 'they live', **chorromos** 'poverty', **viyátsa** 'life', **zhuklêski** 'dog's', **wóya** 'right', **zakóno** 'law', **themêsko** 'country's', **derécho** 'right' (North American and French-Kalderash word from Spanish).

Óide parrudyan man pe l'love Amerikáchi — Oh, you traded me for American money

Chíro bezax te avel. — May it be your sin.
Tu zhanglan ke me tut kamáva — You knew that I loved you
Tu zhanglan ke me tut mangáva — You knew that I wanted you
Núma nas tu, chi míla ánda mánde — But you had no pity for me
Chíro bezax, te avel. — Let this be your sin.
Óide tu shindyan man po yilo — Oh, you cut me to the heart
Ánda mánde tu kerdyan dilo — You made a fool out of me
Xoxadyas man, thai meklas man — She deceived me and abandoned me

Chíro bexax, te avel. — May it be your sin.

The chorus is in English:

Oh love is as warm as the ruby
Love is as yellow as gold
Here in my arms and my love for you
You'll find the ruby and the pearl.

This was originally a Machwáya song from California attributed to *Sylvia and the Four Panthers*, a local Los Angeles group in the late 1950s who made a record with it included in the medley, and it is still popular in the US and Canada. The Machwanítska **chíro** for Kalderash **tíro** has been retained even by Kalderash singers in its many versions.

Lesson twelve

Word list

andre	inside, in
angáli	embrace
búrrnêx (f.)	handful
chink (f.)	sneeze
dab (f.)	blow
dúma	talk, speech
gáta	end, completion, finish
i-	too, also
muiyal	face up (adverb)
opral	upwards, from the top (adverb)
pálpale	back, back again (adverb)
rrûl (f.)	fart

The past perfect or pluperfect tense

To translate 'I had' as in 'I had seen', add **< -as >** to the past tense form. If the past tense form ends in a vowel, as in **gêlo** 'he went', add **< -sas >**.

With **dikh-** 'see':

dikhlém-as	I had seen
dikhlyán-as	you had seen
dikhlás-as	he/she had seen
dikhlyám-as	we had seen
dikhlyán-as	you had seen
dikhlé-sas	they had seen

Plus

aviló-sas	he had come
avilí-sas	she had come
avilé-sas	they had come

The above are generally used with the form of the verb for the continuous past to express the following types of sentences (this will be explained in more detail in later lessons):

Te dikhlémas lês me phenávas túke   If I had seen him I would have told
                                           you (I was telling you)

Compound verbs

Compound verbs in Romani, for example, **chumidav** 'I kiss (I give kiss)' or
kándav 'I obey (I give ear)' are complete verbs and simply take the appropriate
conjugations like any other verb of their type.

Compound verbs with separable adverbs and nouns

Romani also has a large number of compound verbs with separable adverbs
which differ from one dialect to another and are sometimes based on calquing
(copying) from the surrounding non-Romani language. There are also analytic
compound verbs with separable nouns which are common to many related
dialects in different countries.

Examples with separable adverbs from North American-Kalderash (the word
list at the start of this lesson gives the meanings of these adverbs and nouns):

Avav pálpale	I come back, I return (**avav** with **palpale**)
Dav andre	I get in, gain entry (**dav** with **andre**)
Dav angle	I come to the front, forward (**dav** with **angle**)
Dav pálpale	I reply, give back (**dav** with **pálpale**)
Del opral	It is overflowing (**del** with **opral**)
Dyas bul opre	It overturned, turned bottom up (**del** with **bul opre**)

Examples with separable nouns commonly used in widely dispersed Kalderash
dialects:

Dav chink	I sneeze (I give sneeze) (**dav** with **chink**)
Dav dab	I hit, strike (**dav** with **dab**)
Dav-dúma*	I speak (I give talk) (**dav** with **dúma**)

Some other compounds are:

Aven andre!	Enter! (plural imperative)
Dav and angáli	I embrace, hug
Dav gáta	I finish, complete
Dav pûnrró	I kick (give foot)
Dav rrûl	I pass wind

---

*   The two elements are not usually separated by a noun, pronoun, adjective or other word.

Dav swáto	I promise
Dav yag	I set fire to, ignite, shoot (a gun)
Dem andre	I entered, got inside
Zhav andre	I enter, I go inside

The verb **del** is used in this way, as follows:

| Del o brêshùn | It is raining (it gives rain) |
| Del o iv | It is snowing (it gives snow) |

Other nouns and pronouns can be combined with **kerav** 'I do, make' and **lav** 'I take':

Keren drôm	They make way, get out of the way (they make road)
Kerav pále	I do again
Lav búrrnêx	I grab, grasp, take hold of (I take a handful)
Lav pa mánde	I undress (I take off me)
lav pe mánde	I wear (I take on me)

Examples

Dem dab e basúna le chokanésa	I hit the basin with the hammer
Dem lês dab ándo mui	I hit him on the mouth
Dêm pûnrró le zhuklês ánde bul	I kicked the dog in the rear end
Dyas andre andral e filástra	He got in through the window
Kerdem pále mai êkh dáta	I did it again one more time
Keren drôm, shavorrále!	Get out of the way, kids!
Wo dyas zórali chink	He sneezed loudly (gave a loud sneeze)

Verb conjugations in < il > and < ol >

Look back at Lesson three and review the forms in the present tense of **lipil** and **farbol**. Some Kalderash and Lovari speakers use longer, but regular, forms. Instead of **lipiv** 'I stick' and **farbov** 'I paint' they retain the **< isar >** and the **< osar >** in the present tense which gives **lipisarav** 'I stick' and **farbosarav** 'I paint'. This is especially true of Romanian-Kalderash speakers. A few such longer forms exist in North America and are sometimes used transitively to separate them from the reflexive forms which use the short form of the verb with the reflexive (accusative) personal pronouns. Examples from North American-Kalderash:

| **tristol-pe** | he/she is becoming sad (intransitive/reflexive) |
| **tristosarel la** | he is making her sad (transitive) |

Lip- 'stick'

Short form	Long form
lipiv	**lipisarav**
lipis	**lipisares**
lipil	**lipisarel**
lipis	**lipisaras**
lipin	**lipisaren**
lipin	**lipisaren**

Farb- 'paint'

Short form	Long form
farbov	**farbosarav**
farbos	**farbosares**
farbol	**farbosarel**
farbos	**farbosaras**
farbon	**farbosaren**
farbon	**farbosaren**

The past tense is the same for both forms:

lipisardem	I stick
volisardyan	you loved
farbosardyas	he painted
ramosardyam	we wrote
pushkisardyan	you shot
farbosarde	they painted

All the above are athematic verb stems but the **< iv >** and **< ov >** endings can also be attached to thematic Romani nouns to make verbs like this example: **shuriv** 'I stab' from **shuri** 'knife' which is a thematic noun.

There are exceptions to the above rule, however, in **thol** 'he puts, places' and **mothol** 'he tells, says'. These never have **< sar >** in either the present or past. The past is **thodem** 'I put, did put', **thodyan** 'you put', etc. and **mothodem**, **mothodyan**, etc.

Transitive and intransitive forms of verbs in < iv > and < ov >

There are two forms of all verbs in **< iv >** and **< ov >**, the transitive and the intransitive. One example is **ansuril** 'he marries':

Ansuril pêske shavês	He is marrying his son, getting his son married (transitive)
Ansuril-pe	He is getting married (intransitive and reflexive)

The two forms are as follows:

Ansuriv múrre shavês	I am getting my son married (transitive verb form)
Ansuris tíre shavês?	Are you getting your son married?
Ansuril pêske shavês	He is getting his son married
Moritil pêska sha	He is getting his daughter married (a different verb **moritil** for women)
Ansuris amáre shavês	We are getting our son married
Ansurin tumáre shavên?	Are you getting your sons married?
Ansurin pênge shavên	They are getting their sons married

but

Ansurí-ma (ansuriv man)	I am getting married (reflexive with personal pronoun)
Ansurís-tu?	Are you getting married?
Ansuríl-pe	He is getting married
Moritíl-pe	She is getting married (a different verb for women)
Ansurís-ame	We are getting married
Ansurín-tume?	Are you getting married?
Ansurín-pe	They are getting married

In the past tense, the forms already given in this course apply for the first group when used as transitive verbs:

Ansurisardem múrre shavês	I got my son married, married off my son
Ansurisardyan tíre shavês?	Did you get your son married?

The past tense of the intransitive form has a different ending:

Ansurisáilem	I got married, I married
Ansurisáilan	You got married

Ansurisáilo	He got married
Moritisáili	She got married (different verb for women)
Ansurisáilam	We got married
Ansurisáilan	You got married
Ansurisáile	They got married

Compare:

Ansurisardyas pêske shavês barvalya familyása	He married his son into a rich family
Ansurisáilo barvalya Gazhyása	He married a rich non-Romani woman

The command forms (imperatives) for this intransitive form of the verb are **ansurisáwo!** 'get married!' (singular) and **ansurisáwon!** 'get married!' (plural).

Kako (continued)

As mentioned earlier, **kako**, **kakya** and the others can be used on their own to mean 'this man', 'this woman' etc. While the learner is advised to use the form **kako mursh** 'this man' etc., the following sentences are commonly heard from native speakers:

Prinzhares kakalês?	Do you know this man?
Avili kodolênsa	She came with those people

The following is also heard in songs, proverbs and sayings:

Zhávtar í-me* kakalênsa zháltar í-wo kodolênsa
I depart with these people and he departs with those people

Reading exercise
A Canadian-Kalderash folk tale recorded in 1963 from Waso Russel Demitro

Sas êkh Gazho thai Gazhi hai nas lên raklorre. Dine hai rrugisáile ka o Del te del le, o Del, rakliorre.

   Dya(s) o Del, avilo lênde hai pendya(s) lênge, "Dikhen e níva le kukurozôski. Zhan ánde níva thai len kukurúzo ánda e níva tha mangen yêkh raklorro. Len yêkh kukurúzo thai mangen mai but raklorre.

---

*   **í-me** and **í-wo** mean 'I also' and 'he also'. The **< i- >** is a prefix meaning 'also, too'. It is a
     Romani idiom that defies an exact English translation and can be used in normal conver-
     sation where the meaning is clearer, for example, **í-tu zhas?** 'are you also going?' or **í-me**
     dikhlem lês 'I too saw him'.

Len yêkh kukurúzo pe swáko raklorre kai mangen."

Lya(s) o Gazho hai e Gazhi thai gêlé ánde níva le kukuruzôski, hai line dui kukurúzurya hai shude le ánde níva.

Ánda le dui kukurúzurya avile yêkh raklorro hai yêkh rakliorri, rupune balênsa hai sumnakune dandênsa.*

Translation

There was a Gazho and a Gazhi and they had no children. They made a decision and prayed to God that he give them, God, children.

God got started, he came to them and told them, "See the corn field. Go into the field and take a corn cob from the field and ask for one male child. Take one cob and ask for more children. Take one cob for each child you want."

The husband took himself and the wife and they went into the corn field, and took two cobs of corn and threw them into the field.

Out of the two cobs of corn came one male child and one female child, with silver hair and with golden teeth.

(The complete text of this folk tale was published in the *Journal of the Gypsy Lore Society*, Volume XL11 Parts 3-4, 1969, pp.95–9.)

Kalderash texts
An evening prayer (Canadian-Kalderash)

Ánde ki míla, Dévla, hai Swuntonya Maríyo, hai sógodi Swíntsurya kai si ándo Raiyo. Ándo tíro kíno hai tíro zhávo kai tsirdyan pe gadya lúmiya, yertisar amên amáre bezexa thai arakh amên katar o nasvalimos, katar e yag, katar o pai, katar le prêpêdyéli, katar le chor, hai katar amáre dush-máya, hai katar o bêng hai katar lêske manusha, hai katar le rai, te na keren amênge báyo, hai arakh amên po swáko drôm, hai pe swáko ker-rárya hai pe swâko páso ándo amári viyátsa. Hai nayis-túke, Dévla, so kerdyan amênge pe gadya lúmiya hai duryar o nasvalimos pa amênde.[†]

---

*   Notes: **rrugisáile** 'they prayed', **dya(s) o Del** 'God took pity (on them)', **níva le kukurozôski** 'corn field', **kukurúzo** 'Indian corn, corn-on-the-cob', **rupune** 'silver', **sum-nakune** 'golden' (both plural describing **bal** 'hair' and **dandênsa** 'teeth').

†   Notes: **ki** 'your' (variant form of **ti míla** 'mercy', **sógodi** 'whatever', **swíntsurya** 'saints', **Raiyo** 'Heaven', **kíno** 'agony', **zhávo** 'sorrow', **tsirdyan** 'you suffered', **yertisar** 'pardon', **bexexa** 'sins', **arakh** 'protect', **nasvalimos** 'sickness', **prêpêdyéli** 'accidents, disasters', **dushmáya** 'enemies', **bêng** 'devil', **rai** (here) 'policemen', **báyo** 'harm', **kerráriya** 'path-way', **paso** 'step', **duriar** 'remove', **gadya** variant pronunciation of **kadya** 'that'.

Translation

In your pity, God, and Saint Mary, and whatever Saints that are in Heaven. In your torment and your sorrow that you endured in this world, pardon us our sins and protect us from sickness, from fire, from flood [water], from disasters, from thieves, and from our enemies, and from the devil and from his people, and from the police, that they will not make trouble for us, and protect us on every road and on every path and at every step in our life. And thank you, God, what you have done for us in this world and remove sickness from us.

Blessing on the Pomanáki Síniya

The **Pomána** table is a feast at which the memory of a dead Rom/Romni is honoured by the family, relatives and the local community. A **Pomána** (mourning period) usually lasts one year for an elder or an adult but must be in units of three: three months, six months, nine months or one year. A **Pomána** table is held at the termination of each three-month unit as well as the start of the **Pomána** following the funeral.

Kháma, Shóna, thai Dévla. Ashun ma! Kakya síniya kai dáva ángla Kutári/Kutárka, te avel ángla lêste/láte ándo Raiyo hai te avel lêske (láke) prôsto o them hai e lúmiya kai xan ánda gadya síniya.Te aven lênge po lêngo sastimus thai te ningerel lês/la, o Del lêske(láke), ándo Raiyo. Hai nayis-túke, Dévla, so kerdyan amênge pe gadya lúmiya.*

Translation

Sun, Moon, and God. Hear me! This table that I give before So-and-So, may it appear before him/her in Heaven and may the local community and the outsiders who eat from this table become humble. May it bring health for them and may his/her God transport him/her into Heaven. And thank you, God, what you have done for us in this world.

American Kalderash song
Voliv Tut Ages 'I love you today'

Voliv tut ages   I love you today

---

*   **Notes: Kháma** 'Oh Sun', **Shóna** 'Oh Moon', **Dévla** 'Oh God' (all in the vocative), **ashun ma!** 'hear me' (note the imperative singular implying a Trinity), **Kutári** 'So-and-So' (masculine), **Kutárka** 'So-and-So' (feminine), **avel prósto** 'become humble', **o them** (here) 'the Romani people from the locality', **e lúmiya** (here) 'the people (Roma) from other localities', **sastimus** 'health'.

Voliv tut tehára	I'll love you tomorrow
Voliv tut mai but	I'll love you much more
Desar mai anglal.	Than ever before. [Repeat verse]
Khel, khel, khel thai gilaba	Dance, dance, dance and sing
Khel, khel, khel thai gilaba	Dance, dance, dance and sing
Av, av, av vésolo!	Be, be, be happy!
Av, av, av vésolo!	Be, be, be happy! [Repeat verse]

These words are mixed into the instrumental festive dance **Báso** which is performed at Kalderash weddings and other group gatherings and the singers mix in English translations of the verses.

Proverbs

Shukar si kriyánga pêske pateryánsa, mai shukar si Rrômní pêske shavênsa*
A branch is beautiful with its leaves, a woman is more beautiful with her children

Na chungarde ánde xaying, shai te avel te piyes mai yêkh dáta
Don't spit in the well, it may happen that you drink (there) once again

Te shines yêkh Rrôm ánde desh kotora[†], chi mudares lês, núma keres deshe Rromên
If you cut a Rrom into ten pieces, you won't kill him, but you will create ten Roma

Kána símas tsinorro, piyávas múrro thudorro, akana ke barilem, piyáva múrro táxdai byérya[††]
When I was a little boy, I used to drink my milk, now that I have grown up, I drink my glass of beer

Kalderash saying

Ame, o Rrómano them si yêkh baro kopáchi kai si lês but kriyênzhi thai swáko kriyánga si êkh nátsiya kai si la but vítsi
We, the Romani people are a large tree that has many branches and each branch is a nation that has many clans

---

*   **kriyánga** 'bough', **patrya-** 'leaves', **pateryánsa** 'with leaves'.
†   **kotor** (m.sing) 'piece', **kotora** (m.pl).
††   **barilem** 'I have grown up', **taxdai** 'glass', **byérya** 'beer'.

Lesson thirteen

Long and short forms of the present tense

Look at the following table:

Short form	Long form
mangav	**mangáva**
manges	**mangésa**
mangel	**mangéla**
mangas	**mangása**
mangen	**mangéna**

So far in the lessons the short forms have mainly been used. In Kalderash, the long forms are used in folk tales, songs, poems and in very formal, rhetorical speech by elders, for example, during the **Kris-Rromani** or Judicial Assembly of Elders which deals with issues of Romani law.

Uses of long and short forms

dikhav	1) I see; 2) I'll see
dikháva	1) I see (in songs and in rhetorical speech); 2) I'll see (ditto)
kam-dikhav	I shall see (everyday speech)
kam-dikháva	I shall see (rhetorical speech and in folk tales, songs and poetry)

Rhetorical speech as used during the Kris-Romani by a witness addressing the assembly

Shavále, Rromále! Me avilem kai kakya kris te phenáva tumênge kh' me, o Wáso, o shav le Zlatchósko, mangáva te phenáva tumênge so me zhanáva ánda kadya buki kai si ángla amênde ages ánde kakya kris hai te dáva tumênge sya so me zhanáva ánda kadya buki kai azbal o Miláno thai pêsko zhamutro, o Spiráko, o shav le Dulésko. Te meráva thai te pharruváva te na phenáva tumênge o chachimos. Antúnchi te avel kerdo!

Translation

Young men, male adults! I have come to this trial to inform you that I, Zlatcho, son of Waso, want to inform you [of] everything that I know about this matter which is before us today, in this trial and to present for you all that I know about this matter which concerns Milano and his son-in-law, Pete, the son of Dule. May I die and disintegrate if I do not tell the truth. So let it be done!

'Who' and 'which'

When 'who' and 'which' join two phrases, the forms **ka** (m.) and **kai** (f. and pl. of both genders) are used, for example:

Prinzhares le manushês ka avel akana? Do you know the person who is coming now?

Dikhlem la zhuvlya kai lyas le love I saw the woman who took the money

O khiral ka si pe skafedi si kêrnó The cheese which is on the coffee table is bad

Ashundem le Rromên kai akushline lês I heard the Roma who cussed him out

A sentence like 'Where is the man to whom you gave the letter?' is simplified in Romani to:

Kai si o Rrôm ka dyan o lil lêste? Where is the man to whom you gave the letter (him)?

This can also be put another way:

Kai si o Rrôm káste dyan o lil? Where is the man to whom you gave the letter? (**káste** 'to whom')

Many speakers use **kai** for both genders in the singular:

Kodo si o Rrôm kai avilyas ánda o Franzúzo That is the Rom who came from France

Gadya si e sheyorri kai khelel-pe shukares That is the young girl who dances beautifully

Kon si o Rrôm kai beshel khote? Who is the Rom who is sitting there?

Kon (a nominative singular pronoun) has no plural except **kai** which is only used as a relative pronoun and cannot be interrogative. **Kon** can be used as a relative pronoun in certain types of sentences and meanings where **ka** could also be used and additionally, **kon** can imply a plural when inflected in the singular:

O zhukel kon ródel arakhel o kokalo	The dog who seeks finds the bone
Le zhukla kai róden arakhen le kokala	The dogs who seek find the bones
Káske shavorre si kodole ándo kóltso?	Whose children are those in the corner?
Káske mobíliya si parkime avryal e ófisa?	Whose cars are parked outside the office?

Interrogatives

Che?	What, which? (not declined nor inflected)
Che fyal Rrôm san?	What kind of Rom are you?
Che fyal kiral plachal tu?	Which kind of cheese pleases you?
Savo?	Which? (inflected for gender and number and has oblique forms)

Nominative:

Savo mobíli si tiro?	Which car is yours?
Savi zhuvli si e Mára?	Which woman is Mary?
Save love chorádyile?	Which money was stolen?

Oblique:

Save Rrômèsa des-dúma?	Which Rom are you speaking to? (instrumental)
Savya Rrômnyátar ashundyan kodya?	From which woman did you hear that? (ablative)
Save Rromênge si o xabe?	For which Roma is the food? (dative)

The genitive case

The **< 's >** as in 'the boy's hair' or 'the workman's tools' is expressed in Romani by the following endings which are attached to the oblique stem of the noun. This is the most difficult case ending to understand, especially when it is used in conjunction with modifying adjectives and personal pronouns:

-ko	raklêsko, dadêsko	after a masculine singular noun
-ko	raklyáko, Maráko (Mary's)	after a feminine singular noun
-go	raklêngo, dadêngo	after a masculine plural noun
-go	raklyángo, sheyángo	after a feminine plural noun

The genitive case ending must be declined according to the gender and number of the object(s) possessed by the subject:

le raklêski piramni	the boy's sweetheart (f.)
la raklyáko piramno	the girl's sweetheart (m.)
le raklêske gada	the boy's shirts
le raklêsko phral	the boy's brother (m.)
le raklêske phrala	the boy's brothers (m.pl.)
le raklêsko dad	the boy's father (m.)
le raklênge dada	the boys' fathers (m.pl.)

Modifiers used with oblique nouns in the genitive case must be inflected for gender and number as with any other case:

le bare raklêsko shoro	the big boy's head
la barya raklyáko shoro	the big girl's head
múrre pralêsko zhukel	my brother's dog
múrra phenyáko zhukel	my sister's dog
múrre pralêske zhukla	my brother's dogs
múrra phenyáke zhukla	my sister's dogs
múrre phralêngo zhukel	my brothers' dog
múrre phralêngi zhukli	my brothers' bitch

More examples

le raklêsko gad	the boy's shirt
le raklênge gada	the boys' shirts
le zhukêsko kokalo	the dog's bone
le Babêski zhuvli	Bob's wife
la Maráko Rrôm	Mary's husband
la sheyáke bal	the girl's hair (hair is plural in Romani)
le Rromêngo mobíli	the car belonging to the Roma

While the genitive case ending agrees with the thing possessed in gender and number, the adjective or pronoun is inflected to the oblique because it modifies an inflected noun, just as it would for any of the other case endings. To put this another way, the adjective or pronoun is inflected to match the gender and number of the noun in the genitive. The noun in the genitive, like an adjective, is inflected to match the gender and number of the thing possessed.

Examples with adjectives

Nominative:

Le bare Rrômèsko mobíli	The important Rom's car
La barya Rrômnyáko mobíli	The important woman's car
Le bare Rromênge mobíliya	The cars of the important Roma

Singular genitive oblique:

Kindas le grastês le bare Rrômèsko	He bought the important Rom's horse
Kindas la grasnya le bare Rrômèski	He bought the important Rom's mare
Kindas le grastên le bare Rrômèske	He bought the important Rom's horses
Kindas le grastes la barya Rrômnyáko	He bought the important Romni's horse
Kindas la grasnya la barya Rrômnyáki	He bought the important Romni's mare
Kindas le grastên la barya Rrômnyáke	He bought the important Romni's horses

Plural genitive oblique (behaves as the above in the plural forms):

Kindas le grastên le bare Rromênge	He bought the horses of the important Romani men
Kindas le grasynyan le bare Rrômnyánge	He bought the mares of the important Romani women

Kásko 'whose?'

Kásko also changes for feminine and plural:

Kásko shav san tu?	Whose son are you?
Káski búkfa si?	Whose book is it?
Káske mobíliya si kodole?	Whose cars are those?

Test whether you have understood

Translate into Romani:

1.   my wife's hat
2.   the caravan's window
3.   the caravans' windows

The genitive case is difficult for non-Romani speakers to understand and to use. The basic rule is to keep it simple like the Roma themselves do because a series of nouns using the apostrophe plus 's' cannot be strung together as in English, for example, 'I saw Yanko's sister's boyfriend's brother.' In Romani, we would begin at the other end of the sentence as follows:

Dikhlem le phralês, le piramêsko, la phenyáko, le Yankóski

I saw the brother (accusative) of the boyfriend of the sister of Yanko

As can be seen here, the definite articles and genitive case endings must agree with the noun they modify. The use of such complicated sentences is generally avoided, even by Roma, who have idiomatic ways of getting around them. In daily speech the following examples are typical:

Dikhlem le Yankóski Rrômní ánde wúlitsa   I saw Yanko's wife in the
                                                 street

Lake zhamutróski piramni sas lása   Her brother-in-law's
                                                 girlfriend was with her

Sas la láko zhukel po shelo lása   She had her dog with her
                                                 on a leash

This avoids trying to say 'I saw Yanko's wife's brother-in-law's girlfriend's dog on a leash on the street.' These patterns can be learned from native speakers and through familiarity with the language.

Genitive case as an adjective

Unlike the other case endings, the genitive case of nouns can be used like an adjective and it follows the same rules as thematic adjectives, for example, **stákla** 'glass' has a genitive in **stakláko** and a 'glass window' would then be **stakláki filástra**. **Motúra** 'broom' has a genitive in **moturáko** so 'a broom handle' would then become **moturáki pori**. **Pecháta** 'spot, splotch, patch', with a plural in **pechêtsi**, gives the genitive plural of **pechêtsèngo** 'having spots, patches, piebald'. A piebald horse would then be **pechêtsèngo grast**.

Constructions like these can become compound nouns in themselves and the plurals would become **stakláke filástri** 'glass windows', **moturáke porya** 'broom handles' and **petchêtsènge grast** 'piebald horses'.

Examples

kashtênge-shinipéya	sawdust, shavings (wood's cuttings)
filastráke-khosáriya	windshield wipers (window's wipers)
gurumnyángi-gozhni	cow manure (cows' manure)
pechêtsèngi-grasni	piebald mare
zudêske-grópi	wall plugs (wall's holes, if a single wall)
zudênge-grópi	wall plugs (if in general for any wall, use plural)

This form of the genitive case is also used to create adjectives which have a different meaning than other adjectives with derivatives from the root or stem of the noun:

From **súmnakai** (m.) 'gold':

Si la sumnakune bal	She has golden hair (colour of gold) (adjective)
Si lês sumnakásko lántso	He has a gold chain (made of gold) (genitive adjective)

From **grast** (m.) 'horse':

Si lês grástuni fátsa	He has an equine face (resembling a horse)
Phirdyas ánde l' grastêski khul	He walked in horse droppings (belonging to a horse)

From **sastri** (m.) 'iron':

Si tut sastruno yilo	You have an iron heart (the quality of iron)
Si lês sastrêski budáka	He has an iron pickaxe (made of iron)

From **kasht** (m.) 'wood':

Wo si Rrôm kashtalo	He is a wooden Rom (unable to speak Romani)
Kindem kashtêski síniya	I bought a wooden table (made of wood)

You must also watch for the following types of seemingly confusing sentences:

O grastêngo-pravarimos si ándo gryázhdo	The horse fodder is in the barn

Grastêngo here is the adjective part of a compound noun used in the nominative.

Lênge grast xale amáre grastêngo pravarimos   Their horses ate our
horses' fodder

Here the genitive case ending indicates to which horses the fodder belonged.

Kindem mobilênge-shûni   I bought automobile tyres

Where **mobilêngo** is an adjective modifying tyres in a compound noun.

Chordyas múrre mobilêske shûni   He stole my car's tyres

The genitive case ending is used here to show that the tyres belonged to my
car. But:

Chordyas wúni mobilênge shûni   He stole some car tyres

This is a compound noun with the adjective and the noun inflected to the plural
nominative.

Pharruli yêkh shûna múrre mobilêski   One of my car's tyres blew
out

The genitive case here shows that the tyre that blew out belonged to my car.

Genitive case combined with adjectives

Since the genitive case can serve as an adjective, it can be combined with
other adjectives to create compound adjectives, for example, **kovlo-yilêsko**
'soft-hearted'. When used as descriptive adjectives and the verb 'to be', both
elements are inflected for gender and number:

kovlo-yilêsko si   he is soft-hearted
kovli-yilêski si   she is soft-hearted
kovle-yilêske si   they are soft-hearted

When these compounds are used to modify an object in a sentence, the adjective must be inflected to an invariable ending in **< e >** and the genitive adjective
in the component must be inflected for gender and number of the object(s).

Nominative:

Wo si kovle-yilêsko mursh   He is a soft-hearted man
Woi si kovle-yilêski zhuvli   She is a soft-hearted woman
Won si kovle-yilêske zhene   They are soft-hearted people

When used to modify inflected nouns, the genitive element of the compound
must be inflected like a thematic adjective to agree in gender and number with
the inflected noun it modifies.

Oblique:

Dem-dúma le kovlé-yilêske murshêsa   I spoke with the soft-hearted man
Dem-duma la kovle-yilêska zhuvlyása   I spoke with the soft-hearted woman
Dem-dúma le kovle-yilêske zhênènsa   I spoke with the soft-hearted people

When **< bi- >** is used with a genitive adjective, for example, **bi-yilêsko** 'heart-less, without compassion', the genitive adjective follows the rules for thematic adjectives.

Nominative:

bi-yilêsko mursh   a heartless man
bi-yilêski zhuvli   a heartless woman
bi-yilêske zhêné   heartless people

Oblique:

Dikhlem le bi-yilêske murshês   I saw the heartless man
Dikhlem la bi-yilêska zhuvlya   I saw the heartless woman
Dikhlem le bi-yilêske zhênèn   I saw the heartless people

For the rules of the genitive case of the abstract noun in **< imos >** as an adjective and a compound adjective, see Lesson seventeen.

Prepositions

A list of the most common prepositions in this dialect. Note that some are also adverbs:

an	a short form of **ándo** and **ánde** in this list
and-	in, inside (see **ándo** and **ánde**)
ánda	about, because of, from, by
ánde	before feminine nominative nouns and nominative plurals of both genders
ándo	before a masculine nominative noun
ángla	in front of
inkyal	across
ka	to (**ka o zudo** 'to the well', **kai síniya** 'to the table')
káring	towards
katar	from, from where, from wherever
mashkar	between, among
pa	about, concerning

pála	1) after, behind; 2) by (adverb); 3) with (in North American-Kalderash)
pásha	near, beside, close by
pe	on (with feminine singular and for both genders with nominative noun plurals)
po	on (with masculine nominative nouns)
prótivo	against, up against
sar	like, as, how
tela	under, underneath
vash	for
vi	also
zhêkùn	until
zhi-ka	until, up to

Examples

An 'in' is a short form of **ánd-** and is used in such expressions as **Phendem lês wórta an lêsko mui** 'I told him straight to his face'.

Ka 'to' becomes **kai** before feminine nouns and **ka le** or **ka l'** before plural nouns:

Zhav ka o Târánto	I'm going to Toronto
Zhal kai shkóla	He is going to school
Phirel pa l' gava	He is travelling through the countryside (small towns)

Note that the prepositional case could also be used in place of the above:

Zhav le Târantóste	I am going to Toronto

Pa has many idiomatic meanings:

Den-dúma pa l' love	They are talking about money
Lem múrre tsáliya pa mánde	I took my clothes off
Pelo pa e síniya	It fell off the table
Tradem pa América	I drove through the US

Pála has the general meaning of 'behind, after' but in North American-Kalderash it has a meaning of 'with' in some types of sentences. It also means 'by' in such expressions as 'one by one' in many Kalderash dialects:

Phir pála mánde	Walk behind me
Háide pála mánde!	Come with me!

Zha pála lêste!	Go after him!
Gêlé andre trin pála trin	They went in three by three
Yêkh pála yêkh xayisáile	One by one they perished (**xayil-pe, xayisái-lo** 'perish')

Pe means 'on' but it must take the following forms:

Beshel po grast	He is sitting on a horse (with masculine nouns)
Tho lês pe síniya	Place it on the table (with feminine nouns)
Sovel pe l' phaleya	He is lying on the floor (with plural nouns)

Vi, **zhêkùn** and **zhi-ka** are used as follows:

Vi me shai zhav	I too can go
Azhuker kathe zhêkùn me avav pálpale	Wait here till I come back
Phirdyas ándo pai zhi-ka korráte	He walked into the water up to his neck (**korr** (f.) 'neck')
Musai te azhukeras zhi ka l' pansh	We have to wait here until five (o'clock)

You will find other examples of the use of prepositions throughout the lessons.

The prefix < wáre >

This prefix can be combined with words like **kána** 'when' and **kon** 'who' as follows. The most commonly used are listed here:

kána	when	**wárekana**	whenever, at whatever time
kanagodí	whenever	**warekanagodí**	whenever, no matter when
kai	where	**wárekai**	somewhere, anywhere
kaigodí	wherever	**wárekaigodí**	wherever else, whatever other place
kásko	whose	**wárekasko**	whoever's, whomever's
katar	from where	**wárekatar**	from wherever
kon	who	**wárekon**	somebody, anybody, whoever
sar	how	**wáresar**	somehow, however
savorre	everyone	**wáresavorre**	whatever people, whomsoever (pl.)
sávo	which	**wáresavo**	whichever
so	what	**wáreso**	anything, something
sóstar	why	**wáresostar**	for whatever reason, for some (any) reason

The suffixes < ivar > and < var >

but	much, many	**butívar**	often
wúni	some	**wunívar**	sometime, sometimes
sóde	how much	**sódevar**	however many times

< war > also means 'times' as in **trin-war-desh** 'three-times-ten' or **pansh-war-dui** 'five-times-two' and can be used as a comparative with adjectives:

Dui-war mai baro si	It is two times bigger
Trin-war mai xansi sas	It was three times smaller
Si lês trin-war le love kai si man	He has three times the money I have

It can be suffixed to numerals as follows:

yêkhwar	once
dúiwar	twice
trínwar	thrice
shtárwar	four times

The above can also become adverbs:

yêkhwarès	once
duwares	twice (not **duiwares**)
triwares	thrice (not **trinwares**)
shtarwares	four times

Useful nouns

Family and kinship terms can differ from one Kalderash or Vlax-Romani dialect to another. The most common terms in North American-Kalderash are listed here. I have omitted the immediate family which has already been covered in previous lessons and word lists (father, mother, brother, sister, son and daughter).

Singular	Plural	
bibi	**bibya**	aunt
bori*	**borya**	1) sister-in-law (brother's wife); 2) daughter-in-law (son's wife)

*   **bori** is a temporary status in a Kalderash family. When a girl marries, she generally
      spends a period of time living at the home of the parents of her husband. During this
      period she is called a **bori** 'bride, daughter-in-law' and is more or less an apprentice wife.
      After she has born her first child, she and her husband are then free to leave and set up

boryorri	**boryorra**	newly-married bride
fína	**fíni**	goddaughter
fíno	**fínurya**	godson
gláto	**gláturya**	male baby, infant son
gláta	**gláti**	female baby, infant daughter
kak	**kaka**	uncle
kirivi	**kirivya**	godmother
kirivo	**kirive**	godfather
kumnáta	**kumnáti**	sister of a spouse
kumnáto	**kumnáturya**	brother of a spouse
mami	**mamya**	grandmother
nipóta	**nipótsi**	1) niece; 2) granddaughter
nipóto[*]	**nipóturya**	1) nephew; 2) grandson
nyáma	**nyámi**	female relative
nyámo	**nyámurya**	male relative
pápo	**pápurya**	grandfather
parintíya	**parintíyi**	parentage, ancestry
parínto	**parínturya**	male parent, ancestor[†]
pásho	**páshurya**	husband of a wife's sister
shey-bari[††]	**sheya-barya**	eldest daughter
sókra	**sókri**	mother-in-law
sókro	**sókrya**	father-in-law
vára	**várya**	female cousin
véro	**vérya**	male cousin
xanamik	**xanamícha**	co-father-in-law (father of a son or daughter's spouse)

Footnote * cont.

    for themselves. She is now referred to as a **Rrômní** 'wife-mother' by her peers since adult status only comes with motherhood and fatherhood. Her husband's mother now refers to her as **shey** 'daughter' and her sisters-in-law as **phey** 'sister'.

[*]   To clarify grandson, the Kalderash use the following terms: **shavêsko-shav** 'son of my son' (the grandson who remains in his father's extended family) and **sheyáko-shav** 'son of my daughter' (who will become part of his father-in-law's extended family).

[†]   The word **dad** 'father' is also used to mean 'ancestor, forefather' and **le dada** is used to mean 'the forefathers, the male ancestors'.

[††]   The eldest daughter replaces the mother as housekeeper and supervisor of her siblings when the mother is sick or temporarily not able to perform this function herself. She has a specific role in the family hierarchy.

xanamíka	**xanamíchi**	co-mother-in-law (mother of a son or daughter's spouse)
zhamutro	**zhamutre**	1) brother-in-law (sister's husband); 2) son-in-law (daughter's husband)

Mashtívo is an athematic adjective which means 'step' or 'adopted' and which can be used to form compound nouns for step or adopted family members. It is inflected like **prôsto** (see Lesson three):

mashtívo-shav	(plural **mashtívi shave**)
mashtívo-shey	(plural **mashtívi sheya**)

One more term which should be mentioned here is **zhamutro ánde tsêra** which has no English equivalent. If a boy wishes to be married among the Kalderash and some other Vlax-Romani groups, and he or his father do not have the money for the bridal offering (**darro**) he can marry the girl and spend a period of time with the family of the bride working with her father to pay off the bridal offering. This status is called **zhamutro ánde tsêra** 'son-in-law in the tent'. In this case, he is a sort of hostage to the bride's family until the full amount of the bridal offering is paid. It is not generally considered to be the ideal arrangement by the Roma but I have seen cases of it and heard of it from others.

Other terms related to personal identity

kumpaníya	1) an economic unit living in a given location or territory, not necessarily related. The **kumpaníya** claims the territory and excludes other Roma who are not members. They can become so by requesting membership which is usually under the jurisdiction of the local territorial representative or **Rrôm Baro**; 2) a travelling community working as an economic unit
nátsiya	nation (the broad divisions of Vlax-Roma, i.e. Kalderásha, Machwáya, Lovára etc. Each nation contains many clans)
vítsa	clan, extended group of families descended patrilineally

Shey-bari – a Kalderash song from Mexico

Ói, shey-bari	Oh, eldest daughter
So me te kérav ánda túte?	What can I do about you?

Ói, shey-bari	Oh, eldest daughter
Múrro shóro tu dilyardyan	You have made my head crazy
Ói, shey-bari	Oh, eldest daughter
So me te kérav ánda túte?	What can I do about you?
Múrro yílo pharradyan	You broke my heart
Múrro shóro dilyardyan	You have made my head crazy
Óide, Dévla, shey-baríyo	Oh, God, eldest daughter
Tu phendyan man	You told me
Ke tu chi mai lésa	That you won't drink any more
Núma araki	But last night
Tu makilan*	You got drunk
Ói, shey-bari	Oh, eldest daughter
So me te kérav ánda túte?	What can I do about you?
Nai man, Dévla, so kerav,	God, there is nothing I can do about it,
Ánda túte pharruvav	Because of you I am falling apart
Óide, Dévla shey-baríyo	Oh, God, eldest daughter (repeat first verse)

(The Spanish verses have been omitted. Song recorded privately on cassette tape in the early 1990s by the late "Mexican George".)

The Romani national anthem – Opre Roma 'Arise Roma'

Djélem djélem lúngone drômènsa
Maladílem báxtale Rromênsa
Ái Rromále, kátar túmen áven
Le tsêrènsa báxtale drômènsa
Vi-man sas u[†] bári familíya
Thai mudardya la E Kali Lêgíya
Ái Rromale, Ái Shavale (repeat twice)
Áven mánsa sa lumiyáke Rroma
Kai putáile le Rrománe dróma
Áke vryámya, úshte Rrôm akána
Ame xutása míshto kai kerása
Ái Rromale, Ái Shavale (repeat twice)

---

*   **makyol-makilo** 'get drunk' from the thematic adjective **mato** 'drunk'. An alternative verb form exists in **matyol-matilo**.

†   **u** indefinite article from Zarko's Yugoslavian Romani dialect.

Translation

I have travelled over long roads
I have met with fortunate Roma
Oh Romani adults, Oh Romani youth [repeat twice]
Oh Roma, from wherever you come
With tents along fortunate roads
I too once had a large family
But the Black Legion [Nazis] murdered them
Come with me, Roma of the world
To where the Romani roads have opened
Now is the time – stand up Roma!
We shall succeed where we make the effort
Oh Romani adults, Oh Romani youth

(Words composed by the late Zarko Jovanovic, a Romani Holocaust survivor, and adopted at the First World Romani Congress, London, 8 April 1971. The melody is based on a traditional Serbian-Romani song but in the anthem it is in march-time.)

Answers to questions in this lesson

1.	**múrra Rrômnyáki stagi**
2.	**le vôrdônèski filástra**
3.	**le vôrdônènge filástri**

Lesson fourteen

More about numbers

When cardinal numbers are used on their own referring to people or animals who are the object of an action, they take accusative case endings which then serve as the oblique stem in other cases excluding the vocative, as shown below:

Sóde manusha avile?   How many men came?
Dikhlem don   I saw two (accusative)

The forms in the accusative are as follows:

1. **yêkhès**	9. **enyan**
2. **don**	10. **deshên**
3. **trinên**	20. **bishên**
4. **shtarên**	30. **triandan**
5. **panshên**	40. **shtar-war-deshên**
6. **shovên**	50. **pindan**
7. **iftan**	1,000. **miyan**
8. **oxton**	1,000,000. **milionên**

These words behave like other nouns when they have case endings:

Si tut yêkh, so keres shtarênsa?   You have one, what will you do with four (of them)?

Gêlém avre panshênsa   I went with five other (men)

Arakhlem le trinên   I found the three of them

but note

Woi si shey le hiftánsa shukarimatánsa   She is a girl with the seven beauties (folk tale)

This type of construction is used more often when the adjective is in apposition (follows) the noun it modifies:

Wo si o Rom, o barvalo   He is the Rom, the rich one
Dem-dúma le Rromêsa, le barvalêsa   I spoke with the Rom, the rich one
Dem-dúma la Rromnyása, la barvalyása   I spoke to the Romani woman, the rich one

Dem-dúma le Rromênsa, le barvalênsa I spoke to the Roma, the rich ones

Numeral adjectives

When numbers are used as adjectives they have the following oblique inflections:

yêkhé	before masculine nouns in the oblique
yêkhá	before feminine nouns in the oblique
yêkhé	before plurals of both genders in the oblique
do, done	two
trine	three
shtare	four
panshe	five
shove	six
hiftatone	seven
oxtotone	eight
inyatone	nine
deshetone	ten

From eleven to nineteen use the forms above combined with **dêsh-u-** (number in the oblique).

bishe	twenty

From multiples of ten from twenty to one hundred inflect only the number at the end of the compound: **bish-ta-yêkhé** and so on.

triyándone	thirty
píndone	fifty
shêlé	hundred
mílone	thousand
mílyone	million

Examples

Yêkhá tilarása chi kines khánchi ages	With one dollar you can't buy anything today
Yêkhá bulása nashti bêshes pe done grastênde	With one rear end you can't ride on two horses (i.e. you can't be in two opposing camps at the same time)

Si lês vôrdòn done grastênsa	He has a caravan with two horses
Mardyas-pe hiftatone raklênsa	He fought with seven non-Romani boys
Shêlé Gazhêndar chi daráva	I am not afraid of 100 non-Roma (poem)

Fractions

filtári (m.)	quarter
yêkh filtári	one quarter
dopashin (f.)	half (noun), **do-pash** (adjective inflected for gender and number)
trin-filtárya	three-quarters

Examples with 'half'

Do-pash is inflected when used as an adjective with nouns in the oblique but it is not declined in the nominative.

Noun:

Lyas pêski dopashin	He took his half
Arakhlem le dui dopashina	I found the two halves

Adjective in the nominative:

Do-pash Rrôm si	He is half-Romani (one non-Romani parent. The noun **Rrôm** is used here)
Xalyas do-pash o mas	She ate half the meat

Adjective in the oblique:

Gêlótar dopashe le masêsa	He left with half of the meat
Nashlótar dopasha la marikyása	He ran away with half of the cake (**mariki** 'cake')
Gêlótar dopashe le Rromênsa	He left with half of the men
Gêlítar do-pashe le Rrômnyánsa	She left with half of the women

Units of measure, amounts, distance, etc.

Singular	Plural	
dêsêtína	dêsêtíni	acre
sêntimètro	sêntimètra	centimetre
dáimo	dáimurya	dime (ten cents)
tilára	tilêri	dollar
duzína	duzíni	dozen
panshêngi	panshênge	five-dollar bill
pínda sênturya		fifty cents
pindáki	pindáke	fifty-dollar bill
pûnrró	pûnrré	foot/feet
galóno	galóiya	gallon
grámo	grámurya	gram
do-pash duzína		half a dozen
shêláki	shêláke	hundred-dollar bill
sapûsh (m.)	sapûsha	inch
kilomêtro	kilomêtra	kilometre
mêtro	mêtra	metre
míya/míla	míyi, míli	mile
drámo	drámurya	ounce
do-pash butêlka	do-pash butêlchi	pint (of beer)
fúnto	fúntsi	pound
chêtwèrto	chêtwèrturya	quart
cheréko	cherékurya	quarter (of beef)
fránka	fránchi	quarter (25 cents)
deshêngi	deshênge	ten-dollar bill
hiliyáda	hiliyádi	ton
bish-tilára-súmnakai		twenty-dollar gold piece
harshûno	harshûnurya	yard
líra (f.)	líri	pound (sterling)
shîlíngo (m.)	shîlíngurya	shilling
yêkh líra		one pound
dui líri		two pounds
yêkh péni		one penny
dui péni		twopence

In North America, the word **líra** with a plural in **líri** is a counting unit based on the one-time value of gold at US $50 per ounce. Thus **desh líri** means ten times fifty dollars or $500. **Líra** also has the meaning of 'pound of gold'. The same term is used in Europe with a different monetary value applied to the **líra.** In Romanian, the word *líra* means one pound sterling so the word is actually a Romanian loan word in Romani. The song *Lúma Maj* (*Lúma Maı*) recorded by *Kalyi Jag* in Hungary has the line, **_triyánda líri me dav túke, Lúma Mai_** which translates as 'I'll offer you thirty *liri, Lúma Maı*' in reference to a bridal price. (*Chantes Tziganes de Hongrie*, Playa Sound, Audovis Distribution, 1993.) There is no word for guinea but it can be expressed as **yêkh líra thai yêkh shîlíngo** (one guinea) and ten guineas **desh líri thai desh shîlíngurya** (ten pounds and ten shillings).

Quantities

but	many, a lot, a lot of, much
desya but	too much, too many, very much, very many
mai but	more
mai xansi	less
sa, sya*	all (inflected to **sare** and **sarya** in the oblique)
sórro	all (as an adjective **sórro ryáto** 'all night' or **sórro ges** 'all day')
tsirra	a few, small amount of
tsirratsítsa	a very small amount of
xantsi	less
xordo	small amount of, small (adjective)
zaloga	small amount, a little (also means 'slightly' as an adverb)
zalogítsa	trifling amount

Examples

Avile but zhêné kai sláva	A lot of people came to the feast
Dem lêske tsírra love	I gave him a little money
Mangel sa kai si man	He wants all I have
Sa gêlèntar	They all left
Phabardyas sa pêske love	He wasted all his money

---

*   Examples of **sa** when inflected in the oblique:

    Gêlótar sare le xabenésa   He went away with all the food (**xabe** (m.) 'food')

    Gêlítar sara la marikyása   She went away with all the cake (**mariki** (f.) 'cake')

    Nashlótar sare le lovênsa   He fled with all the money (**love** (m.pl.) 'money')

Rromníyo, grizhosar zaloga!	Hey, wife, clean up a little bit!
Lem mai xansi lêstar	I got less than him
mai but wôrka mai xansi	more or less
mai but de shêl tilêri	more than a hundred dollars (usually used with **de** in this meaning)
mai xansi de shêl tiléri	less than a hundred dollars (usually used with **de** in this meaning)
xorde love	small change, small amount of coins
Dilyardyas lês thai mêklas	She made a fool of him and left him with
lês xorde lovênsa ánde posuki	small change in his pocket (skinned him alive)

'Each other', 'one another'

yêkh-avrês (m.)	each other	**yêkh-avrèn** (m.pl.)	one another
yêkh-avrya (f.)	each other	**yêkh-avryan** (f.pl.)	one another

Chi den-dúma yêkhé-avrêsa	They don't talk to each other (two men)
Chi den-dúma yêkhá-avryása	They don't talk to each other (two women)
Akushline yêkhé-avren	They swore at one another (more than two men)
Akushline yêkhé-avryan	They swore at one another (more than two women)

Sometimes the reflexive pronouns **pês** and **pên**, both of which are usually contracted to **pe**, are used instead of the words 'each other' and 'one another':

Volin-pe	They love each other (they are in love)

'Another'

As a noun:

mangel aver	he wants another, another one (if masculine gender)
mangel avrya	he wants another, another one (if feminine gender)
Zhanes avrên kai zhanen?	Do you know others who know (this)?

As a pronoun this means 'an other' and is declined for gender and number in the nominative and inflected to the oblique:

Aver sas kai gilabadyas	It was another person who sang (nominative)

Nas woi kai muli, avrya sas   It wasn't she who died, it was another (nominative)

There is no change for gender in the nominative singular but the plural is subject to root inflection:

Avre sas kai akushline lês   It was others who insulted him

The oblique forms are subject to root inflection for gender and number:

Chi dikhlem avrês	I didn't see any other person (m. accusative)
Chi dikhlem avrya	I didn't see any other person (f. accusative)
Avrêsko sas	It belonged to somebody else (m. genitive)
Avryáko sas	It belonged to another woman (genitive)
Avrêngo mobíliya si	The cars belong to other people (genitive pl.)
Gêlótar avrênsa	He departed with other people (instrumental pl.)

Aver can also sometimes mean 'else' as in 'somebody else':

Volil wárekon avrês	She loves somebody else (accusative)
Volil wárekon avrya	He loves somebody else (accusative)
Sas wárekon aver kai kerdyas	It was somebody else who did it (nominative)

Music

In Europe, Romani musicians do not use the same terminology as the English-speaking world:

Europe	English
Do	C
Re	D
Mi	E
Fa	F
Sol	G
La	A
Si	B
Do	C
Madjóre	Major
Minóre	Minor
Gili ánde La Madjóre	A song in A Major
Gili ánde Re Minóre	A song in D Minor

Useful musical words and expressions

ámpo (m.)	amplifier (shortened form of **amplafikatóri**, plural **ámpurya**)
ándo gláso	in tune, in voice
báso	base, rhythm
gili (f.)	song, tune
kapêlmáistoro	band leader (plural **kapêmáistorya**, also **primash** in Lovarítska)
kidári (m.)	pick-up (plural **kidáriya**)
kórdo	chord (plural **kórdurya**)
kiyáiya	tuning screw (plural **kiyáiyi**)
lavutári (m.)	violinist, musician (plural **lavutárya**)
máistoro-muzikánto	virtuoso, master musician (plural **máistorya-muzikánturya**)
mêlodíya	melody (plural **mêlodíyi**)
mikrofóno	microphone (plural **mikrofónurya**)
morki (f.)	skin of a drum (plural **morkya**)
muzíka	music
muzikánto	musician (plural **muzikánturya**)
nilóno	nylon string (plural **nilónurya**)
plástiko	pick, plectrum (plural **plástichi**)
shtrángo	plug-in cord (plural **shtrángurya**)
sistéma-sonóri	sound system (plural **sistémi-sonórya**)
skamin (m.)	bridge of a stringed instrument
vuchimos (m.)	action (height of strings from top of body at the 12th fret on a guitar)
xóro	band, choir, music group (plural **xórya**)
zhútso	steel string (plural **zhútsurya**)
Tyi gitára nai ándo gláso	Your guitar is not in tune
Tyo skamin chi beshel wórta	Your bridge is out of adjustment (does not sit right, out of alignment)

Instruments

While Roma may play any existing instrument, the following are those most usually found in popular and folk music Romani groups:

bragi (f.)	metal milking pot used as a drum (plural **bragya**)
buzúki (m.)	Greek bouzouki (plural **buzúkya**)

dáfi (m.)	Turkish or Arab tambourine with animal skin and double bells (plural **dáfya**)
darbúka	metal drum with skin or plastic skin (plural **darbúki**)
daúli (m.)	large skin drum played along with a **zúrna** (q.v.) (plural **daúlya**)
flúyera	flute (plural **flúyerya**)
gitára	guitar (plural **gitári**)
gormónya	piano accordion (plural **gormónyi**)
harmónika	electric organ or piano accordion (plural **harmónichi**)
klarinêto	clarinet (plural **klarinêturya**)
laúto	fretted lute (plural **laúturya**)
lávuta	violin (plural **lávuti**)
mandolíno	mandolin (plural **mandolínurya**)
saksafóno	saxophone (plural **saxafónurya**)
sázi	saz (plural **sázya**)
sinzizáto	synthesizer (plural **sinzizáturya**)
swiráika	orchestral tambourine (plural **swiráichi**)
tambúra	type of mandola resembling an "Irish bouzouki" (plural **tambúri**)
tóba	drum (plural **tóbi**)
tobash (m.)	drummer (plural **tobásha**)
tobáshka (f.)	drummer (plural **tobáshki**)
trompéta	trumpet (plural **trompéti**)
tsímbalom	cymbalom (singular usually used for plural)
úti (m.)	oud, fretless lute (plural **útya**)
zúrna	double-reed shawm (plural **zúrni**)

Subjunctive mood

While there is no subjunctive verb tense in Romani, there is a subjunctive mood which separates two conjugated verbs by the particle **< te >**. This is used to express the infinitive of the verb, as in 'to come', 'to eat', etc.

Mangav te zhav	I want to go
Mangel te zhal	He wants to go
Mangav te aves	I want you to come
Kai manges te zhas?	Where do you want to go?
So manges te kerav?	What do you want me to do?
Mangen te avas	They want us to come
Mangle te bashavas	They wanted us to play music

Pushlem látar te khelel-pe	I asked her to dance (**khelel-pe** 'she dances', a reflexive transitive verb)
Kam-shunav lês te gilabal	I shall hear him sing

< na > is used for 'not'

Mangav te na avel	I don't want him to come (I want him not to come)
Phen lêske te na kerel	Tell him not to do (it)

< Te > as an optative particle (expressing a wish or desire) must also be used for the following types of expressions in Romani (look out for these in the songs, folk tales and other material in this course):

Te avel tehára	I hope he comes tomorrow (may he come tomorrow)
Te lel lês o bêng	May the devil take him

It is also used to translate the following types of expressions where the present participles of verbs are used in English:

Te gilabav si múrri plácha	I enjoy singing (singing is my pleasure)
Ashundem la te gilabal	I heard her singing
Ashundem wárekon te marel po wudar	I heard somebody knocking on the door
Dikhlem lês te xal	I watched him eating
Dikhlem lês te avel	I saw him coming, approaching

Test whether you have understood
Translate:

1.   We want them to eat with us
2.   He asks me to sell him my horse (the ablative noun case must be used with the verb to ask)

Reading pieces
Proverbs
Yêkh dilo kerel but dile thai but dile keren dilimáta
One fool makes many fools and many fools create stupidity

Te xines-tu ánde Breyíla xines-tu* ánde Bukarêshti
If you disgrace yourself in Breyila, you'll disgrace yourself in Bucharest

Kai si thuv, kothe vi[†] si yag
Where there is smoke, there is also fire

A folk tale in Canadian Kalderash-Romani

This folk tale was recorded in 1962 from Waso Russel Demitro in the old, traditional style of rhyming metre. Waso was one of the last extant in Canada among the elders in the 1960s who could still remember these old stories. None of his five sons or three daughters could repeat them. The translation is inserted between paragraphs.

Yéla, e fárma-katárka 'Yela the witch'

E Yéla sas fárma-katárka hai woi sas she bari, hai woi sas buzhangli, hai butêndar sas piradi. Woi beshélas po brégo le Daryevêsko hai katélas hai gilabálas hai sáni tsírma woi tsirdélas hai ánda móste woi phenélas, "Háiden, háiden, shavorrále, te dikhen e Yéla. Dikh, aven le dui phrala. Waresávo kon notíla inkyal o Daryévo thai-vi káring, kódo-vi te lel e Yéla."[††]

Yela was a weaver of spells [witch] and she was an eldest daughter, and she was cunning, and by many she was courted. She was sitting on the bank of the Danube and knitting and a thin strand she was drawing and from her mouth she was saying, "Come on, come on, boys, to see Yela. Look at the two brothers. Whichever one of you who swims across the Danube and towards here, that one will take [marry] Yela."

O Márko, o phral o mai baro phendyas, "Háide, háide, phrála, te dikhas la Yéla!"

Marko, the bigger (older) brother said, "Come on, brother, let's go see Yela!"

O phral o mai terno phenéla, "Na zha, phrála, sav ka Yéla, ke woi si shey-bari, hai woi si buzhangli hai butêndar sas phiradi."¶

---

*   **xines-tu** 'you soil yourself'.

†   **vi** means 'also', another form of < i- > as in **i-me zhav** 'I too am going'.

††   **fárma-katárka** 'witch, weaver of spells', **brégo** 'bank', **Daryévo** 'Danube', **katélas** 'she was weaving', **sáni tsírma** 'thin strand', **tsirdélas** 'she was drawing', **háiden** 'come', **notíla** 'swims', **káring** 'towards', **kódo-vi** 'that one indeed'.

¶   **sav ka Yéla** 'all the way over to Yela', **shey-bari** 'eldest daughter', **buzhangli** 'cunning', **butêndar** 'by many', **phiradi** 'wooed, courted'.

The younger brother says, "Don't go, brother, over to Yela, because she is an eldest daughter, and she is cunning and she has been courted by many."

O Márko, wo chi pakyála, thai kai Yéla wo kai zhála. Pa pêste pêske tsáliya léla hai ándo Daryévo wo xutéla. Inkyal po Daryévo wo nakhéla hai pálpale wo amboldéla. Kána pásha o mólo areséla Yéla astaréla tai gilabála hai sáni tsírma woi tsirdéla. O Márko o pai lel lêske wast hai lêske pûnrré hai o Márko tasóla.*

Marko, he didn't believe, and towards Yela he went. He took off his clothing and into the Danube he jumps. Across the Danube he crosses and turns to look behind him. When he reaches close to the shoreline, Yela begins to sing and a slender strand she draws. The water takes (numbs) his hands and feet and Marko drowns.

O Geórgi, o phral o mai terno ándo pai xutéla pêske phralês te ankalavéla Kána lêste areséla. Wo sas mulo. Po tsirmorro lês ankalavéla hai kána pála lêste mai dikhéla, la Yéla chi mai dikhyóla.†

Georgi, the younger brother jumps into the water to rescue his brother. When he reaches him, he is dead. With a small rope he gets him out and when he looks behind him again, Yela is no longer visible.

Hai o Geórgi so keréla? Lês po grast thóla tha lês nigerel khere lês te angropóla hai solax wo léla, la Yéla wo te mudaréla.††

And Georgi what does he do? He puts him (Marko) on his horse and carries him home to bury him and an oath he takes to kill Yela.

Dui bêrsh sa Bálkano wo phiréla tha la Yéla chi mai arakhéla. Ánde Bukarêshti wo areséla ka o Stánko, o Rrôm o barvalo hai o báro kakyavári.¶

---

*   pakyála 'believes', inkyal 'across', amboldéla 'turns', mólo 'shore', astaréla 'starts', lel
     'takes', tasóla 'drowns'.

†   ankalalvel 'take out', tsirmorro (here) 'a thin rope', pála lêste 'behind himself, over his
     shoulder', chi mai dikhyóla 'was not to be seen any more'.

††   nigerel 'carries', khere 'home' (adverb), angropóla 'bury', solax 'oath, vow'.

¶   kakyavári 'kettlesmith, metal smith' (from kakyavi/kakavi 'kettle'. The < ári > suffix is
     common to denote a trade, for example, pushkári 'gunsmith' from púshka 'gun').

For two years he travels all the Balkans and never finds Yela. He arrives in Bucharest at Stanko's, the rich Rom and the renowned kettlesmith.

"Mai drobroi tu, Káko Stánko," wo mothóla

"Greetings, Uncle Stanko," he says.

"Nayis-túke, Geórgi," o Stánko wo phenéla, "pála sóste avilyan khate?"

"Thank you, Georgi," Stanko says, "for what reason have you come here?"
(Continued in the next lesson)

According to Waso Russel Demitro, Yéla was a **djúli** or 'spirit of the forest', a type of **víla** 'fairy' or **keshali** 'nymph who spins spells with silk thread' who had assumed human form as a beautiful woman to lure men to their deaths. Not all these **djúlya** or **keshalya** are evil in Kalderash folklore. They can use their magic for good or evil depending on the circumstances. In Kalderash folklore, **fárma-katárka** means 'a weaver of spells' and the root is **fárma** 'drugs, medication' so means a woman who has the ability to work with herbs and natural products to cure sickness, assist childbirth and work sympathetic magic which is called **fármichi** from **farmáko** 'spell'. It can be roughly translated as 'white witch'. In Marko's case, it might be theorized that he got what was coming to him since his intentions were somewhat less than honourable, even if the punishment was extremely drastic.

Waso Russel Demitro was born in the US, from immigrant Kalderash parents, and was brought to Canada by his family. He told me he learned this story from his father which would locate it in the Balkans, and the mention of the Danube and Bucharest would more than suggest Romania. This type of **paramíchi** or folk tale died out with the urbanization of the Kalderash in Canada and the US. Roma still tell stories but no longer in rhyming metre.

A twenty-dollar gold piece – an American-Kalderash song

Ai bish-tilára súmnakai	
Bish-tilára-súmnakai	A twenty-dollar gold piece [repeat twice]
Sa ándo súmnakai	All in gold [repeat twice]
Kakya sheyórri	This girl
Kai me voliv	That I love
Kakya sheyórri	This girl
Woi kai me voliv	She that I love [repeat twice]
Thai láko dad	And her father
Thai láki dey	And her mother

Won chi kamen	They don't want
Chi kamen te den	They don't want to give her (in marriage)
Chi kamen te den	They don't want to give her (repeat verse twice)
Bish-tilára súmnakai	A twenty-dollar gold piece (repeat twice)
Sa ándo súmnakai	All in gold (repeat twice)

More verses are ad-libbed by the singer.

Answers to questions in this lesson

1.   **Mangas te xan amênsa**
2.   **Pushel mándar te bikinav lêske múrre grastês**

Lesson fifteen

The adverb

The adverb is formed by adding **< es >** to the stem of thematic adjectives ending in a stressed **< o >**. If **kovlo** means 'soft' then **kovles** means 'softly', for example, **o pai zhal kovles** 'the water flows softly'.

Examples

baxtalo	fortunate	**baxtales**	fortunately
chacho	true, real	**chaches**	truly, really
dilivano	stupid	**dilivanes**	stupidly
polokorro	slow	**polokorres**	slowly

Note these two:

Gazhikano	non-Romani	**Gazhikanes**	like a/the non-Roma
Rromano	Romani	**Rromanes**	like a Rom, like the Roma

Thematic adjectives ending in a consonant add **< es >**:

shukar	beautiful	**shukares**	beautifully

Athematic adjectives ending in an unstressed **< o >** retain the **< o >** and add **< nes >**:

múndro	wonderful	**mundrones**	wonderfully

Plural adverb

There is also a plural adverb ending in **< en >** which is not heard in all dialects but which I have recorded from some middle-aged and elderly native speakers in North America as late as 2003. This can usually be ignored since most Roma, especially in Europe, do not use it:

le paiya zhan kovlen	the waters flow softly
phirénas polokorren	they were walking slowly
keren-pe(n) dilivanen	they are behaving stupidly

Comparison of adverbs

Kako mobíli zhal zurales	This car goes fast
Kodo mobíli zhal mai zurales	That car goes faster (more fast)
Kuko mobíli zhal o mai zurales	Yonder car goes the fastest (the most fast)

There are some adverbs which are complete in themselves. Some of these are also adjectives and prepositions, for example:

dur	far	**O drôm zhal dur**	The road goes far
fêrdi	only	**Fêrdi dikhlem le Babes**	I only saw Bob
fúgo	quickly	**Zha fúgo!**	Go quickly!
ivya	freely, gratis	**Dêm andre ivya**	I got in free
mishto	well, splendidly	**Mishto kerdyan**	You did well
rano	early	**Telyardyas rano**	He left early

Mai mishto and **mai gorde** mean 'better' and 'worse':

E Mára gilabal mishto	Mary sings well
E Ána gilabal mai mishto	Anne sings better
E Rayída gilabal o mai mishto	Edith sings the best
E Tína gilabal chorres	Tina sings badly
E Dára gilabal mai gorde	Dora sings worse
E Pavléna gilabal o mai gorde	Pauline sings the worst

Wórta has many meanings including 'straight', 'right', 'directly', 'justly', 'fairly' and can also be used as an adjective:

Zha wórta!	Go straight, straight ahead!
Chachimos, so phenav?	Isn't it true what I say? (question)
Wórta!	Right! (in answer to a question)
Nai wórta so kerel	It's not right what he is doing
Phendem lês wórta ándo lêsko mui	I told him straight to his face
Nai wórta so phenav?	Isn't that right, what I am saying?
Gindas le love wórta	He counted the money fairly

The word **sar** 'like' is also used to express adverbial meaning in phrases:

Del-dúma Rromanes sar o pai	He speaks Romani fluently (like water)
Del-dúma sar e bráshka	He speaks hoarsely (like a frog)
Kerel-pe sar o dilo	He is acting stupidly (like an idiot)
Ker sar me kerav?	Do as I do?

The instrumental case of nouns can sometimes serve as an adverb:

Vryamyása ame das-ame lása	Eventually, we'll get used to it (**vryamyása** 'with time')
Del-dúma zorása	He speaks with power, convincingly (**zor** (f.) power, strength)

This gives a different meaning than the following:

Del-dúma zorales	He speaks loudly (adverb)

Nouns in the genitive case used with the privative particle **< bi- >** can also sometimes serve as adverbs:

Del-dúma bi-zoráko	He speaks without power, unconvincingly (the privative particle **< bi- >** is explained later in this lesson)

Sometimes adverbial meaning is expressed by idiomatic constructions:

Thon pênge barimáta pe pênde	They are behaving ostentatiously (they are placing their importance on themselves)
Amboldisáilo e bul opre	It turned upside down (bottom up)
O grast phirélas páplale bulása	The horse was walking backwards (back by the rear)

Word list

List of commonly used words in Kalderash including some which are multifunctional and can serve as adverbs, prepositions or conjunctions:

ambóri	maybe, perhaps
anúmi	on purpose, deliberately
ánde wúrma	finally, at last
Che fyal?	What sort of? What kind of? Which kind of?
chi mai	anymore, no more
defyal	at all, in no way, really, anyhow
desya	very, too, overly (**desya dur** 'too far')
i-, vi-	also, too (usually prefixed to pronouns or nouns)
intáini	to no purpose, without reason, for nothing
ivya	free, without charge or payment
kadiki	so, this (usually with **de**, for example, **kadiki de baro** 'this big')

kadya	thus, like this, so
kâsevó*	so, such, so much
khatênde	nowhere, anywhere
kodya	thus, like that, so
mai	ever
mai anglal	before, in front of, ahead
mai angle	forward, in front of
mai do gáta	nearly, almost
mai palorral	later, afterwards
núma	even, but
pôrma	then
samuchi	nearly, almost (**Samuchi mulo** 'He almost died')
sar	how, like, as
sáyêkh	always, forever
shai-vi	perhaps, maybe
Sóde?	How much? (interrogative and relative)
Sodya?	How many? (interrogative and relative)
sogodi	however many, so many, whatever
swágdar	forever, always
wárekai	anywhere, somewhere
wunívar	sometimes

Examples

Mai anglal te zhav	Before I leave
Mulo tsírra mai palorral	He died a little later
Le sogodi so manges	Take however many you want
Zha mai angle	Go forward (adverb)
Zha mai angle mándar	Go in front of me (preposition)

Many adverbs, some of which are also prepositions, end in a stressed **< é >**:

agore	towards the edge
andre	inside
angle	forward, ahead

---

*   **kâsevó** has many meanings and is subject to gender and number:

Kâsevó si sar o vitiyázo   He is so much like a hero
Kâseví si sar e lulugi   She is so much like a flower
Kâsavé si sar le ánzhêlya   They are so much like angels

aworde	over here, this way
khere	home
mashkare	into the middle, in among
opre	up, upwards, upstairs
tele	down, downwards, downstairs

Similar to this group are the following:

Djurdjevdáne	St George's Day
Krechune	at Christmas
Kurkone	on Sunday(s)
Patradjine	at Easter
Santane	on St Anne's Day
Savotune	on Saturday(s)
Zhune	on Christmas Eve

There are also a large number of adverbs with the ending **< al >** implying direction, location, etc. which will be found throughout the lessons, for example, **andre** 'inside, in' gives **andral** 'from inside, from within' as in **Ashundem andral e kumpaníya** 'I heard from inside the community.' Some of these are multifunctional and the following are typical:

agoral	at the end of, edge of
andral	from inside
anglal	in front of, before (usually as **mai anglal**)
avryal	from outside
awordal	from over here, from this place
choryal	sneakily, stealthily
dural	from afar, a long way off
inkyal	across, over
kheral	from home
kruyal	around, round about
mashkaral	in the middle
muiyal	face up, upside down
opral	from above, from the top of
palal	at the rear, behind
palorral	later, afterwards (usually with **mai** as in **mai palorral**)
pálpale	back, back again
pashal	nearby, close by
stêngál	to the left, on the left (side)
telal	underneath

Examples

Avilo andral	He came from inside
Kerav lês mai palorral	I'll do it later
O pai pikyal opral	The water is leaking from above
Phirdem mai anglal	I walked forward, ahead, in front of
Avilo dural	He came from far away
Musai te zhas mai anglal	We must move ahead (adverb)
Gêlótar mai anglal ke areslem	He left before I arrived (conjunction)

The privative particle

The productive privative particle **< bi- >** means 'without' or 'un' and serves to give words the opposite meaning. It is prefixed to adjectives, adverbs and, in one exceptional case, to a noun.

Examples with adjectives:

baxtalo	lucky	**bi-baxtalo**	unlucky
pharo	heavy, difficult	**bi-pharo**	light, easy

Adjectives with this prefix are still inflected for number and gender in in the oblique:

bi-baxtalo mursh	an unlucky man
bi-baxtali zhuvli	an unlucky woman
bi-baxtale rakle	unlucky boys

Examples with adverbs:

pakivales	honourably	**bi-pakivales**	dishonourably
Kerel-pe(s) pakivales	He behaves honourably		
Kerel-pe(s) bi-pakivales	He behaves dishonourably		

Examples with a noun:

baxt	luck	**bi-baxt**	bad luck
Che bi-baxt!	What bad luck!		

Prekazhime sim, sya bi-baxt pe mánde I am jinxed, (it's) all bad luck on me

When **< bi- >** is prefixed to a noun inflected to the genitive case, it gives the meaning of 'without'. Since these nouns in the genitive case can also be used as adjectives, **< bi- >** can be prefixed as it is with other adjectives to give **bi-grastêsko** 'without a horse' and **bi-grastêngo** 'without horses'. These adjectives must then be inflected for gender and number in the nominative and the oblique, for example, **grast** 'horse' and **grastêsko** 'belonging to a horse'.

Examples

bi-manrrêsko	without bread
bi-lovêngo	without money, broke
Ame ashilyam vôrdônènsa thai bi-grastênge	We were left with caravans and without horses
Rrôm bi-grastêsko nai Rrom	A Rom without a horse is not a Rom
Rrôm bi-shibáko nai Rrôm	A Rom without tongue is not a Rom (i.e. a Rom who doesn't speak Romani is not a Rom)

When used like the above example, this use of **< bi- >** serves as the opposite of the instrumental case, but if 'the' or 'my' or another modifying word comes between 'without' and the person or thing, then this word has the **< sa >** ending and must be in the instrumental case.

With examples like these, **bi** stands alone as a word in itself:

bi le manrrêsa	without the bread
bi lêske lovênsa	without his money

Note also the following:

bi-mánsa 'without me', **bi-tusa**, **bi-lêsa**, **bi-lása**, **bi-amênsa**, **bi-tumênsa**, **bi-lênsa**

Examples

Nashti kerav e buki bi-túsa	I can't do the work without you
O djédjêsh gêlótar bi-mánsa	The train left without me

But be aware that when **< bi- >** is used with personal pronouns and the meaning is insulting or sarcastic, the following forms are used. Some speakers do not make a clear distinction between the previous pattern using the instrumental and that following:

bi-mángo	without me
bi-túko	without you
bi-lêsko	without him

bi-láko	without her
bi-amêngo	without us
bi-tumêngo	without you (pl.)
bi-lêngo	without them

Examples

Dilo san. Tu zhas bi-mángo!	You're crazy. You'll go without me!
Sa meren bokhátar bi-mángo	They'll all die from hunger without me
Te na azhutin man, kerav lês bi-lêngo	If they won't help me I'll do it without them
Mek zhántar. Shinas e kris* bi-lêngo!	Let them depart. We'll reach a verdict in the trial without them!

Bi can also be used with verbs, as in the following examples:

Rodem pe swáko rêgá† bi te dikhav khánchi	I looked everywhere without seeing anything
Rodem, rodem, bi te arakhav la	I searched, I searched, without finding her

Thematic inchoative and passive verbs ending in < yol >

Words ending in **< yol >** in the 'he' form have slightly different endings from those ending in **< ol >**. Refer back to Lesson nine where these forms are explained in detail.

mothov	**lolyovav**	I go red, become red (blush)
mothos	**lolyos**	you go red
mothol	**lolyol**	he goes red
mothos	**lolyos**	we go red
mothon	**lolyon**	you go red
mothon	**lolyon**	they go red

Try making all the forms of **baryol** 'he/she gets bigger, grows'. These verbs are formed in two ways:

(1) Those derived from thematic adjectives such as **lolo** 'red' and **baro** 'big' which give **lolyol** 'he gets red, blushes' and **baryol** 'he grows, gets big';

---

*   **Shinas e kris** 'We'll cut the trial (reach a verdict)'.

†   **pe swáko rêgá** 'on every side, all around, everywhere'.

(2) Those derived from past participles of thematic verbs such as **mudardo** 'killed' which gives **mudárdyol**.

Examples

kingo	wet	**kingyol**	he gets wet
bango	bent	**bangyol**	it gets bent
mudardo	killed	**mudárdyol**	he is killed, gets killed
kirado	boiled	**kirádyol**	it gets boiled
dikhlo	seen	**díkhyol**	it gets seen, is seen

Athematic verbs ending in **< il >** and **< ol >** have their own reflexive forms and cannot serve to create the **< yol >** verbs like those for thematic verbs. See Lesson twelve for athematic verbs, transitive and intransitive/reflexive forms.

Reading pieces

Yela the witch (continued from Lesson fourteen)

"Avilem la Yéla te arakhav hai la te mudarav."

"I came to find Yela and to kill her."

"Tu, na róde la Yéla, ke e Yéla tut mudaréla. Sóstar tu la Yéla ródes?"

"You, don't search for Yela, because Yela will kill you. Why are you looking for Yela?"

"Ke* mudardyas múrre phralês."

"Because she killed my brother."

"Ánde Breyíla tu te zhas. Othe tu la Yéla arakhes. E Póla si fárma-katárka tha woi si láki gazderítsa†."

"You must go into Breyila. There you will find Yela. Pola is a weaver of spells and she is her mentor."

Ka e Póla o Geórgi gyas hai baro mangin ka e Pola dyas hai pêsko gor lyas, la Yéla arakhlyas tha wo la mudardyas.††

Georgi went to Pola and gave her a big treasure and he attained his end, he found Yela and he killed her.

---

*   **ke** 'because'.

†   **gazderítsa** 'mentor, teacher'.

††   **Notes: gyas** 'he went' (an old form of past tense used instead of **gêló** because of the need for rhyming metre), **mangin** 'treasure', **lyas o gor** 'and got the information he wanted' (idiom: **dem ándo gor** 'I succeeded', **lyas o gor** 'he took his end (got what he wanted)').

A Pentecostal hymn in French-Kalderash-Romani

(Substitute words for this course are given in brackets)

Te kames e vóya, e cháchi vóya   (**losh** (f.) 'joy')
Mek O Del ándo tyo yilo
Dikhéla tye bezexa   (**bezaxa** (m.pl.) 'sins')
Ai vo chaches yertíla túke,   (**wo** 'he')
Ai angeréla tut pêsa ándo chéri   (**ingaréla, nikeréla** 'carry, transport'
                                      and **Raiyo** 'Heaven')

Te trayis lêsa chachimása.*

Translation

If you want the joy, the true joy
Let God get into your heart
He sees your sins
And he will truly forgive you
And he will transport you into Heaven
So you can live with him with truth.

Canadian-Kalderash round

Éta avêntar dui sheya   Behold the two girls emerging
Le wêrshèstar zêlenyá†   From the forest green
Patriyorránsa ánde l'wast   With leaves in their hands
Thai lulugyánsa ánde l'bal   And flowers in their hair
Xanamíka piyav tyo rat   Co-father-in-law, I drink your blood (honour
                                      you)

Háide amênde swáko ryat   Come visit us every night
Kerav túke gad lolo   I'll make you a red shirt
Chirêshènsa po shoro.   With (embroidered) cherries around the top.

Kalderash table song

Recorded in 1960 from Vanya Kwiek while living and travelling together as
work partners in rural Quebec, Canada.

---

*   French-Kalderash words used in the text: **vóya** 'joy', **mek** 'let', **del ándo** 'comes in,
     enters', **bezaxa** 'sins', **angeréla** 'brings', **chéri** 'sky, Heaven'.
†   Feminine oblique for masculine **zelene** to rhyme with **sheya** at the end of the previous
     line, as is often done in Kalderash songs.

Ángla mánde dui drômá 'Before me [are] two roads'

Molatnívas sórro ryáto	I was having a wild party all night long
Tehára ánde diminyátsa	Until tomorrow morning
Makyovávas amalênsa	I was getting drunk with friends
Xasarávas múrri viyátsa	I was wasting my life
Lem-man, Dále, thai gêlémtar	I made up my mind, Mother, and departed
Ka l' dui drômá me areslem	I arrived at two roads
Yêkh chi dur, yêkh chi pashal	One not far, one not near
D'aresáva	To arrive at
Dikhlem opre, dikhlem tele	I looked up, I looked down
Chi konikas me chi dikhlem	I didn't see anybody [nobody]
Me dikhlem êkh chirikliórri	I saw a little bird
Núma nas gódya chirikliórri	But that wasn't a little bird
Sas gódya múrri deyorri	That was my dear mother
Thai woi rovélas sav d'aswênsa	And she was crying tears
Sav d'aswênsa ratwalênsa	All tears of blood
Thai woi rovélas sav d'aswênsa	And she was crying all tears
Sa balênsa phuterdênsa	With all her hair open [hanging down loose]
Ángla mánde dui drômá	Two roads before me
Thai chi zhanav savo te lav	And I don't know which to take
Wôrka o drôm o Rromano	Either the Romani road
Wôrka o drôm o Gazhikano	Or the non-Romani road
Lem o drôm Gazhikano	I took the non-Romani road
Chi dur, chi páshal me gêlèm	Not far, not near, I went
Ánde bári béda me pelem	I fell into big trouble
Ánde bári béda me pelem	I fell into big trouble
Xalem pûnrró la papináko	I ate a leg of a goose
Ashilémas la rrobiyáko	I spent time [stayed] in jail
Xalem tsumpo le gansakáko	I ate a drumstick of a gander
Ashhilem la temnitsáko.	I spent time in the dungeon.*

* **Notes:** molatnívas 'I was having a wild party' (from **mólatni** 'spree, shindig' in Lovaríts-ka), **amalênsa** 'with male friends' (in Lovarítska), **xasarávas** 'I was losing, wasting', **lem-man** 'I took myself (made my decision)', **konikas** 'nobody' (feminine accusative of **kónik**), **chirikliórri** 'little bird' (diminutive of **chirikli** – diminutives will be explained in the following lesson), **deyorri** 'dear mother', **aswênsa** 'with tears' (**aswin** 'tear'), **béda** 'trouble', **papináko** 'of a goose' (**papin**), **gansakáko** 'of a gander' (**gansáko**). While **gansáko** is male and takes < o > for 'the', a feminine genitive case ending in < áko > has been added to it in the song to rhyme with **papináko** and the other endings.

This song is metaphorical and cannot be translated exactly. The last four lines might seem nonsensical to non-Roma but what they mean is that the singer tried to become assimilated but this only resulted in trouble for him/her. This is the Romani song which appears in *Goddam Gypsy* (Tundra Books, Montreal, 1971, and also in German and Spanish with a forthcoming Czech edition). It is the theme of my novel and its main character, Yanko, is an educated Rom who tries to take the non-Romani road but ends up back with the Roma because of prejudice based on the "Gypsy stereotype".

Vanya's mother, Volga, was Lovára, and some words in the song are from the Lovarítska dialect. Vanya's basic Romani was French-Kalderash spoken by the Rrom-Franzúzurya, then based in Montreuil-sous-Bois, near Paris. According to Vanya's account, he learned this song from his father who lived in Poland until the Nazi invasion. After relatives were massacred by Nazi troops, the family went to Italy where Vanya, a small child, grew up in an internmant camp for Roma until they somehow got to Italian-occupied North Africa. Liberated by the Allies, they then went to Algeria, Spain and finally France after the end of the war. They came to Canada in the 1950s where I met them in my late teens. Vanya went to Poland in 1972 after his parents died in Canada, married a **Romni** and went to live in Stockholm where he died in the late 1980s, according to Mateo Maximoff who knew him.

Lesson sixteen

The diminutives

Thematic diminutives ending in < orro >

The endings **< orro >** (m.), **< orri >** (f.) and **< orre >** (pl.) can be suffixed to many thematic nouns to change the meaning, as will have been seen in various examples in the reading pieces. The basic meaning is 'small' but it often means 'dear'. Sometimes it is used for showing contempt and it is not always possible to translate its exact meaning into English.

It can be used to make something smaller:

grast	horse	**grastorro**	small, young horse
grasta	horses	**grastorre**	small, young horses
shuri	knife	**shuriorri**	tiny knife, penknife
shurya	knives	**shuriorra**	small knives, penknives

To mean 'dear' or to express affection:

Múrro dadorro mulo	My dear departed father
Voliv tu(t) múrri Rrômniorrí	I love you, my dear wife

To show contempt or sarcasm:

Si lês zhuklorro	He has a puny little mutt of a dog
Che bukiorri kerdyas	What a miserable, flea-bitten job he did

These diminutives are inflected for number and gender in the nominative and the oblique like thematic nouns ending in a stressed **< ó >** (m.) and stressed **< í >** (f.):

Dem-pûnrró le zhuklorrês	I kicked the miserable mutt (accusative)
Chumidas pêske Rrômniorrá	He kissed his beloved wife (accusative)
Dav-dúma múrre dadorrêsa	I am speaking to my dear father (instrumental)
Sas lês trin grastorre	He had three young horses (nominative pl.)

Athematic diminutives

With masculine diminutives ending in **< útso >** the final vowel is dropped before the suffix, and the nominative plural is **< útsurya >**:

vôrdônútso	cart, little wagon, wheelbarrow (from **vôrdòn** 'caravan')
wortakútso	beloved partner (from **wortáko** 'partner')
kolegútso	dear colleague (from **kolégo** 'colleague')
murtanútso	wretched tomcat (from **murtáno** 'tomcat')

These are inflected for gender and number in the nominative and the oblique like athematic nouns ending in an unstressed **< o >**:

Shudyas avri le murtanutsos	He threw out the miserable cat (accusative)
Bikinel vordonútsurya	He sells wheelbarrows (nominative plural)

For feminine diminutives ending in **< útsa >** and **< ítsa >** the final vowel is dropped in words ending in a vowel. The nominative plural is **< útsi >**:

birtashútsa	little or young barmaid (from **birtashka** 'barmaid')
wortaikútsa	dear partner (from **wortáika** 'female partner')
kustomankútsa	lousy customer (from **kustománka** 'female customer')
rozítsa	a small, newly-bloomed rose (from **róza** 'rose')
Rozítsa	little Rosie
wuchitêlkítsa	dear teacher (from **wuchitêlka** 'school teacher')
gazdinkítsa	lousy female boss (from **gazdínka** 'boss, manager, owner')

These are inflected for gender and number in the nominative and the oblique like athematic nouns ending in **< útsa >** and **< ítsa >**.

There is also the suffix **< ichóso >** which can be a diminutive or can modify an adjective. These are declined for gender and number and the noun plural is **< ichósurya >**. Example with nouns:

balo	pig	**balichóso**	piglet	plural	**balichósurya**

It is more often used with adjectives defining colours:

parno	white	**parnichóso**	whitish, cream-coloured
kalo	black	**kalichóso**	blackish, dark grey
lolo	red	**lolichóso**	reddish, pink

These behave like athematic adjectives when inflected for gender and number, for example, when taking **parnichóso** 'cream-coloured' as a model:

o parnichóso grast	the cream-coloured horse (nominative)
e parnichóso grasni	the cream-coloured mare (nominative)
le parnichósi grast	the cream-coloured horses (nominative)
le parnichósone grastês	the cream-coloured horse (accusative)

la parnichósonya grasnya	the cream-coloured mare (accusative)
le parnichósone grastên	the cream-coloured horses (accusative)

Difficult words – pe and pa

The words **pe** and **pa** have many meanings in Romani. The main meaning of **pe** is 'on' when used before feminine nouns and plurals, and here the definite article merges with **pe** and disappears:

Tho lês pe síniya	Put it on the table

When **pe** is used with masculine nouns it becomes **po**:

Ashunav o brêshùn po taváno	I hear the rain on the roof

Plural form:

E dosh perel pe l' Rrom	The blame will fall on the Roma

In a few idiomatic constructions, **pe** can mean 'for':

Parrudyan man pe l' daimántsi	You traded me for diamonds (from a song)
Sóde pokindyan pe láte?	How much did you pay for it?

The main meaning of **pa** is 'about':

Den-dúma pa múrro kher	They are talking about my house

It can also mean 'off' or 'from':

Pelo pa o taváno	He fell off (from) the roof
Zhal o pai pa mánde	I am sweating (water is going from me)

Here the masculine definite article is retained.

Both **pe** and **pa** have other (idiomatic) meanings, some of which can be found in the reading material and examples given in this course.

Review

Review the past tense of verbs ending in **< yol >** in conjunction with the tables in Lesson nine. They follow these patterns:

lol- 'blush, grow, go red'	
lolilem	I got red, blushed (from **lolo** 'red')
lolilan	you blushed

lolilo	he blushed
lolili	she blushed
lolilam	we blushed
lolilan	you blushed
lolile	they blushed

márd- 'get beaten (up)'

márdilem	I was beaten (from **mardo** 'beaten')
márdilan	you got beaten
márdilo	he got beaten
márdili	she got beaten
márdilam	we got beaten
márdilan	you got beaten
márdile	they got beaten

Examples

Makilem ándo bírto le Rromênsa thai márdilem ándo marimos le Gazhênsa

I got drunk in the bar with the Roma and got beaten (up) in the fight with the non-Roma

Lolili e Djíta kána ashundyas kodole djúngale swáturya*

Djita blushed when she heard those obscene words

But Rroma kinile thai mudárdile ánde l' kámpurya-kôntsêntráke (note use of **l'** and **kámpo-kônsêntráko)**

Many Roma were tortured and (were) murdered in the concentration camps

Test whether you have understood

Translate into Romani:

1.   He grew big (grew up)
2.   The windows were opened
3.   We were seen

More about forming infinitives and subjunctives

The word **ke** is used like **te** in sentences where one person wants another to perform an action, as compared to sentences where the speaker wants to do something:

---

*   **swáto** 'word', **djúngalo swáto** 'obscenity'.

Mangav te avav	I want to come
Mangav te aves	I want you to come
Mangav ke keres	I want you to do so (this is a command and needs **ke**)
Mangav te ashunes	I want you to listen
Mangav ke ashunes	I want you to listen (command)
Pushav tútar te zhas kai sláva	I am inviting you to the feast
Mangen te zhas kai sláva	They want us to go to the feast

It is also used to introduce a dependent phrase or clause and often **ke** is shortened to an aspirated **kh'** sound, for example:

Zhanav ke wo si barvalo	I know that he is rich
Chi zhanav kh' wo kamel	I don't know what he wants
Chi zhanglan kh' wo si barvalo?	Weren't you aware he is rich? (Didn't you know?)
Chi zhanglem kh' wo avélas kai sláva	I didn't know he was coming to the feast
Chi zhanglem kh' wo chordyas sa kodole love le Gazhêndar kána kêrélas buki ánde fábrika	I didn't know he stole all that money from the Gazhe when he was working in the factory

Ke or **kh** can also be used instead of **vêska** 'because' and **te** 'to':

Xav ke bokhalo sim	I am eating because I am hungry
Xal ke merel bokhátar	He is eating because he is famished (dying of hunger)
Nashti dav túke love kh' nai man	I can't give you money because I have none

More examples

Ashundem la te gilabal	I heard her singing
Dikhlem lên te maren–pe	I saw them fighting
Chi zhanav kh wo gûndíl-pe	I don't know what he is thinking
Te marav lês nai múrro gûndo	I am not planning to beat him up (that I beat him is not my plan)
Phenav o chachimos, te merav	I'm telling the truth, may I die (if I'm not is implied)
Te del o Del	I hope so (may God grant it)

Te bashavav e gitára si múrri plácha   I enjoy playing guitar (that I play the
                                              guitar is my pleasure)

Mangav ke bashaves* e gitára   I want you to play the guitar
                                              (command)

The use of the particles **ke** and **te** is important in Romani and ideally must be
learned by hearing native speakers. More examples are provided in the reading
material and phrases given in this course.

Conjunctions

The commonly used conjunctions are listed here and examples of their use can
be found throughout the lessons:

'ma	but (contraction of **núma**)
ánda kadya	therefore, in that case
ánda kodya	because of that, that's why, for that reason
ápo	so, thereupon
de sar	since
fêrdi	except, but for
kána	while, when
ke (kh/k')	because
nitála	even though, although
núma	but
pála gódo	then, after that, following that
pála kodya	after that, following that
pôrma	then, at that time
sar sas	as if it was
tha	and
thai	and, also
te na	unless
te	so that, in order to
vêska	because
wôrka	or, or else
zhêkùn	since, seeing that, being that way
zhi ka, zhi kai	until
zhîpùn	unless

*   The verb **bashavav** 'I play music' is not commonly used in North America but is widely
     used by central and eastern European-Kalderash and other Vlax-Romani speakers.

A Christmas prayer

This prayer is in the Lovarítska dialect and the words given in italics are written in the Hungarian alphabet.

Nayis le Devlêske, *hody* areslam kádo báro Krechúno. Te aresas *mindig* lês zorása, sastimása, na kâsevé chorre *modesa*, yêkhh tsirra mai lashe *modesa*, grastênsa, vurdonênsa, shukare borénsa. Te aresas le shukare *chaladonsa*. Kon dur mashkar amênde, te azhutil lês o Svúnto Del mashkar amênde, T'aves baxtalo.*

(A Hungarian-Lovari song now widely sung in America and Europe because of music CDs in Romani produced in Europe.)

O Phúro Rrôm 'The old Rom'

Kéren shavorrále drôm	Get out of the way kids
Te khelel o phúro Rrôm	So that the old Rom can dance
Ái lári lári lári lári lai lai lai	[nonsensical chorus like 'tra la la']
O phuro Rrôm kai khelel	The old man who (that) is dancing
Amara borya te del	Will give us our daughter-in-law
Ái lári lári, etc.	
Dui, dui, desh-u-dui	Two, two, ten times two
Chumidav me láko mui	I kiss her mouth
Ái lári lári, etc.	
Láko mui si rupuno	Her mouth is silver
Hai o státo sumnakuno	And the [her] body is golden
Ái lári lári, etc.	
Yoi, te merav	Oh, may I die
Te na o chachimos phenav	If I do not tell the truth
Ái lári lári, etc.	
Láko mui si rupuno	Her mouth is silver
Hai o státo sumnakuno	And the [her] body is golden

---

*   Hungarian words: ***hody*** 'that' (pronounced **hodj**), ***mindig*** 'always', ***mod*** 'manner', ***chalad*** 'family' (also in Kalderash as **chêlyédo**). These examples show why a native speaker of Romanian- or North American-Kalderash might have trouble even understanding another Vlax-Romani dialect very closely related to his/her own because of (in this case) the use of Hungarian loan words and roots.

    Romani words: **aresel** 'arrive', **Krechúno** 'Christmas', **kâsevé** 'so, such a', **chorro** 'poor', **yêkh tsirra** 'a little', **bori** 'bride, daughter-in-law' (with a male ending of **borênsa** but it should be **boryánsa**).

Ái lári, lári, etc.
Kéren shavorrále drôm   Make way, kids
Te khelel o phúro Rrôm   So that the old Rom can dance
Ái lári lári, etc.
Bish-tha-yêkh rêg málavla   Twenty-one sides he strikes (kicks)
Kána o phúro khélela   When the old man dances
Ái lári, lári, etc.
Málav, Mo, e chismesára   Strike the boots hard, old man!
Te ashunen la zhi tehára   So they can hear them until tomorrow
Ái, lári, lári, etc.
Amari si amari   Ours is ours
Amari terni bori   Our young daughter-in-law
Ái lári lári, etc.*

Answers to questions in this lesson
Past tenses review:

lolilo	**márdilo**
lolili	**márdili**
lolilam	**márdilam**
lolilan	**márdilan**
lolile	**márdile**

1.	**Barilo**
2.	**Le filástri phutérdile**
3.	**Ame dikhlam**

---

*   **Notes: rupuno** 'silver' (adjective), **státo** 'body, statue, shape', **sumnakuno** 'golden',
málavla a contraction of **malavéla** 'strike, strike out, kick out, stomp', **chizmesára** 'high
boots (Hungarian style. **Chizmesára** means 'a pair of boots' but the word is singular in
Romani), **Mo** 'Old man, Elder' (a vocative used only in direct address), **zhi** 'until'.

Lesson seventeen

Enclitics replacing the verb 'to be'

Another way of saying 'is' or 'are' is the use of enclitics. **Si** can be replaced by the following words (enclitics) which mean nothing by themselves:

lo he is
la she is
le they are

They are only used in certain types of sentences, usually with adjectives, interrogatives and prepositions:

baro lo	he is big	**bari la**	she is big	**bare le**	they are big
opre lo	he is upstairs	**opre-la**	she is upstairs	**opre le**	they are upstairs
andre lo	he is inside	**andre la**	she is inside	**andre le**	they are inside
po drôm lo	he is on the road	**po drôm la**	she is on the road	**po drôm le**	they are on the road
kai le?	where are they?	**opre le**	they are upstairs		

Do not imitate these forms, but try to use **si** instead. These enclitics are best learned by hearing them from native speakers.

The genitive case of the abstract noun in < imos >

The genitive case of the substantive ending in **< imos >** also serves as an adjective:

merimos death **merimásko** belonging to death, having to do with death

This then becomes the equivalent of English words ending in **< ing >** in examples such as 'the dying flowers' or 'their dying customs'. These adjectives are declined for gender and number in the nominative and the oblique:

o merimásko guruv	the dying bull
e merimáski gurumni	the dying cow
le merimáske guruva	the dying bulls
le merimáske gurumnya	the dying cows (cattle)
e merimáski yag	the dying fire
le merimáske lulugya	the dying (wilting) flowers
O rashai rrugisáilo* le merimáske Rrômèske	The priest prayed for the dying Rom
Tradine la merimáska Rômnyá kai shpíta	They drove the dying Romni to the hospital

More examples as an adjective:

O shudrimos si mudarimásko	The cold is murderous (lethal)
Kodo si o mudarimásko mobíli	That's the killer car (one that somebody was killed in)
Le rai arakhle e mudarimáski púshka	The police found the murder weapon (gun)
Le tiburóya† si mudarimáske mashe	Sharks are killer fish

It can also be combined with another adjective:

Xamásko, the genitive of **xamos** 'act of eating, feeding' is combined with **lasho** 'good' to create a compound adjective in **lasho-xamásko** 'good to eat, delicious':

Lasho-xamásko si	It is delicious (referring to meat (m.) noun in Romani)
Lashi-xamáski si	It is delicious (referring to an apple (f.) noun)
Lashe-xamáske si	They are delicious (referring to grapes (pl.) noun)

In the above sentences, there is no object. The two adjectives are referring to something which is understood by the speakers, as in:

Kames te xas ítome†† mas?	Do you like to eat spiced meat?
Ya, lasho-xamásko si	Yes, it's delicious

But when the two adjectives are used with an object in a sentence, the adjective

---

*   **rrugil-pe** 'he prays' (intransitive verb) (**rrugisáilo** is the past tense).

†   **tiburóno** 'shark'.

†† **itome** 'spiced', **itol** 'he spices'.

which modifies the genitive adjective must be in the masculine singular oblique since it is modifying an inflected masculine noun, even though this is serving as an adjective in this instance. The genitive adjective must agree in gender and number with the noun it modifies:

O lashe-xamásko mas	The delicious meat
E lashe-xamáski phabai	The delicious apple
Le lashe-xamáske phaba	The delicious apples
Woi peklas lashe-xamasko mas	She cooked delicious meat
Xalem lashe-xamáski phabai	I ate a delicious apple
Baryarel lashe-xamáske phaba	He grows delicious apples

Note the following compound adjective:

shtaré-rêgèngo	square
shtaré-rêgèngo kotor kasht	a square piece of wood
shtare-rêgèngi níva	a square field
shtare-rêgènge plóchi	square tiles
Wusharadyas le paleya	He covered the floor with square
shtare-rêgènge plochênsa	tiles

It can be used in compound nouns to incoin (create) new nouns in Romani. In such compounds, the adjective is declined as an adjective and the noun inflected for gender and number in the nominative and the oblique:

amblayimásko-kasht	gallows (hanging tree)
drabarimásko-skamin*	fortune-telling chair
gilabayimáski-chirikli	nightingale (singing bird)
nashimáske-grast	race (running) horses
perayimáske-cheraya	shooting (falling) stars

When the nominative compound is inflected to the oblique, the genitive adjective behaves like a thematic adjective and the noun in the compound is inflected:

Kindyas nashimáske-grastês	He bought a racehorse (accusative case)
Kindyas nashimáske-grastên	He bought racehorses (accusative)
Phiravel pêske nashimáske-grastêsa	He travels with his racehorse (instrumental)
Dikhlan e zûn le nashimáske-grastêski?	Have you seen the racehorse's saddle? (genitive)

*   A special chair kept in fortune-telling parlours for non-Romani customers.

Dikhlan e zûn la nashimáska-grasnyáki Have you seen the racing mare's saddle?

In this last example the word 'horse' is in the genitive singular to agree with **zûn** (f.) 'saddle', and the genitive adjective **nashimásko** is in the oblique to modify the inflected noun part of the compound, 'horse', which is masculine. With **grasni** 'mare' the noun in the compound is feminine so the genitive adjective modifies a feminine noun. The definite article is inflected according to the gender of the noun in the compound, and the number if the noun is in a plural inflection.

O zhukel daral le nashimáske grastêstar   The dog fears (from) the racehorse (ablative case)

Here, the word **grast** in the compound is inflected to the masculine singular ablative case ending and the genitive adjective is in the oblique masculine singular to agree with the gender of **grast** which is masculine.

Past participles of verbs

The past participles of thematic Romani verbs are formed from the verb stem of the past tense:

phaglem	I broke	**phaglo**	broken
phabardem	I burned	**phabardo**	burnt

Athematic verbs which end in **< isardem >** or **< osardem >** in the past, change to **< ime >** or **< ome >**:

volisardem	I loved	**volime**	loved
farbosardem	I painted	**farbome**	painted

These past participles are used as adjectives.

Thematic past participles like **paglo** are declined for gender and number in the nominative and the oblique:

o paghlo skamin	the broken chair
e phagli síniya	the broken table
le phagle mobiláriya	the broken furniture (**mobilári** (m.) 'piece of furniture')
So keres la phaghlya sinyása?	What will you do with the broken table?

Athematic past participles like **volime** or **farbome**, when used as adjectives, do not change and always have the same form in the nominative and oblique for gender and number:

múrro volime phral	my beloved brother
gêlèm múre volime phralêsa	I went with my beloved brother
Akushlas múrra volime phenya	He insulted my beloved sister

An oblique form of these thematic past participles in **volimene** has vanished in North American-Kalderash, nor have I heard it from French- or Romanian-Kalderash. It may be retained in some European dialects.

Athematic adjectives ending in unstressed < o >

The following are paradigms of loan adjectives ending in an unstressed **< o >** from Lesson three, using **múndro** 'wonderful' as an example:

Nominative form		Accusative form
O múndro raklo avel	The wonderful boy is coming	**Dikhav le mundrone raklês**
E múndro rakli avel	The wonderful girl is coming	**Dikhav la mundronya raklya**
Le múndri rakle aven	The wonderful boys are coming	**Dikhav le mundrone raklên**
Le múndri raklya aven	The wonderful girls are coming	**Dikhav le mundrone raklyan**

Most of this group of adjectives behaves like **múndro** except for those ending in **< go >** like **drágo** 'dear, beloved' plus a few other exceptions. In North American-Kalderash, any not listed below will usually behave like **múndro** and would be understood by European speakers of Kalderash.

Nominative		Accusative
Múrro drágo phral avel	My beloved brother is coming	**Dikhav múrre dragone phralês**
Múrri drágo phen avel	My dear sister is coming	**Dikhav múrra dragonya phenya**
Múrre drázhi phrala aven	My dear brothers are coming	**Dikhav múrre dragone phralên**

Múrre drázhi phenya aven   My dear sisters are coming   **Dikhav múrre dragone phenyan**

Remember that the oblique forms shown for all adjectives are those used with nouns having case endings.

Other loan adjectives which behave like **drágo** are **ântrégo** 'complete, whole, entire' and **krúgo** 'round'.

List of exceptions to the general rules given for múndro and drágo based on North American- and French-Kalderash

Adênko 'deep'
Masculine and feminine nominative singular is **adênko**
Masculine and feminine nominative plural is **adênchi**
Masculine oblique singular is **adênkone**
Feminine oblique singular is **adênkonya**
Oblique plural for both is **adênkone**

Chápeno 'hard, stiff'
Masculine and feminine nominative singular is **chápeno**
Masculine and feminine nominative plural is **chápenya**
Masculine oblique singular is **chápenone**
Feminine oblique singular is **chápenenya**
Oblique plural for both is **chápenone**

Dívlio 'wild, untamed'
Masculine and feminine nominative singular is **dívlio**
Masculine and feminine nominative plural is **dívli**
Masculine oblique singular is **dívlione**
Feminine oblique singular is **dívliona**
Oblique plural for both is **dívlione**

Hamishágo 'jealous, envious'
Masculine and feminine nominative singular is **hamishágo**
Masculine and feminine nominative plural is **hamishéguri**
Masculine oblique singular is **hamishágone**
Feminine oblique singular is **hamishágonya**
Oblique plural for both is **hamishágone**

Hárniko 'hard-working, industrious'
Masculine and feminine nominative singular is **hárniko**
Masculine and feminine nominative plural is **hárnichi**

Masculine oblique singular is **hárnikone**
Feminine oblique singular is **hárnikonya**
Oblique plural for both is **hárnikone**

Krêtso 'curly, frizzled'
Masculine and feminine nominative singular is **krêtso**
Masculine and feminine nominative plural is **krêtsi**
Masculine oblique singular is **krêtsone**
Feminine oblique singular is **krêtsonya**
Oblique plural for both is **krêtsone**

Lêzno 'cheap, inexpensive' and **strázhno** 'dangerous'
Masculine and feminine nominative singular is **lêzno**
Masculine and feminine nominative plural is **lêzni**
Masculine oblique singular is **lêznone**
Feminine oblique singular is **lêznonya**
Oblique plural for both is **lêznone**

Ôblo 'round'
Masculine and feminine nominative singular is **ôblo**
Masculine and feminine nominative plural is **ôbli**
Masculine oblique singular is **ôbloné**
Feminine oblique singular is **ôblonyá**
Oblique plural for both is **ôbloné**

Prósto 'common, ordinary, humble, contrite'
Masculine nominative singular is **prósto**
Feminine nominative singular is **prósti**
Nominative plural for both is **prósturi** or **prósti**
Masculine and feminine oblique singular is **prósti**
Oblique plural for both is **próstone** or **prósturi**

Skúrto 'short'
Masculine and feminine nominative singular is **skúrto**
Masculine and feminine nominative plural is **skúrtsi**
Masculine oblique singular is **skúrtsone**
Feminine oblique singular is **skúrtsonya**
Oblique plural for both is **skúrtsone**

Slóbodo 'free, unfettered, at liberty'
Masculine and feminine nominative singular is **slóbodo**
Masculine and feminine nominative plural is **slóbodji**

Masculine oblique singular is **slóbodjone**
Feminine oblique singular is **slóbodjonya**
Oblique plural for both is **slóbodjone**

Stêngo 'left' (as in direction and left hand) and **lúngo** 'long'
Masculine and feminine nominative singular is **stêngo** and **lúngo**
Masculine and feminine nominative plural is **stèndji** and **lúndji**
Masculine oblique singular is **stêngone** and **lúngone**
Feminine oblique singular is **stêngonya** and **lúngonya**
Oblique plural for both is **stêngone** and **lúngone**

Vorrúto 'disgusting'
Masculine and feminine nominative singular is **vorrúto**
Masculine and feminine nominative plural is **vorrútsi**
Masculine oblique singular is **vorrútsone**
Feminine oblique singular is **vorrútsonya**
Oblique plural for both is **vorrútsone**

Xlútro 'cunning, astute'
Masculine and feminine nominative singular is **xlútro**
Masculine and feminine nominative plural is **xlútri**
Masculine oblique singular is **xlútrone**
Feminine oblique singular is **xlútronya**
Oblique plural for both is **xlútrone**

The directions

The adjectives of direction also serve as nouns and adverbs in Kalderash.

As nouns, all masculine gender:

Lanórdo	North
Lasúdo	South
Lasári	East
Lamári	West

As adjectives:

The genitive case ending of the directions as nouns serve as adjectives. They are declined for gender and number in the nominative and inflected for gender and number in the oblique:

lanordósko, lasudósko, lasarêsko, lamarêsko

O Lanordósko cheran	The North Star
E Lanordóski balwal	The North wind
O iv avilo lanordêska balwalása	The snow came with the North wind

As adverbs:

lanórdo, lasúdo, lasári, lamári

Giving directions

wórta	straight	**zha wórta**	go straight, straight ahead
chacho	right	**bangyar ka o chácho**	turn right
stêngo	left	**bangyar ka o stêngo**	turn left
pe cháchi rêg	on the right side	**pe stêngo rêg**	on the left side

Noun plus noun genitives

In expressions such as 'a piece of bread' there is no word equivalent to 'of' in English, nor are any of the nouns inflected to the genitive case to express 'of '. Study the following examples for typical constructions:

kotor manrro	piece of bread
Ashélas khote kotorêsa	He was standing there with a piece of
manrro ándo wast	bread in his hand (note **kotor** in the instrumental case)
táxdai chai (cháyo)	a cup of tea
páchka tsigêri	a pack of cigarettes
trin páchki tsigêri	three packs of cigarettes
páchka kárti	a pack of cards
posuki phérde love	a pocketful of money
wast-phérdo xúrde love	a handful of change
yêkh gono angar	one bag of coal
dui gone angar	two bags of coal
trin gone pherde love	three bags full of money
Gêlótar trine gonênsa pherde love	He went away with three bags full of money
yilo pherdo volimos	a heart full of love
yile pherde dushmaníya	hearts full of enmity

Fast Romani song from the former Yugoslavia in 9/8 rhythm
Áka avel e Vérka 'Here comes Little Vera'

Áka avel e Vérka	Here comes Little Vera
E Vérka e kaludjérka	Vera the chaste [repeat both lines]

Chorus

Áiya Vérka	Hey, Vera
E Vérka e kaludjérka	Vera the chaste
Xoxadya la o ladjári	The sailor deceived her
Le lóle papuchênsa	With a pair of red shoes [repeat chorus]

Verse

Sa e Rroma phénen	All the Roma say [**e** replaces **le** here]
Ke nasvali e Vérka	That Vera is sick [repeat line]
E Vérka e kaludjérka	Vera the chaste [repeat verse]
	[repeat chorus]

Verse

Áka aven e Rróma	Here come the Roma
Te mandjen e Vérka	To ask Vera [repeat line]
E Vérka e kaludjérka	Vera the chaste [repeat verse]
	[repeat chorus]*

This song has been included to show the similarity between Romani dialects. It would be understood by almost any native speaker of Vlax-Romani anywhere in the world.

Modern Kalderash-Romani

A telephone conversation between a Romanian-Romani refugee and myself in Toronto, 2002 to serve as an example of how modern Kalderash is spoken:

Sar san, Káko, te aves baxtalo. So mai keres?
How are you, Uncle? What are you up to?

---

*   Notes: **Áka avel** 'here comes', **kaludjérka** 'nun, chaste woman' (Vera was taken advantage of by a sailor who gave her an expensive pair of red shoes in return for her affections), **ladjári** 'sailor' (from **ladjíya** 'boat'), **papuchênsa** 'with red slippers' (from **papúchi**, pl. of **papúka**, 'a woman's shoe, slipper'. Note the use of the masculine ending < **ensa** > in the plural for a feminine noun, the singular is **papukása**), **mandjen** for **mangen** 'they want', **e** is an alternative form of **le** (plural definite article) in many European dialects of Vlax-Romani but it is not used in North American-Kalderash.

Buki, buki, swáko ges mai but buki, desya but buki. Tasavel ma.
Work, work, every day more work, too much work. It is smothering me.

Sar san tu, manúsha, tyi familíya?
How are you, Sir, your family?

Mishto sam, Nayis Devlêske. Ei Káko, ashundyan so nakhlo le Ishwanêsa?
We are fine, thanks to God. Hey, Uncle, did you hear what happened to [with] Ishwan?

Chi ashundem khánchi. So nakhlo? Núma sávo Íshwan? Zhanav but mashkar le azilánturya.
I didn't hear anything. What happened? But which Ishwan? I know a lot [of Ishwans] among the refugees.

O Íshwan kai bashavel o sinzizáto, ánda e Transilvániya, terno Rrôm. Avilo katar e Anglíya ánde kôntáina, wo thai pêski familíya.
Ishwan who plays the synthesizer, he is from Transylvania, a young man. He came from England in a container [shipping crate], he and his family.

Prinzharav lês akana. So nakhlo lêsa?
I know him now. What happened to him?

Ándo phandayimos. Avile le shingale mashkaral la ratyáko hai phandade lês ánde ditêntsiya. Wo, pêski zhuvli thai pêske shavorre. Mangen te traden le pe strázha pálpale ánde Rumúniya. So shai keras te azhutis le?
In custody. The immigration officers came in the middle of the night and arrested him. He (him), his wife and children. They want to deport them back again to Romania. What can we do to help them?

Sas lên krisi, tárdyulash, ánde imigrátsiya?
Have they had an adjudication hearing at [Canadian] immigration?

Ya, nêgatívo sas. Normálo. Mangénas te keren 'appeal' zhanes.
Yes, it was negative. As usual. They wanted to make an appeal, you know.

Sóstar chi kerdine gadya? Nai lên zhutóri?
Why didn't they do that? Don't they have a lawyer?

Na, nas dósta vákto. Mukisáile katar lêngo apartamênto hai avilo yêkh lil ka o phurano adréso. Chi mai dikhle kodo lil. Phendya lênge godo lil te zhan ánde imigrátsiya te den swáto pa lêngo késo. Ápo chi gile thai e imigrátsiya kerdine ákto te traden le pe strázha. So shai keras akana?
No, there was not enough time. They moved from their apartment and a letter came to their former address. They never saw that letter. That letter told them to go to the immigration department to discuss their case. So they didn't go and the immigration [people] issued an official order to deport them. What can we do now?

Musai te arakhas xlútro zhutóri kai kerel buki le azilantênsa. Núma trobul lês but love. Chi den khánchi o 'Legal Aid' vash kakya buki. Si lês love o Íshwan? O zhutóri kam-pushel dui, trin míyi tilêri, anglal, tu zhanes kodya? Sa xanzhwale si. Griyátsa! Chi keren khánchi bi-lovêngo.
We must find a smart lawyer who works with refugees. But he will need a lot of money. Legal Aid doesn't give anything for this work. Does Ishwan have any money? The lawyer will ask for two, three thousand dollars up front, you know that. They are all greedy. Disgusting! They won't do anything without money.

Nai lês but. Núma si lês súmnakai, lántsurya, kola, zhanes.
Not much. But he has gold, chains, stuff, you know.

Te del o Del kh' si lês dósta.
I hope he has enough.

Te del o Del
I hope so too.

Ashun! Me akharav wúni zhutóriya thai akharav tu pálpale tehára. Mishto? Musai te keras wáreso fugása te na traden le pálpale.
Listen! I will call some lawyers and call you back tomorrow. O.K.? We must do something quickly so they don't send them back.

Nayis túke, Káko. Azhukerav tyo swáto. Devlésa. Mai lashi tyi ryat.
Thank you, Uncle. I will wait for your call. So long for now (remain with God). Good night.

I-tu, manúsha. Mai lashi tumári ryat. Devlésa!
You too, Sir. Good night. Stay with God!*

---

* **Notes: káko** 'Uncle', term of respect for an elder in the community, **tasavel** 'drowns, smothers', **manúsha** 'Sir', term of respect for a middle-aged man or one older man to another older man, **nakhlo** 'happened', **le(n)** 'them' (**lên** is often shortened to **le** in conversation), **phandayimos** 'enclosure, detainment', **shingale** 'police, especially immigration police' (literally 'horned ones' or 'devils'), **mashkaral** 'in the middle of', **zhuvli** 'wife, woman, female', **traden pe strázha** 'send under guard, deport', **pálpale** 'back, back again', **azhutis** 'we help', **krisi** 'hearing, court appearance', **zhutóri** 'lawyer', **dósta vákto** 'enough time' (**vákto** 'time' used in Romanian-Kalderash instead of **vryámya**), **mukisáile** 'they moved, vacated' (**mukin-pe** 'they move'), **den swáto** 'to discuss (give word)', **késo** 'case' (from English), **ápo** 'so', **xlútro** 'shrewd, smart', **xanzhwale** 'itchy, greedy', **azilantênsa** 'with refugees' (**azilánto** 'refugee'), **trobul** 'need', **vash** 'for', **tiléri** 'dollars', (**tilára** 'dollar'), **anglal** 'forward, up front', **lántsurya** '(gold) chains', **kola** 'stuff, assets', **Te del o Del** 'May God grant (I hope so)', **wúni** 'some', **wáreso** 'something', **fugása** 'in a hurry, quickly', **azhukerav tyo swáto** 'I'll wait to hear from you' (idiom), **I-tu** 'you too', **mai lashi tumári ryat** 'good night' (plural to him and his family).

Spoken Romani generally uses short, concise sentences, rather than long rambling narratives as in English. For example:

Múrro phral avilyas ka o Târánto o kurko nakhlo. Kerélas but buki thai khino sas. Mangélas te hodenil-pe tsirra mai anglal te astarel pêsko nevo kôntrákto.

My brother came to Toronto last week because he had been working hard and was tired and he wanted to relax a little bit before starting his new contract.*

An episode in the forgotten Romani Holocaust

Narrative in a bar in Hamilton, Ontario, 2004

Tu zhanes, manúsha, so nakhlo e Romênsa ándo maripe. O Antonêsku tradyas but, but Rróma

You know, Sir, what happened with the Roma during the war. Antonescu sent many, many Roma

katar e Romúniya kai Transdinístrya, tu zhanes kai sas kodo them? Sas ánde Ukrayína pashal o Búgo.

from Romania to Transdinistria, you know where that country was? It was in the Ukraine, near the River Bug.

But Rróma trádyile kothe. Nas le xabe, nas dóftorya, nas baráchi, khánchi. Mule but Rróma.

Many Roma were sent there. They had no food, no doctors, no barracks, nothing. Many Roma died.

Núma ashun! Kána avile le Nyámptsurya. Kidine but Rróma thai ladine le ándo vapóri ánde

But listen! When the Germans came. They collected many Roma and loaded them into a steamer on the sea,

máriya, e Káli Máriya, zhanes, pashal e Odésa. Hay thodine ándo vapóri hârtíya, dêrzi, swáko fyal kova kai phabarel.

the Black Sea, you know, near Odessa. And they placed inside the ship, newspaper, rags, every kind of thing that burns.

Atúnchi dine yag o vapóri, sa e Rroma andre, thai sa phabárdyile.

Then they set fire to the steamer, all the Roma inside and they all got incinerated.

---

*   **Notes: kurko naklo** 'last week', **khino** 'tired', **hodenil-pe** 'rest, relax', **tsirra** 'a little', **mai anglal** 'before'.

Me zhanav. Wúni lêndar sas múrre nyámurya, múrre kak, múrre vêrya. Me zhanav.

I know. Some of them were my relatives, my uncles, my cousins. I know.

Me símas tsinorro shavorro kána nakhlo godo núma me zhanav ke chachipe. Chi xoxavav túke, manúsha.

I was a very young boy when that happened but I know it is the truth. I am not lying to you, Sir.

Sas o Hítler kai kerdyas gadala djúngali buki.

It was Hitler who did this ugly deed.

The narrator of this story was Xúlyo, a Romanian-Romani refugee in Canada aged 68. He could not remember the date except that it was during the Second World War and many of his relatives were victims. He heard the story from living relatives. The dialect is Romanian-Kalderash and is that shown in this course except for the plural definite article in **< e >** instead of **< le >** and the nominalizing suffix in **< pe >** plus a few idiomatic expressions common to his dialect.

Lesson eighteen

Review

Review the following basic pattern for thematic verbs:

Present indicative	Past (continuous)	Past tense
me marav	**marávas**	**mardem**
tu mares	**marésas**	**mardyan**
wo/woi marel	**marélas**	**mardyas**
ame maras	**marásas**	**mardyam**
tume maren	**marénas**	**mardyan**
won maren	**marénas**	**marde**

As well as the short form of the present tense there is also a long form: **maráva**, **marésa**, **maréla**, **marása**, **maréna**, **maréna**.

The use of this long form varies with different dialects but it is basically another form of the present tense and serves the same function. Its other uses are shown in the lessons.

In the past tense some verbs have special forms in 'she' and 'he' which end in stressed vowels:

avilo	he came
avili	she came
avile	they came

Imperative of thematic verbs

The imperative singular is usually the root of the verb (see Lesson five for exceptions):

ker	do
av	come

The imperative plural is the same as the third person plural in the present tense:

keren	do
aven	come

Future tense of verbs

Prefix **< kam- >** to the present tense, for example, **kam-avav** 'I shall be'.

The verb 'to be'

Present	Past
me sim (sôm*)	**símas (sómas*)**
tu san	**sánas**
wo, woi si	**sas**
ame sam	**sámas**
tume san	**sánas**
won si	**sas**

Special forms for 'to be':

nai	is not, are no
nas	was not, were not
manas	there was not, none

Pluperfect tense of thematic verbs

This is formed by adding **< -as >** to the past tense or **< -sas >** if the past tense ends in a vowel, for example:

mardem-as	I had hit
avilém-as	I had been

ker- 'do'	
kerdém-as	I had done
kerdyán-as	you had done
kerdyás-as	he/she had done
kerdyám-as	we had done
kerdyás-as	you had done
kerdé-sas	they had done

*   Variant forms used by some speakers. You may hear these forms but you do not need to learn them, just be aware that they exist.

Use of the prefix < kámas- >

< **Kámas-** > can be used to express 'would' to form a conditional present tense. It can be used with verbs in the present tense (as < **kam-** > is used with the future tense) and means 'would see':

kámas-dikhav   I would see
kámas-dikhes   you would see
kámas-dikhel   he/she would see
kámas-dikhas   we would see
kámas-dikhen   you would see
kámas-dikhen   they would see

< **Kámas-** > can also be used with the past tense to create a conditional past tense:

kámas-dikhlem   I would have seen
kamas-dikhlan   you would have seen
kámas-dikhlas   he/she would have seen
kámas-dikhlam   we would have seen
kámas-dikhlan   you would have seen
kámas-dikhle   they would have seen

These conditional verb tenses are used to express sentences such as the English 'I would have come tomorrow if I had not come yesterday.' Phrases of this type differ from one dialect to another since there are often various ways of expressing this type of sentence construction in Romani, as the two examples below indicate:

Kámas-avilem tehára te na avilémas araki
I would have come tomorrow if I had not come yesterday (note use of **na** instead of **chi** as the negative)
Símas te avav tehára te na avilémas araki
I was supposed to come tomorrow if I had not come yesterday

Examples (recorded in the 1960s and 1970s in Montreal)

Kámas-kindem o mobíli te avilésas man le love
I would have bought the car if I had had the money
Te zhanglémas, kámas-phendem túke
If I had known, I would have told you

Tu, te na avilyánas* desya dilo, chi-mai kámas-sluchayil-pe kodya
If you had not been so silly, that would not have happened
Woi, te avilísas khote, me kámas-dikhlem la
If she had been there, I would have seen her

Other examples (recorded 2000-03)

Kodo Rrôm, te na piyélas desya but, chi kámas-meklas lês pêski zhuvli
That Rom, if he wasn't drinking so much, his wife would not have left him
Te kerdyánas tiri buki mishto sa kámas-anklisto mishto
If you had done your job properly, everything would have turned out all right
Sar zhanglémas me te kámas-pharraven o djuléshi?
How was I to know they would destroy the meeting?

The continuous past tense can also be used in some of these expressions, typical of refugee Roma-speaking Vlax-Romani dialects from central and eastern Europe:

Me kerávas kadya buki te zhanglémas so te kerav
I would have done that (thing) if I had known what to do
Merélas bokhátar, kodo thulo balo, te mekélas lês pêski zhuvli
He would die of hunger, that fat pig, if his wife were to leave him
Shai-vi te pokinélas túke le love te zhanélas ke trobúlas[†] tu
Perhaps he would have paid you the money if he had known that you needed it
Te zhanávas, phenávas túke
If I had known, I would have told you
Le skini mudarénas lês te na nashlótar
The skinheads would have killed him if he hadn't run away

These sentences will give some idea of how to form pluperfect-conditional expressions, however, different dialects may have alternative ways of doing this.

Transitive athematic verbs

Transitive athematic verbs follow the same general rules as thematic verbs. The following points should be noted.

*   **avel** 'to be, become'.

†   **Trobul** is what is called a 'defective verb' and it exists only in two forms in most Kalderash dialects: **trobul** 'it is needed' and **trobúlas** 'it was needed'. It can also have the prefixes **< kam- >** and **< kámas- >**.

Their present tenses are formed in **< il >** and **< ol >** (see Lesson twelve for further details on this and the following rules):

vol- 'love'   **voliv, volis, volil, volis, volin, volin**
farb- 'paint'   **farbov, farbos, farbol, farbos, farbon, farbon**

The imperative forms include **< sar >** in the singular and **< sar- >** in the plural:

Singular   Plural
volisar   **volisaren**
farbosar   **farbosaren**

The past tense includes **< isar- >**:

volisardem	I loved	**farbosardem**	I painted
volisardyan	you loved	**farbosardyan**	you painted
volisardyas	he/she loved	**farbosardyas**	he/she painted
volisardyam	we loved	**farbosardyam**	we painted
volisardyan	you loved	**farbosardyan**	you painted
volisarde	they loved	**farbosarde**	they painted

The past continuous tense (imperfect tense):

volívas	I used to love
farbóvas	I have been painting

The pluperfect tense takes the same suffixes as thematic verbs:

volisardémas	I had loved
farbosardémas	I had painted

The prefixes can also be used with athematic verbs:

kam-voliv	I shall love
kam-farbov	I shall paint
kámas-voliv	I would love
kámas-farbov	I would paint
kámas-volisardem	I would have loved
kámas-farbosardem	I would have painted

Intransitive athematic verbs

Intransitive athematic verbs become reflexive and must be used with oblique (accusative) personal pronouns. In the present tense, the oblique pronouns are used as the object of the verb:

Voliv múrri Rrômní	I love my wife (transitive)
Voliv-man	I love myself (intransitive)
Farbol o kher	He is painting the house (transitive)
Farbol-pe	She is applying make-up (painting herself) (intransitive)

Imperatives:

Singular	Plural	
ansurisáwo	**ansurisáwon**	get married
farbosáwo	**farbosáwon**	apply make-up

In the past tense, there is a different conjugation:

volisáilem	I loved myself	**farbosáilem**	I applied make-up
volisáilan	you loved yourself	**farbosáilan**	you applied make-up
volisáilo	he loved himself	**farbosáilo**	he applied make-up
volisáili	she loved herself	**farbosáili**	she applied make-up
volisáilam	we loved ourselves	**farbosáilam**	we applied make-up
volisáilan	you loved yourselves	**farbosáilan**	you applied make-up
volisáile	they loved themselves	**farbosáile**	they applied make-up

In the past continuous, the oblique personal pronouns are retained in the intransitive:

volívas man	I was loving, used to love, myself

The prefixes **< kam- >** and **< kámas- >** are used as with the transitive athematic verbs and the oblique personal pronouns are retained in these tenses:

kam-voliv man	I shall love myself
kámas-voliv man	I would love myself
kámas-volisáilem	I would have loved myself

Pluperfect tense:

volisailémas man	I had loved myself

Possession (to have)

Taking the first person singular, possession is expressed as follows:

Present tense	**Si man grast**	I have a horse
Past tense	**Sas man grast**	I had a horse

Past continuous	**Avélas man grast**	I used to have a horse
Future tense	**Kam-avel man grast**	I shall have a horse
Conditional	**Kámas-avel man grast**	I would have a horse
Past conditional	**Kámas-avilósas man grast**	I would have had a horse
Optative	**Te avel man grast!**	Oh, that I might have a horse!

With these constructions, if the object possessed is plural, the plural forms of the verb 'to be' must be used instead of the singular as shown above:

Si man love	I have money
Sas man love	I had money

There is no change here because **si** means 'there is' and 'there are'. In the following five examples, the verb 'to be' is in the third person plural:

Avénas man love	I used to have money
Kam-aven man love	I will have money
Kámas-aven man love	I would have money
Kámas-avile man love	I would have had money
Te aven man love!	May I have money! (optative with **< te >**)

Nouns

Basic pattern for thematic items:

Masculine	Feminine	Plural masculine	Plural feminine	
bakro	**bakri**	**bakre**	**bakrya**	subject (nominative)
bákra	**bakríyo**	**bakrále**	**bakryále**	direct address (vocative)
bakrês	**bakrya**	**bakrên**	**bakryan**	object (accusative and oblique stem)

The following five case endings are formed on the oblique stem:

bakrêske	**bakryáke**	**bakrênge**	**bakyánge**	for, to (dative)
bakrêste	**bakyáte**	**bakrênde**	**bakryánde**	at, to (prepositional/locative)

bakrêstar	bakryátar	bakrêndar	bakryándar
			from (ablative)
bakrêsa	bakryása	bakrênsa	bakryánsa
			with (instrumental)
bakrêsko	bakryáko	bakrêngo	bakryángo
			of (genitive)

Inanimate nouns are not usually inflected to the accusative. They can have vocative cases and they must be inflected with the dative, prepositional, ablative, instrumental and genitive cases. Their plurals and oblique stems are given in the tables in Lesson seven.

Adjectives

Basic pattern for thematic items:

Masculine	Feminine	Plural
baro	bari	bare (nominative)
bare	barya	bare (oblique)

Words which end in a consonant have the following endings only:

shukar (subject of action, singular and plural for both genders) becomes **shukare** (m.) and **shukareya** (f.), for example, **le shukare raklêsa** 'with the handsome boy' and **la shukareya raklyása** 'with the beautiful girl'. The nominative and oblique forms are the same for masculine and feminine plurals in **shukare**.

Note that with nouns which do not have a case ending, the subject (nominative) form of the adjective is used:

Me dikhav baro, shukar kher   I see a large, beautiful house

Idiomatic expressions

Because Romani has been an unwritten language, without literature until the latter twentieth century, and Roma have basically been an illiterate, marginalized population, many expressions cannot be translated word for word from English. These must be expressed by idioms and metaphorical translations, for example, the following sentence in English could easily be translated word for word into any other literary language: 'He is coming to the end of his career'. However, the Romani translation would be:

Pêsko kham beshel   His sun is setting

On the other hand, 'He is just beginning his career', would be:

Pêsko kham anklel   His sun is rising

It is important to listen for such idioms from native speakers and record them. Here are several common idioms widely used in Canada and the US and usually understood by European-Kalderash speakers. There is a large number of such idioms in every Vlax-Romani dialect.

Pharrulo lêsko yilo	His heart exploded (had a heart attack)
O swiyádêro xal múrro shoro	The (pneumatic) drill is driving me crazy (eating my head)
Shudyas pêski gláta	She suffered a miscarriage (threw out her baby)
Gêlótar te avel	He went out to regain his composure and return
Xalyas pêski baxt	He ruined his ability to be successful (ate his own luck)
Xalyas pêsko manrro	He has enjoyed life to the fullest (he has eaten his bread)
Mulo terno, bi te xal pêsko manrro	He died young, his life unfulfilled
Kako vôrdòn piyel desya but bênzína	This station wagon is using (drinking) too much petrol

In this course, only one or two meanings have usually been assigned to verbs but many Romani verbs have a wide variety of meanings which must be learned from native speakers. These alternative meanings and idiomatic uses will not usually be found in dictionaries of Romani. They can vary between closely related dialects and are often calqued from the non-Romani language of the speakers.

Examples

Beshav 'I sit'

Kai beshes?	Where are you staying/living (sitting)?
Me beshav pe gadya buki	I am in control of that situation (sitting on it)

Beshel pe bul ánde buki	He's taking no action about the matter (sitting on his backside)
Beshlem trin bêrsh ánde Kanáda	I lived (remained) three years in Canada
Beshélas po grast	He was riding his horse
O cháiniko beshel pe síniya	The teapot is resting on the table

Mudarav 'I kill'

Mudar e lámpa	Extinguish the lamp
Mudarde o ilêktriko	They turned off the hydro power
Mudarde múrro permíto	They annulled my permit
Mudarel múrro shêfto	He's ruining my business
Phuterdem kako fóro thai chi mangav te mudarel lês kónik	I opened this town and I don't want anybody to ruin it (said by a local Rom-Baro at a **diwáno** 'meeting')
Sar mudarel pêski vryámya?	How does he pass the time?
Mudardyas pêske chánsurya	He has blown his chances
Mudardem o ádo ánde hârtíya	I terminated the advertisement in the paper
Mudardyas o takimos	She brought down the fever
Mudardyam o buzherimos	We stopped the gossip

Nakhavav 'I swallow, pass'

Nashti nakhavav kodole manush	I can't stand (stomach) those people
Nakhade o motsyúne	They put through (passed) the motion
Chi nakhade lên pa e gránitsa	They wouldn't let them through the border
Chi nakhavav mai but xoli lêndar	I won't take any more aggravation from them
Nakhadyam lên ándo móbili	We sped past them (outstripped them) in the car

Xav 'I eat'

Xalyas sa pêske tsáliya	He has worn out all his clothes (literally: eaten them)
Xalem dósta xoli lêndar	I have put up with (eaten) enough aggravation from them
Xalyas pêski xoli	He has expended his anger
Xalyas but kíno ánde rrobíya	He endured much suffering in prison

Xalyas but daba ándo marimos	He received a lot of punches during the fight
Xan-pe	They are arguing (eating one another)
Xale sa pênge love	They spent all their money

There are a large number of idiomatic expressions using the verb to 'give'. Many can be found throughout the lessons but the following are typical:

Del anglal	He comes forward
Del opral	It is overflowing (giving from above)
Dyas-tele	It collapsed (gave down)

Sometimes idioms are formed in Romani by copying expressions or word order from the non-Romani majority language of the speakers. Typical are the following:

North American-Kalderash:

Phiravel skútsome tsáliya*	He's a sharp dresser

French-Kalderash:

Pharradyas man o yilo	*Elle m'a brisée le coeur* (she broke me the heart)

In most other Kalderash dialects this would be:

Pharradyas múrro yilo	She broke my heart

Constructions based on spiritual beliefs

Until recently, Kalderash Roma were influenced by animistic beliefs in spirits in water, trees, the earth, etc. These beliefs have even been applied to things like cars, electricity, alcohol and drugs which are seen as forces that act on their own outside of human control. This is reflected in the expression which in English would be 'He drowned' where Kalderash Roma will often say **Tasadyas les o pai** 'The water drowned him.' You could also say **Tasádyilo** 'He got drowned, he drowned'.

Not all these transitive forms allocating blame to the force or thing responsible can be expressed by inchoative or passive verbs. Other common expressions include:

---

*   **phiravel** 'he wears (clothes)', **skutsome** 'sharp' as in a sharp knife.

Lyas lês e rrakíya	The whisky took him (he got drunk)
Mudardyas la o shtrafyaiyimos	Lightning killed her (she was struck by lightning)
Mudardyas lês o ilêktriko	Electricity killed him (he died from an electric shock)
Mudardyas lês lêsko mobíli*	His car killed him (in the accident)
Mulo o ilêktriko	The electricity died (there was a power failure)
Mulo pêsko mobíli	His car broke down (died)
O parrno xalyas lêsko shoro	Cocaine destroyed him (ate his head)
O pimos xalyas lêsko shoro	Drink (alcohol) destroyed him (he became an alcoholic)
O póno mudardyas lên	The plague killed them (they died of the plague)
O Rráko xalyas lês	Cancer ate him (he died of cancer)

Brief history of the Romani language

The basic vocabulary of the Romani of Indo-Aryan origin is probably about 1,000 words (root elements) which are multiplied by suffixes and other grammatical devices to create a much more extensive list. The vocabulary has been, and continues to be, augmented by loan words. It might not be amiss to point out that only about twenty percent of English is Anglo-Saxon, the rest is composed of loan words (athematic items) from Celtic, Scandinavian languages, French, Greek, Latin, and words from just about every other language in the world from kimono to potato, from boomerang to puttees. On the other hand, an estimated sixty percent of the basic Romani vocabulary is of Indo-Aryan origin, ultimately from Sanskrit.

When the Romani people left India and came to other countries they met new ideas and saw new plants and animals, so in some cases they borrowed

---

*   A car that has killed somebody in an accident, or in which somebody died as the result of an accident, is called **mudarimásko mobíli** 'killer car' in North American-Kalderash. No Roma will knowingly buy such a car and will sell it to **Gazhe** 'non-Roma' if somebody died in it. I have witnessed **krisa** 'trials' where the allocation of guilt was the issue in a case where a family was suing the owner of a vehicle in which one of their family was killed in an accident after borrowing the car from its owner, now charged with the responsibility for this person's death. The issue was if they could they prove the owner knew the car had previously been involved in a fatal accident.

the word from the people in the new country. Some words which they probably brought from India disappeared because the animals, plants or purely Indian items of the past did not exist in the new countries they encountered. A few examples include: **dîz** 'fortress, castle' from Persian, **grast** 'horse as a beast of burden' from Armenian, and **petalo** 'horseshoe' and **molivi** 'lead' from Byzantine Greek.

In the south Balkans, new words for unfamiliar objects and other athematic items entered Romani, such as **púshka** 'firearm', **lovína** 'ale' and **porum** 'onion'. In Wallachia and Moldavia (present-day Romania) the Vlax-Roma who suffered over 500 years in slavery added a new battery of words derived from this experience, such as **klávo** 'slave', **kláviya** 'slavery', **kíno** 'suffering', **kurbash/korbáchi** 'lash/knout', **shîba** 'whipping', **lántsurya** 'chains', **yúgo** 'neck yoke/cangue' and finally **slobuzhénya** 'emancipation, freedom' in 1864.

As the Kalderash moved out of Romania and travelled through Europe they again added new words, which constant migration and intermarriage then spread among the communities in many countries. Typical are **têliga** 'carriage' from Russian, **djédjêsh** 'train' from Hungarian, **stígla** 'brick' from German and **hatázheno** 'floor of a building' from French. In Canada and the US, the Vlax-Romani immigrants added words to express new concepts and give new meanings to old Romani such as **karnivalash** 'carnival man', **mobíli** 'automobile', **drabarimos** 'reading/fortune-telling business', **dukáto** 'lawyer', **shâto** 'big shot', **blôko** 'city block', **gangstêri** 'gangster', **ófisa** 'fortune-telling parlour', **drôsto** 'drugstore', **blastêri** 'sand blaster', **rilífo** 'welfare', **tirrúmo** 'tea room', **pônko** 'punk', and many more.

For European Roma, the Romani Holocaust brought in new words for this attempted genocide, such as **Hitlêri** 'Hitler', **Fashísmo** 'Fascism', **kámpo-konsêntráko** 'concentration camp', **o mudarimos le Romêngo** 'the extermination of the Roma', **baráka** 'hut housing inmates', **sóba-gasóski** 'gas chamber', **phabayitóri** 'crematorium', **blokári** 'kapo' and **Kali-Legíya** 'Gestapo'. Under Communism, new words became necessary such as **Komisário** 'Commissar', **fábrika** 'factory', **Pártiya** 'Party' and **Sosialísmo** 'Socialism'.

In the former communist countries, now the new democracies, new words are again entering Romani such as **rasísmo** 'racism', **skini** 'skinhead', **persekútsiya** 'persecution', **azílo** 'asylum', **azilánto** 'refugee' and **shingale** 'immigration police'. As technology advances, more words are entering Romani such as **gramafóno** 'record player, stereo', **tilifóno** 'telephone', **televízhono** 'television', **mobílo** 'mobile phone', **sinzizáto** 'synthesizer', **komputéri** 'computer' and dozens of others.

Sometimes Roma form new words, like compound nouns, from Romani root elements.

With two nouns:

burr-kanrro	thorn bush (pl. **burr-kanrre**)
mashûnka-púshka	machine gun (pl. **mashûnka-pûshki**)

With a noun modified by an adjective (see also Lesson thirteen, compound nouns from genitive adjective plus noun):

baro-gav	capital city (pl. **bare-gava**)
kále-shtákli	black glasses/sunglasses
kanrralo-masho	perch, spiny fish (pl. **kanrrale-mashe**)
kúchi-khelitórka	shake dancer, hootchy-kootchy dancer (in a carnival) (pl. **kúchi-khelitórki**)

With a noun combined with a verb:

mashûnka kai ramol	writing machine, typewriter (pl. **mashûnki kai ramon**. Literally: 'machine that writes' and 'machines that write')
mashûnka kai xalavel	washing machine (pl. **mashûnki kai xalaven**)

Romani also borrows from other languages to create new words when needed. The **< iv >** verbs are one example:

Musai te faksis lênge kakya informátsiya	We must fax them this information (**faksil**)
Spreyisardem e fárba po mobíli	I spray painted the car (**spreyil**)
votisardem lêske	I voted for him

New nouns are constantly borrowed and are being adopted internationally:

Singular		Plural
azílo	asylum/refugee status	
bateríya	battery	**bateríyi**
dentísta (m.)	dentist	**dentísti**
dôftoro	doctor	**dôftorya**
êdukátsiya	education	
fákso	fax	**fáksurya**
fóto-kópiya	photocopy	**fóto-kópiyi**
Internêto	Internet	

karburéta	carburator	**karburéti**
konfêrèntsiya-internashionálno	international conference	
lumiyáki-miriyázha	worldwide web	
Nátsiya-Rromani	Romani nation (concept of the Roma as a non-territorial nation)	
Romanestan (f.)	Originally a Romani homeland but now the concept of a non-territorial nation	
shantíra	construction site	**shantíri**
stifikáto	certificate	**stifikáturya**
tíro	transport truck	**tírya**
univêrsitário	university	**univêrsitárya**
zastávo	flag	**zastávurya**

Often, when a new athematic noun is taken into Romani, it then undergoes incoining to create even more words. The original word for 'truck', taken from American/Canadian-English, developed as follows:

tróko	truck
trokútso	pick-up truck (diminutive)
trokash	truck driver
trokáshka	truck driver's wife or female truck driver
trokashútsa	truck driver's daughter
trokashítska	truck drivers' CB radio language (slang)
trokiv	to truck, send by truck (transitive verb)
trokime	trucked, sent or brought by truck (past participle and adjective)
trokimos (m.)	act of shipping by truck, shipment by truck

New athematic adjectives are also being formed with the suffix **< no >** as follows:

nashyonálno	national
ofishiyálno	official
sosiyálno	social
spêsiyálno	special

New words for the continents and nation states have also entered Romani. Some examples are:

Áfrichi (f.pl.)	African continent (literally: the Africas)
Américhi (f.pl.)	the Americas

Amérika	USA
Anglíya	Britain
Azíya	Asia
Fránsiya/Franzúzo	France
Itáliya	Italy
Ivrópa	Europe
Kanáda	Canada
Mêksiko	Mexico
Nyámptso	Germany
Rumúniya	Romania
Shpániya	Spain
Shwédiya/Shwédo	Sweden
Sud-Américhi (f.pl.)	the Latin American countries in South America
Ungáriya	Hungary

Nationalities and ethnic groups

Romani has also coined new words for nationalities, ethnic groups and non-Romani languages. Some examples are given here. The plurals and oblique stems for these can be found in the tables in Lesson seven.

Masculine singular	Feminine singular	
Amerikáno	Amerikánka	American
Ânglézo	Ânglezáika	Englishman/woman
Franzúzo	Franzuzáika	Frenchman/woman
Gêrko	Gêrkáika	Greek
Hindúko	Hindukáika	Hindu
Indiyáno	Indiyánka	Native-American person
Ivropáno	Ivropánka	European
Kalorro	Kalyorri	Black person
Kanadáko	Kanadáika	Canadian
Kitáitsa (m.)	Kitaitsáika	Chinese person
Mêksikáno	Mêksikánka	Mexican
Nipôntso	Nipontsáika	Japanese person
Nyámptso	Nyamptsáika	German
Rúso	Rusáika	Russian
Sêldjúko	Sêldjukáika	Turk
Zhúdovo	Zhudováika	Jewish person

Languages

The suffix **< ítska >** usually identifies a language in Kalderash-Romani:

Baiyashítska	Beásh language (a dialect of Romanian spoken by some Romani groups)
Churarítska	Churára dialect of Romani
Kalderashítska	Kalderash dialect of Romani
Franzuzítska	French
Inglezítska	English
Lowarítska	Lovára dialect of Romani
Machwanítska	Machwáya dialect of Romani
Môdyarítska	Hungarian
Nipôntsítska	Japanese
Rusítska	Russian
Shpaniolítska	Spanish
Vlaxítska	Romanian
Xoraxanítska	Muslim Romani (non-Vlax dialects spoken by Turkish and Muslim Roma)
Zhudovítska	Yiddish

but

Gazhikanes	Like a non-Rom, in the manner of a non-Rom (adverb)
Rromanes	Like a Rom, in the manner of a Rom (adverb)
Del-dúma Gazhikanes	He speaks in a non-Romani language
Del-dúma Rromanes	He speaks in Romani

Adjectives of nationality and ethnicity

These can usually be identified by the suffix **< ítsk >** which is declined for gender and number in the nominative and inflected for gender and number in the oblique. Taking the nominative singular of **Franzuzítsko** 'French' provides the following forms:

Franzuzítsko	Masculine and feminine nominative singular
Franzuzítska	Masculine and feminine nominative plural
Franzuzítskone	Masculine oblique singular
Franzuzítskonya	Feminine oblique singular
Franzuzítska	Masculine and feminine oblique plural

Some others are:

Gêrkítsko	Greek
Môdyarítsko	Hungarian
Nyamptsítsko	German
Niponsítsko	Japanese
Vlaxítsko	Romanian
Xoraxanítsko	Turkish
Zhudovítsko	Jewish

How much has Romani changed since the Roma arrived in Europe? History tells us that the Roma first appeared north of Romania in the fifteenth century AD. The following specimens of Romani were recorded in England in 1542 by Andrew Borde as examples of what he called "Egipt Speche" in his *Boke of the Introduction of Knowledge*. I have read these sentences to Roma in North America and to European Roma and they understand them perfectly, as do I. It might be wondered how many North Americans or even English people would understand the commonly spoken English of 1542?

Borde's Romani (phonetic spelling)	Modern English translation
Lachi tiri divés	Good (your) day, good day to you
Katar maila báro fóros?	How many miles (to the) big city?
Mishto-avés baro foros	Welcome (to the) big city
Mol pes, lovína?	Will you drink wine, ale?
Avava tusa	I will come with you
Besh telé, pi!	Sit down, drink!
Pi, pi, Devlesa!	Drink, drink , with God's blessing!
Chaye, de mai manro, lovína!	Girl, give more bread, ale!
De mai mas!	Give more meat!
Chaye, awordé tusa!	Girl, over here with you!
De man pabái ta ambrol!	Give me an apple and a pear!
Ach mishto	Keep well (stay cool)
Lachi rat tute	Good night to you

Battery of commonly used expressions in Kalderash

Besh tele	Sit down (to one person)
Beshen tele	Sit down (to more than one person)
Cháxo!	Ugh! Yuck!
Cháxo, che chorrobíya!	Yuck, how weird!
Che cháso si?	What time is it?

Che chorrobíya!	How odd!
Che fyal Rrôm san?	What kind of Rom are you?
Che vítsa san?	What clan are you?
Gryátsa!	Yuck! (expression of disgust)
Háide andre	Come in (to one person)
Háiden andre	Come in (to more than one person)
Kai tumáre grastên?	Where are your horses? (Where is the toilet? Man to man)
Kai zhan le ranya?	Where do the ladies go? (Where is the ladies' room? Woman to woman)
Kai zhas?	Where are you going?
Káski san tu?	Whose daughter are you?
Kásko san tu?	Whose son are you?
Katar aves?	From where do you come?
Me bushov … …	My name is … …
Mishto, nayís-túke	Fine, thank you
Nai bári djéla	It's not important
Sar bushos tu?	What's your name?
Sar san?	How are you?
Si tut yag?	Do you have a light? (fire)
So mai kerdyan?	What have you been up to?
So mai keres?	What are you up to?
So nakhlo?	What happened?
So zhal?	What's happening?
Sodya bêrshèngi san?	How old are you? (how many years own you) (to a woman)
Sodya bêrshèngo san?	How old are you? (to a man)
Triyánda bêrshèngi sim	I am thirty (thirty years own me) (if a woman)
Triyánda bêrshèngo sim	I am thirty (if a man)
Pansh-war-dêsh-thai-oxto bêrshengo sim	I am fifty-eight years old (a man)
Yertisar man	Pardon me

Remember, if a female speaker uses an adjective, this must be in the feminine form:

Bokhali sim	I am hungry (woman speaking)
Bokhalo sim	I am hungry (man speaking)
Bokhale sam	We are hungry (referring to all men, all women or mixed group)

Other Romani dialects (non-Vlax dialects)

Comments on other Romani dialects with which I have some familiarity because of the influx of speakers of these dialects to Canada as refugees, and with whom I have been interacting as a member of the Romani Community Centre in Toronto:

Sinti dialects

The Romani dialects spoken by the Sinti groups in western and central Europe are too far removed to be fully intelligible to native speakers of Vlax-Romani dialects, although some communication is possible at a basic level.

Romúngere dialects

The Romúngere dialects were historically spoken in Hungary but have now almost disappeared in that country. They are still spoken in Slovakia, the Czech Republic and now in Canada by the recent influx of Slovak-Roma refugees. These are non-Vlax dialects and the pronunciation and word order differs to a large extent but some communication is possible between native speakers of Vlax-Romani and Romúngere-Romani. The stress seldom falls on the last vowel in Romúngere dialects, for example, **Te áves baxtálo. Tu san lácho Rómano chávo** for Kalderash instead of **Te aves baxtalo. Tu san lasho shavorro Rromano** 'May you be lucky. You are a good Romani young man'. However, the massive amount of loan words from Hungarian, German, Slovak and Czech make this dialect difficult to understand for Vlax-Roma unless they speak a Slavic language. Yerli-Romani speakers from the former Yugoslavia and Bulgaria have an easier time understanding Romúngere in Romani because they also speak Slavic languages. One feature of Czech- and Slovak-Romani is the use of the third person singular to form an infinitive. Instead of saying **Me kámav te djav**, **Tu kámes te djas**, etc., as would speakers of Kalderash and other Romani dialects, they employ the third person singular as follows: **Me kámav te djal**, **Tu kames te djal**, etc. 'I want to go', 'You want to go'.

Yerli dialects (South Balkan non-Vlax-Romani)

This group of dialects is closer to Vlax-Romani excluding loan words and some grammatical differences. The best source on the Macedonian-Yerli-Romani is *Romani Gramatika* by Saip Jusuf. While the Romani is written in the Serbo-Croatian alphabet and is readable to anyone familiar with the alphabet and phonetics of Serbo-Croat, the grammatical explanations are Serbian in the Cyrillic alphabet.

There is also a currently available dictionary of Yérli-Romani, Stavov, Atanas, 1999, *Gypsy-English/English-Gypsy Dictionary*, New York, Hippocrene Books, Inc. I have gone over this dictionary with three native speakers now in Toronto who claim it is fairly accurate despite some obvious errors. The author's claim that this dialect can be used with Romani speakers "all over the world" is definitely not accurate. This dialect is not compatible with Kalderash and other Vlax-Romani dialects spoken in Europe and the Americas, nor with Romúngere, Sínti, Xaladítka and other dialects. It could be useful to anyone planning to learn a Bulgarian-Yerli-Romani dialect but it would have to be used in conjunction with a grammar reference since its grammatical rules are not synopsized and do not follow the rules of Kalderash and related Vlax-Romani dialects.

Gurbeti

The Gurbeti-Romani dialect spoken in Sarajevo seems to be midway between a Vlax-Romani dialect and the Yerli dialects with features common to both. It is readable in print and was used extensively by Hedina Sijercic, the former editor of *Romano Lil,* our NGO magazine in Toronto, who was herself a Gurbeti speaker from Sarajevo.

Welsh-Romini (Romnimus)

The last inflected form of British-Romani survived in Wales until at least the mid-twentieth century or even later but is now believed to be extinct. The only source is Sampson, John, *The Dialect of the Gypsies of Wales*, (Oxford University Press, 1924) which is written in English. Here is a specimen translated from the dedication (written in the Devanagari alphabet) and I have also included the Kalderash equivalent for comparative purposes:

Welsh-Romani

Ki Boro dakai but bershende dudyerdas mo drom akai tha akana asala pre mandi peske brishindeskeriate.

Kalderash equivalent

Ka Boro kon desar but bershêndar sikadyas múrro drom khate tha akána asála pe mánde pêska brichiriyátar.

Translation

To (George) Borrow who many years ago illuminated (showed) me my path here and who now smiles (laughs) at me from his rainbow.

Para-Romani

This term has been introduced by non-Romani linguists who write about Romani dialects. It is so far the only descriptive or definitive term for this type of speech. Para-Romani dialects have one thing in common – the speakers have lost the inflected Romani grammatical structure and simply use a certain number of Romani root elements mixed into the languages of the country they live in, usually in the regional vernaculars or the sub-standard forms of these languages. The pronunciation of Para-Romani follows that of the surrounding language which it uses as a vehicle. Below are examples of the only two I am familiar with through interaction with native speakers in Canada and, in the case of Anglo-Romani, also in Britain. Para-Romani is spoken in Britain, France, Spain, the Basque provinces, Portugal, Italy and Greece, and elsewhere by certain sub-groups of Romanis by emigration in the Americas, Australia and New Zealand.

Anglo-Romani example

Mandy's **joll**in into the **gav** to **deek** the **Gawja** about **atch**in the **vardo** on his **poov**
'I'm going into the town to see the non-Romani man about camping my wagon on his land'

The last form of English-Romani to survive with some inflected forms appears to have been in the US. I knew some older native speakers in Canada, or who came through Canada with the Carnivals in the late 1950s and the early 1960s, and who had been born in the US and Canada in the last two decades of the nineteenth century. English Romani families in the US claim ancestors who arrived at least as early as 1840. This form too has become extinct and been replaced by a Para-Romani as in the example shown above.

Scottish traveller cant (non-Romani cant words in italics)

I'll **djal** the **drôm** with the *hurley* the *morgen* to **deek** the **Gadjo**s out in the *muckery* about some *graft*
'I'll go on the road tomorrow morning with the truck to see the non-Romanis out in the countryside about some work'

Irish traveller cant

This is not a Para-Romani register. The speakers call it 'gammon' or 'cant'. I have heard it spoken and find it totally incomprehensible. Many speakers, however, do understand Anglo-Romani or Scottish cant as well as their own non-Romani cant. It has erroneously been called 'Shelta' but no speaker I have questioned on the road ever heard of this word. What has been written on it is mainly a rehashing of earlier works by non-Romani scholars going back to the original sources which are now long-outdated and questionable. There are sounds in Irish cant which are not English or Romani.

Equivalents of Kalderash words in other dialects

The following words in the left-hand column used in Kalderash will not normally be understood by speakers of non-Vlax dialects since many of these Kalderash words are from Romanian. Suggested alternatives for use with non-Vlax-Romani speakers are given in the third column. These need not be learned but are placed here for reference for those who may be interacting with central or eastern European-Romani communities.

Kalderash	English	Central and eastern Europe
ánde diminyátsa	in the morning	**ánde evín**
araki	yesterday	**ich**
cháso	hour	**óra**
chi	negative particle	**na (Na djanav** for **Chi zhanav)**
del-dúma	he speaks	**vakyarel/vachyarel, del sváto** (Bosnia)
dey	mother	**dai**
djédjêsh (m.)	train	**vlak** (Bulgaria) **tren, vonat**
doryávo/rivêri	river	**lên** (m.)
farbol	he paints	**makhel, boinel**
filástra	window	**prózorets** (f.)
fóro	town	**diz, ziz** (f.) (fortress in Kalderash)
fúrka	fork	**bunéla (furkéri** (m.) 'pitchfork')
gáta	ready	**gotov**
Gazho	non-Rom	**Gádjo, Xálo** (Sínti)
ginel*	he reads	**chetinel, drabarel, irinel**

*   **ginel** actually means 'he counts' in Kalderash. Some speakers do use this but **chitol** 'he reads' is much more common. In Romanian Vlax-Romani, the verb **drabarel** 'he/she reads' is now becoming popular and has appeared in Romani-language primers for children and teenagers. In North American-Kalderash, **drabarel** means 'she tells fortunes, reads palms', etc., (literally: 'does readings'). 'I write' in Kalderash is **ramov** with a past tense in **ramosardem** 'I wrote'. In some European Vlax-Romani dialects, 'I write' is **skribisaráv** with a past tense in **skribisardem**.

hakyarél	he understands	**axalel, razumil**
ka l'pansh	at (5) o'clock	**panzh chas, panzh óri**
kai	where	**kate**
kasht (m.)	tree	**rukh**
ke	because	**sóske-to**
khántchi	nothing	**níkach, níchi**
kolompíra	potatoes	**kartófi** (f.)
kónik	nobody	**níkon** (metathesis from **kónik**)
kuch	dear	**skúpo**
kuchi	cup	**chásha**
kukashtára	toilet	**kabinéta**
lávuta	violin	**gáyga, bashadi**
Lúwine	on Monday	**Ponedêlnikos**
mai	more	**po**
manai	there is not (no)	**náne** (Romúngero/Karpáti)
Martsune	on Tuesday	**Vtórnikos**
meázol	he looks like	**prepinel**
mishto	good, all right	**laches, shukar**
míya	1,000	**hiliyáda** (Bulgaria), **êzera** (Hungary)
mobíli	automobile	**matóra**
murtáno	male cat	**mátchko**
mútsa	female cat	**mátchka**
na	particle	**ma** (as in **ma zha** for **na zha** 'don't go' in Kalderash)
nai (m.)	finger, toe	**angúsht** (f.)
núma	but	**áma, táma** (Xaladítko, Russian dialect)
phutrel	he opens	**pharavel**
porrárro	glass	**chásha**
posuki	pocket	**djépo**
púshka	gun	**yagalo**
ramol	he writes	**pishinel, chinel**
Sar bushos?	How are you called?	**Sar akharen tut?**
shávo	Romani boy	**chávo**
shey	Romani girl	**chai**
shon (m.)	month	**másek**
si	he/she is, etc.	**hi, hin** (Romúngero, Gurbéti and Sínti among others)

sláva	feast, holiday	**báro dives**
sóde	how much	**kíbor**, **kítsi**, **kázom**
sóstar	why	**sóske**
stántsya	station	**gára**, **stánitsa**
tehara	tomorrow	**táysa**
than (m.)	bed	**páto**
thol	he puts	**chuvel**
tisírra	a little	**xáritsa**, **fríma**
trobul	it needs	**kámpel** (Romúngero/Karpati dialect)
tsáliya (f.pl.)	clothes	**drêxi** (f.pl.), **gada** (m.pl.)
tsêra	tent	**katúna**, **chêrga**
tsigára	cigarette	**thuv** (f.), **papiróshka**
tyára	plate, saucer	**chiníya**
vêska	because	**sóske-to**
wáreso	something	**chípas**, **chumúni**
wáso	plate	**cháro**
wortáika	female friend	**amalin**
wortáko	friend, partner	**amal** (m.)
wuzho	clean	**shúzho**
xalavel	he washes	**thovel**
zaháro	sugar	**tsáxar** (m.), **gudlo**, **shukíla**
zakóno	law	**krísi**
Zhowine	on Thursday	**Pevtsine**
zhutóri (m.)	lawyer	**právnikos** (Romúngero/Karpati dialect)

If you find that a word in the first column is not understood by a Rom you are talking to, try the one listed in the third column. This list makes no claims to be complete.

Conclusion

I would like to end this course with what I consider to be one of the most beautiful songs in Romani. Like most popular Romani songs, it exists in many versions and this one was recorded in Toronto in 2003 from a Muslim-Romani refugee originally from Kosovo.

Hêderlézi* (in Yerli-Romani)

Sa e Rróma, Daye	All the Roma, Mother
E bakren chinéna	Are sacrificing lambs
Ame sam chorrórre	We are very poor
Dural besháva	I live far away
Sa e Rróma, Daye	All the Roma, Mother
Amaro baro dives	Our holiday
Amaro baro dives	Our holiday
Hêderlézi.	Hederlezi.
Sa e Rróma, Daye	All the Roma, Mother
Sa e Rróma djilabéna	All the Roma are singing
Sa e Rróma, Daye	All the Roma, Mother
E bakren chinen	They are sacrificing lambs
Ei, ...	Hey, ...
O sa e Rróma, Bábo	Oh, all the Roma, Father
Sa e Rróma, o Daye	All the Roma, Mother
O sa e Róma, Bábo	Oh, all the Roma, Father
Ei, Hêderlézi, Hêderlézi	Hey, Hederlezi, Hederlezi
Djurdjevdáne.	St George's Day.
Sa e Rróma, Daye	All the Roma, Mother
Sa e Rróma keléna	All the Roma are dancing
Sa e Rróma djilabéna†	All the Roma are singing
Amaro baro dives.	Our holiday.
Sa e Rróma, Daye	All the Roma, Mother
Sa e Rróma bashavéna	All the Roma are playing music
Sa e Rróma djilabéna	All the Roma are singing
E bakren chinen.	They are sacrificing lambs.
Ei, ...	Hey, ...
O sa e Rróma, Bábo	All the Roma, Father

* Hederlezi (or Herdelezi) is a festival which takes place from the middle of April to 9 May each year but the main days are 5-6 May which also coincide with Djurdjevdan or the Feast of St George. Hederlezi is celebrated by Muslim Roma and Djurdjevdan by Christian Roma. St George's Day is also celebrated in the US by the Machwáya-Roma, a Vlax-Romani group originally from Serbia, but not by the Kalderash who instead celebrate the Santána – St Anne's Day – on 25 May.

† **gilaban** in Kalderash.

Sa e Rróma, O Daye   Oh, all the Roma, Mother
O sa e Rróma, Bábo   Oh, all the Roma, Father
Ei, Hêderlézi, Hêderlézi Hey, Hederlezi, Hederlezi
Djurdjevdáne.   St George's Day.

A standard Romani alphabet

The World Romani Congress recommends one system for international use (see Cortiade in Bibliography). In my opinion, which is shared by many other Roma, the alphabet recommended by the Congress before the advent of the worldwide mass use of home computers is not suitable. While it is an excellent tool for linguists and scholars, it has peculiar letters and symbols which only exist on a special font designed for this alphabet which is unavailable from commercial sources, for example, in Cyrillic or Japanese fonts. It cannot be written on a standard typewriter or computer keyboard and so defeats the very purpose for which it was intended: a tool to enable Roma to write their own language and to communicate with other Roma and for Roma to write, print and publish material in Romani.

A phonetic alphabet using the letters on a standard computer keyboard would be a much better system. The alphabet used in this course does not need the accents when used by native speakers. These have been used only to help non-Romani speakers to pronounce the words and to get the stress in the right place. I fully believe that the alphabet adopted by the World Romani Congress would never have been adopted in the first place had the people making this decision been journalists, publishers, authors, teachers and people working in the area of mass media communication, and had the decision been made in this age of computers and the Internet. An alphabet and phonetic system more suitable to the technology of the twenty-first century is urgently needed. The phonetic system used in this course, or something along the lines of that devised by Dr Ian Hancock, without accents needing specialized fonts and which is also based on English phonetics, might be a good beginning since English is the language most widely taught in universities and is needed by university graduates in the EU member countries and in the new democracies in the former communist countries of central and eastern Europe.

This lesson completes the *Learn Romani* course.

Opre Rromále! Te aven baxtale!
Rise up proudly Roma! May you be fortunate!

Glossary of Romani words

This glossary is designed as a reference for the student to look up unfamiliar terms as they appear in the course and contains the vocabulary used most often plus a few extra basic words. It does not include words given in lists of verbs, adjectives, prepositions, etc. from the lessons unless these are also used elsewhere in the course. The following abbreviations and indicators are used in the glossary:

Nouns: There are only two genders in Kalderash-Romani. Nouns ending in **< o >** whether stressed or unstressed are masculine. Nouns ending in a stressed **< i >** are feminine. Nouns ending in an unstressed **< i >** or a consonant can be either masculine or feminine and are indicated by (m.) or (f.). Nouns ending in **< a >** are usually feminine like **ponyáva** 'carpet' but some are masculine like **gázda** 'boss'. These exceptions will be indicated by (m.). Plural nouns such as **love** 'money' or **tsáliya** 'clothes' have their gender indicated by (m.pl.) or (f.pl.).

Adjectives: Thematic adjectives are defined by (Them. Adj.) and athematic adjectives are indicated by (Athem. Adj.). All thematic adjectives in the glossary are given in the masculine singular form. **Parno** 'white' would become **parni** if the noun it modified was feminine singular, **parne** for plural nouns of both genders in the nominative and for masculine singular nouns in the oblique, and **parnya** for feminine singular nouns in the oblique. Athematic adjectives are also given in the masculine singular nominative form which is often the same for feminine singular nouns in the nominative. For inflected athematic nouns it will be necessary to consult the lessons. Thematic adjectives ending in **< me >** have only one form and are not subject to gender, number or inflection in the oblique.

Verbs: Verbs are given in the third person singular with the third person past tense provided. All other tenses can be formed by knowing the present and past conjugations in the third person singular. Remember that the third person singular of the present tense means 'he' and 'she' so the entry **beshel** means 'he sits' and 'she sits'. The past tense is **beshlas** which means 'he sat' or 'she sat'. On the other hand, verbs such as **nashel** 'he runs' or 'she runs' have two past tense forms in **nashlo** 'he ran' and **nashli** 'she ran'. Since there is no neutral gender, the English word 'it' must be translated into Romani as 'he' or 'she'.

Other parts of speech: Adverbs, prepositions, etc., are not usually indicated since this is often clear from the English meaning and many of these words have more than one definition and are multi-functional.

The abbreviation q.v. is short for the Latin phrase *quod vide* meaning 'which see'. It is used to make cross-references and directs the student to another part of the text for further information.

A

ába	yet, already (variant of **yába** (q.v.))
ages	today
agore	towards the edge
Ái!	Oh!
akana	now
akanash	presently, right away, very soon
akushel	he curses, insults (past **akushlas**)
amal (m.)	male friend (used in Europe but only known to elderly people in North America)
amalni	female friend (used in Europe but only known to elderly people in North America)
amáro	our, ours
amblavel	he hangs, executes by hanging (past **ambladyas**)
amboldel	he turns around, reverses, turns back (past **amboldyas**)
ambóri	maybe, perhaps
ambrol (m.)	pear
ambrolin (f.)	pear tree
ame	we, nominative pronoun and us/ourselves, variant of **amên** (q.v.) as a reflexive pronoun
amên	us
Américhi (f.pl.)	the Americas (North, Central and South America)
Amérika	United States of America
Amerikáko	American
an	in
anav (m.)	name
and-	in (must have a definite article attached, see **ande/ando** (q.v.))
ánda	because of, about, from, by
ánde	in, into, inside (before a feminine or plural noun)
ánde l'	in, into, inside (before plural nouns of both genders)
ánde vúrma	1) in (at) the end, finally; 2) late

ándo	in, into, inside (before a masculine singular noun)
ándo mizméri	in the afternoon
andre	inside, within (**Andre-lo** 'He is inside' (the house or caravan))
anel	he brings (past **andyas**)
angáli	embrace
ángla	before, in front of (preposition)
anglal	in front, ahead of, before
Anglíya	England
angushtri	ring
ankalavel	he gets out, rescues, extracts (past **ankaladyas**)
anklel	1) it turns out; 2) he gets out, gets on, mounts, turns out, exits, rises (past **anklisto/anklisti**)
anrro	egg
ansuril-pês	he gets married (past **ansurisáilo**)
antúnchi	then, at that time/instant, later, after that
anúmi	on purpose, deliberately
ap	so, well, then, by, upon, therefore
aparáti (f.pl.)	tools, equipment
ápo	variant of **ap** (q.v.)
arakhel	1) he protects, takes care; 2) he meets, encounters (past **arahklas**)
araki	yesterday, last night
archíchi (m.)	tin
aresel	he arrives, reaches (past **areslo/aresli**)
asal	he smiles, laughs (past **asáilo/asaiyas**)
ashel	he stays, stops, remains (past **ashilo/áshili**)
ashunel	he hears, listens (past **ashundyas**)
astarel	he catches, begins (past **astardyas**)
aswin (f.)	teardrop
atúnchi	variant of **antúnchi** (q.v.)
atwéto	answer, reply
áva	yes (variant of **ya** (q.v.))
avel	he comes, he becomes (past **avilo/avili**)
avér-tehára	day after tomorrow
avokáto	lawyer, attorney, barrister
avri	outside
avtsûn (m.)	steel
aworde	here, over here, this way (adverb)

azbal	he touches, it relates to (past **azbáilo/azbáili**)
azhukerel	he waits, awaits, waits for (past **azhukerdyas**)
azilantáika	female refugee claimant, refugee
azilánto	male refugee claimant, refugee
azilánturya (m.pl.)	refugees, asylum seekers
azílo	asylum, convention-refugee status

B

bai (f.)	sleeve
bai	1) surely, will surely; 2) so
bakri	ewe
bakro	ram
bal (m.)	one strand of hair
bal (m.pl.)	hair (**Si lês kale bal** 'He has black hair')
bali	sow
balo	male pig
balval (f.)	1) wind, air; 2) breath, oxygen
bango	bent, crooked (Them. Adj.)
bangyarel	he bends, cripples, distorts, twists (past **bangyardyas**)
bánka	bank
baráchi (f.pl.)	housing, huts, shacks
baráka	hut, barrack, shack, dump
baro	big man, local leader, important man
baro	big, important (Them. Adj.)
barruno	stone, made of stone (Them. Adj.)
barvalo	rich, wealthy (Them. Adj.)
baryol	he grows (up) (past **barilo/barili**)
bashavel	he plays music (past **bashadyas**)
bashno	rooster
basúna	basin, tin or copper mixing bowl for making bread or pastry dough
baxt (f.)	luck, karma
baxtalo	lucky, fortunate, favoured (Them. Adj.)
báyo	trouble, problems, misfortune, disaster
béda	trouble
bêlzùna	blowtorch, propane-gas torch
bêng (m.)	devil, Satan
bênzína	petrol, gasoline (European-Kalderash)

bêrsh (m.)	year
beshel	he sits, stays, resides (past **beshlas**)
bezax (m.)	sin
bi-	1) prefix meaning without (**bi-lovêngo** 'without money') and un- as in **bi-wuzho** 'unclean'; 2) it can turn an adjective into its opposite as in **bi-lasho** 'bad'
bi-baxt (f.)	bad luck, ill fortune
bibi	aunt, female elder
bikinel	he sells (past **bikindyas**)
bíra	beer
birtash (m.)	male bartender
bírto	tavern, bar, saloon
bish	twenty (numeral)
bíshto	twentieth (numeral)
bishtrel	he forgets (past **bishterdyas**)
blúdka	saucer
bokh (f.)	hunger, famine
bokhalo	hungry (Them. Adj.)
bori	1) bride; 2) daughter-in-law; 3) sister-in-law
bráshka	female frog
brégo	bank of a river
brêshùn (m.)	rain
budáka	pickaxe, mattock
búkfa	book
buki (f.)	1) work, business, labour; 2) thing, item, matter
bukyárnichi	workmen, tradesmen
bul (f.)	backside, rump, posterior, bottom, base or underside of an object
bul-opre	bottom up, upside down (adverb)
buntuyil	he riots, agitates, disturbs (past **buntuyisardyas**)
burr (m.)	thicket, bush
burr-kanrro (m.)	thorn bush
búrrnêx (f.)	handful, hold (**Lem búrrnêx lêstar** 'I took hold of it')
bushol	he is called (past **busháilo/busháili**)
but	1) much, many, very (**mai but** 'more'); 2) many people (**But avile** 'Many (people) came')
buzhanglo	cunning, astute (Them. Adj.)
buzherimos (m.)	gossip, apocrypha, grapevine
buzno	male goat

CH

Chaches?	truly, really? (adverb)
chachimos (m.)	truth, justice
chacho	right (as a direction) (Them. Adj.)
chacho	true, real, genuine (Them. Adj.)
chai	variant of **cháiyo** (q.v.)
cháiniko	teapot
cháiyo	tea
châng (f.)	knee
char (m.)	grass
cháso	1) hour; 2) time; 3) clock, watch
che?	which, what?
cheran (f.)	star
chêri (m.)	sky
chi	not, don't (negative particle)
chink (f.)	sneeze
chirikli	female bird
chiriklo	male bird
chismesára	pair of high leather boots
chitol	he reads (past **chitosardyas**)
chokáno	hammer
chor (m./m.pl.)	male thief, thieves
chorel	he steals, swindles (past **chordyas**)
chorimos (m.)	theft, robbery
chorres	badly (adverb)
chorro	poor, bad, inferior, pitiful (Them. Adj.)
chorromos (m.)	poverty
chorrorro	poverty-stricken (Them. Adj.)
choryal	stealthily
choxãní	female ghost
choxãnó	male ghost
chumi (f.)	kiss
chumidel	he kisses (past **chumidas**)
chûng (f.)	knee (variant of **châng** (q.v.))
chungardel	he spits, despises (past **chundardyas**)

D

dab (f.)	blow, punch, bang, thud (**daba** (f.pl.) blows, hammering)
dad	father
dar (f.)	fear, apprehension
daral	he fears, is afraid (past **daráilo/daráili**)
daravel	he frightens, intimidates, terrifies (past **daradyas**)
dáta	time, occasion, date (**mai yêkh dáta** 'once more, once again')
defyal	at all, in no way, anyhow
Del (m.)	God
del	he gives, grants, allows (past **dyas**. **Te del o Del** 'May God grant' (idiomatic) 'I hope so')
del-dúma	he speaks (past **dyas-dúma**)
dêrzi	rags
desar	since, then
desh	ten (numeral)
déshto	tenth (numeral)
desya	too, very (**desya but** 'too much, very much')
Dévla!	God! (vocative case)
Devlésa!	1) Go with God!; 2) Stay with God!
dey	mother
dikhel	he looks, he sees (past **dikhlas**)
dikhyol	he is seen (past **dikhyáilo**, **dikhyáili**)
dilimos (m.)	stupidity, silliness
dilo	silly, foolish, crazy (Them. Adj.)
dilyarel	he drives crazy, makes crazy (past **dilyardyas**)
diminyátsa	morning
díno	gift, present
dino	given, struck (past participle as Them. Adj., for example, **Dino-Devlêstar** 'Smitten from God' (slightly mad))
dívlio	wild, untamed (Athem. Adj.)
diwáno	meeting
do mult	a long time ago (adverb)
dóftoro	medical doctor
doháno	tobacco
do-multano	ancient, antediluvian, in the distant past (Athem. Adj.)
do-pash	half (Them. Adj. like **shukar**)
dopashin (f.)	half

doryávo	river
dosh (f.)	blame
dósta	enough, plenty, sufficient
drabarel	she gives readings, tells fortunes (past **drabardyas**)
drabarimos (m.)	reading, advice (the art of consultation as practised in North America by Kalderash women who work as reader advisers)
drágo	dear, beloved, darling (Athem. Adj.)
drôm (m.)	road
dui	two (numeral)
dúito	second (numeral)
dukáto	solicitor, lawyer (North American dialect)
dukhal	it hurts, aches (**Dukhal man o shoro** 'My head aches', past **dukháilo, dukháili**)
dúma	talk, speech
dur	far, far away, distant
dural	from afar, from far away
dushmáno	male enemy, opponent

DJ

djédjêsh (m.)	train
djéla	thing, matter, object
djuléshi (m.)	business meeting
djungalimos (m.)	ugliness, obscenity, disgraceful behaviour
djungalo	ugly, disrespectful (Them. Adj.)

E

e	the (before feminine nouns)
êkh	variant of **yêkh** (q.v.)

F

fábrika	factory
familíya	family
fárba	1) paint; 2) make-up
farbol	he paints (past **farbosardyas**)
farbol-pe	she applies make-up (past **farbosáili**)
fárma-katárka (f.)	weaver of spells, witch

farmáko	spell
fátsa	1) face; 2) colour
fêrdi	only, except, but
férma	farm
filástra	window, computer screen
fína	goddaughter
fíno	godson
firánga	curtain, drape
fistáno	long (ankle-length) Romani woman's skirt
fóro	city, large town
Franzuzítska	French (language)
Franzúzo	1) Frenchman; 2) France
fúga	haste, speed
fugása	quickly, in a hurry (instrumental case serving as an adverb)
fúgo	quickly, fast (Athem. Adj. and adverb)
fúrka	fork
fyal (m.)	kind, sort (**che fyal** 'what sort of, kind of')

G

gad (m.)	shirt, blouse
gálbi (m.pl.)	gold coins, necklace of gold coins
gansáko	gander
gáta (f.)	end, completion, finish, termination
gáta	ready, finished, completed (Them. Adj. and adverb)
gav (m.)	village, small town
gázda (m.)	boss, owner, manager
gazderítsa	female teacher, mentor
gazdínka	female boss, owner, manager
Gazhe	plural of **Gazho** (q.v.) and of **Gazhi** (q.v.) if mixed gender group
Gazhi	non-Romani woman, wife if non-Romani
Gazhikanes	like the non-Roma (adverb)
Gazhikaníya	non-Romani environment, outside world
Gazho	non-Romani man, husband if non-Romani
Gazhya	plural of **Gazhi** (q.v.)
ges (m.)	day
gi (m.)	1) soul; 2) stomach
gilabal	he sings (past **gilabadyas**)

gili	song, poem
gindil-pe	he thinks (past **gindisáilo/gindisáili**)
ginel	he counts (past **gindas**)
gitára	guitar
gláso	1) voice; 2) tune (**E gitára nai ándo gláso** 'The guitar is not in tune')
gláta	infant female baby, baby girl
gláto	infant male baby, baby boy
glatútsa	newborn baby girl
glatútso	newborn baby boy
gogi (f.)	brain, mind, intelligence
gono	sack, bag
gozhni	manure
gránitsa	frontier, border
grápa	1) hole, pit; 2) wall plug, electric socket
grasni	mare
grast (m.)	horse, gelding
griyátsa!	yuck! (exclamation of disgust)
grizhol	he tidies up, cleans up (past **grizhosardyas**)
groposhévo	grave
guglo	sweet, fresh tasting (Them. Adj.)
gûndo	thought
gunoi (m.)	trash, rubbish, garbage
gurumni	cow
guruv (m.)	bull

H

hai	and, also
Háide!	Come on, let's go, let's get going! (imperative command)
hakyarel	he understands (past **hakyardyas**)
hanol	he does wipe tinning, replating (past **hanosardyas**)
harápo	cannibal ogre (in folk tales)
harmasári (m.)	stallion
hârtíya	newspaper, paper
harzópo	lift, elevator
hêrgéla	herd, herd of
hifta	seven (numeral)
hiftáto	seventh (numeral)

I

i-	prefix meaning 'too' (**i-tu** 'you too')
ifta	seven (numeral) (variant of **hifta** (q.v.))
iftáto	seventh (variant of **hiftáto** (q.v.))
ikonáko	icon, religious statue
ilêktriko	1) electricity; 2) headlight
Inglezítska	English (language)
inkyal	over, across (preposition)
intáini	to no purpose, without reason, for nothing
inya	nine (numeral)
inyáto	ninth (numeral)
Itáliya	Italy
iv (m.)	snow
Ivrópa	Europe
ivya	free, gratis (adverb)

K

ka	1) too (preceding a nominative singular masculine noun); 2) who, that (masculine singular relative pronoun)
ka	who (singular), that (pronoun)
kadiki	so, this (usually with **de**. **Kadiki de baro** 'This big')
káfa	coffee
kai	1) too (preceding a feminine singular or plural nominative noun; 2) who, that (a feminine singular or plural of both genders relative pronoun)
kai	who (plural), that (pronoun)
kai?	where?
kak	uncle, patriarch, elder
kakala	these, these things (feminine gender)
kakala	these, these things (describing feminine plural nouns)
kakale	these, these things (masculine gender)
kakale	these, these things (describing masculine plural nouns)
kako	this (describing masculine singular nouns)
káko	uncle (vocative case)
kakya	this (describing feminine singular nouns)
kakya	thus, so, like this, this way, in this manner
kakyavári (m.)	kettlesmith

Kali-Legíya (f.)   Black Legion, Gestapo
kalo   1) black, dark-skinned; 2) tragic; 3) underground (as in **kali buki** 'underground economy'. Them. Adj.)
kalts (f.pl.)   trousers
kaludjérka   nun, chaste woman, prude
kam-   future prefix (**Kam-avav** 'I shall come')
kámas-   conditional prefix (**Kámas-avav** 'I would come')
kamel   1) he loves, wants; 2) he owes (past **kamlas**)
kamféti (f.pl.)   candy
kámpo   camp
kána?   when? (interrogative and relative) (**desar kána** since when?)
Kanáda   Canada
káring   toward, towards (preposition)
kâsevó   so, such, so much (Them. Adj.)
kasht (m.)   1) wood; 2) tree; 3) coffin
katar   from, from where, from wherever (preposition)
katar?   from where?
katel   she weaves, knits, spins (past **katlas**)
ke   because (often contracted to **kh'**)
kerel   he makes, does (past **kerdyas**)
kerel buki   he works, is working (past **kerdyas buki**)
kêrkó   bitter (Them. Adj.)
kernyol   it wilts, goes bad, decays, rots (past **kernilo/kernili**)
kerrárya   pathway, footpath, path
khaini   chicken, hen
kham (m.)   sun
khamni   pregnant (Them. Adj.)
khánchi (m.)   nothing
khangri   church
khatênde   nowhere, anywhere (adverb)
khelel-pês   1) he dances; 2) he plays (games etc. Past **kheldyas-pês**)
khelitóri (m.)   male dancer
khelitórka   female dancer
kher (m.)   house
khere   home, homeward (adverb)
khil (m.)   butter
khino   tired, worn out, exhausted (Them. Adj.)
khul (f.)   excrement, dung, road apples
kídel   he collects, gathers, saves (money) (past **kidas**)

kidino   gathered, collected (past participle as Them. Adj.)

kinel   he buys (past **kindyas**)

kingo   wet (Them. Adj.)

kíno   pain, suffering, torture, torment

kinyol   he is tortured, suffers torment (past **kinilo/kinili**)

kiral (m.)   cheese

kiravel   he boils (past **kiradas**)

kirivi   godmother

kirivo   godfather

kníshka   book (European-Kalderash)

kodo   that, that thing (masculine gender)

kodola   those (describing feminine plural nouns)

kodole   those (describing masculine plural nouns)

kodya   that, that thing (feminine gender)

kokala (m.pl.)   bones, skeleton

kokalo   bone

kola (f.pl.)   stuff, things, valuables (pl. of **kova** (f.) 'thing')

kolégo   colleague

kólkorro   alone

kóltso   corner, street corner

kolumpíra   potato

kolumpíri (f.)   potato (variant of **kolumpíra** (q.v.))

kon?   who?

kónik   nobody, no one, anybody

kôntáina   container, shipping crate

kopáchi (m.)   large tree, giant redwood

korr (f.)   neck, throat

koshtil   it costs (past **koshtisardyas**)

kothe   there, yonder

kotor (m.)   piece, piece of, portion (**kotor manrro** 'piece of bread')

kovles   softly (adverb)

kovlo   soft (Them. Adj.)

Krechúno   Christmas

kris (f.)   trial, court, justice (**Kris-Rromani** 'judicial assembly of Roma, Romani trial', **Kris-Gazhikani** 'non-Romani court or trial')

krisi (f.)   trial, court, justice (European-Kalderash variant of **kris** (q.v.))

kriyánga   bough, branch

krúgo   round (Athem. Adj.)

kruyal	around, round about
kuch	dear, expensive (Athem. Adj.)
kuchi	cup
kui (f.)	elbow
kukurúzo	Indian corn, corn on the cob
kumnáta	sister of a spouse
kumnáto	brother of a spouse
kumpaníya	community of Roma in a town or city; also travelling group
kurko	1) week; 2) Sunday
Kurkone	on Sunday
kúrva	1) prostitute; 2) bitch, bad girl, promiscuous woman
kutári (m.)	so-and-so (unnamed male person)
kutárka	so-and-so (unnamed female person)

L

l'	contraction (elision) of **le** (q.v.)
la	she is (enclitic) (**Avri-la** 'She is outside')
la	her
la	the (before inflected feminine singular nouns)
ladjári (m.)	sailor, boatman, seaman
ladyol	he is loaded into, packed into (past **ladilo/ladili**)
láko	her, hers
lámpa	lamp
langal	he limps (past **langáilo/langáili**)
lántso	1) chain; 2) gold chain
lasharel	he repairs, fixes (past **lashardyas**)
lashimos	goodness, excellence
lasho	good, excellent (Them. Adj.)
lávuta	violin
lavutári (m.)	1) Romani musician; 2) Romani violinist (musicians are a caste among some of the Vlax-Romani groups and consider themselves of higher status than metalsmiths, traders, etc.)
lazhal	he feels shame, is ashamed, is shy (past **lazháilo/lazháili**)
lazhav (m.)	shame, embarrassment, disgrace
le	they are (enclitic) (**Barvale-le** 'They are rich')
le	the (before inflected masculine singular nouns and plural nouns of both genders)
lel	he takes, gets, obtains, receives (past **lyas**)

lên	them
lêngo	their, theirs
lês	him
lêsko	his
lil (m.)	letter
lipil	he sticks, pastes (past **lipisardyas**)
lo	he is (enclitic) (**Andre-lo** 'He is inside')
lolo	red (Them. Adj.)
lolyol	she blushes (past **lolili**)
lônd (m.)	salt
love (m.pl.)	money, monies
lulugi	flower
lúmiya	1) world; 2) humanity, people
Lúndra	London, England (also **Lôndono**)
lúngo	long (Athem. Adj.)
Luwine	on Monday (adverb)
Lúya	Monday

M

ma	me (variant of **man** (q.v.))
ma	my (short form of **múrra** (q.v.), used before inflected feminine singular nouns)
mai but	more, most
Mai drobroi tu?	Greetings, how are you? (idiomatic)
mai yêkh dáta	once more, one more time
mai	1) more; 2) ever
makh (f.)	fly
makhel	he smears (past **makhlas**)
makyol	he gets drunk (past **makilo/makili**)
mal (f.)	field
maládyol	to meet, encounter (past **maládyilo/maládyili**)
malavel	to strike, bang, hit (past **maladyas**)
mami	grandmother
man	me
manai	there is not, there are no
manas	there were no, were not
mangel	he wants (past **manglas**)
manrro	bread

manush (m.)   male person, human being, older man
manushni   woman, female human being, older woman
marel   he hits, beats, strikes (past **mardyas**)
marel-pês   he fights (past **mardyas-pês**)
mariki (f.)   cake (often **tórta** in European-Kalderash)
marime   defiled, polluted, ritually unclean (past participle as Athem. Adj.)
marimos (m.)   fight, fighting, warfare, war
máriya   sea, ocean
Mártsi (f.)   Tuesday
Martsune   on Tuesday (adverb)
mas (m.)   meat, flesh
mashári (m.)   fisherman, fishmonger
mashkar   among, amongst, in the middle, between (preposition)
mashkar (m.)   middle, waist
mashkare   into the middle of
masho   fish
mashtívo   step-, adopted (Athem. Adj.)
mashúnka   machine
mato   intoxicated (Them. Adj.)
maxrime   European variant of **marime** (q.v.)
me   I (nominative personal pronoun)
meázol   he looks like, resembles (past continuous **meazólas**)
mekel   1) he leaves, abandons; 2) he lets, allows, permits (past **meklas**)
melalo   dirty (Them. Adj.)
merel   he dies, expires (past **mulo/muli**)
merimásko   dying, wilting, moribund (Them. genitive adj.)
merimos (m.)   death
mi   short form of **múrri** (q.v.)
mil   thousand (numeral)
míla   pity, mercy
minúto   minute
minútsi   minutes
mishtipe (m.)   favour, good deed, kindness (East European-Kalderash)
mishto   well, fine, excellently, all right, O.K. (adverb)
mishtomos (m.)   favour, good deed, kindness (French and North American-Kalderash)
míya   1) thousand (numeral); 2) mile

mizméri (m.)   afternoon, noon

mo   my (short form of **múrro** (q.v.))

mobilâriya (m.pl.) furniture

mobilêski-shûna (f.) car tyre

mobíli (m.)   car, automobile

mol (f.)   wine

mólo   shore, shoreline, harbour, mole

morel   he rubs, scrubs, polishes (past **morrdyas**)

môritíl-pês   she gets married (past **môritisáili**)

mothol   he tells, says (past **mothodyas**)

motsyúne (m.)   motion (as raised at a meeting)

mudárdyol   he is killed, murdered (past **mudárdyilo/mudárdyili**)

mudarel   1) he kills, murders; 2) he extinguishes (past **mudardyas**)

mudarimásko   murderous, lethal (genitive adj.)

mudarimos (m.) murder, massacre, slaughter

mui (m.)   mouth, face

muiyal   face up, upside down (adverb)

mukhel   1) he lets, allows, permits; 2) he leaves, abandons (past
                    mukhlas) (cognate of **mekel** (q.v.))

mukil-pês   he moves, relocates (past **mukisáilo/mukisáili**)

mulo   dead man, corpse, ghost in general (see also **choxãnó**)

mulo   dead, deceased (Them. Adj.)

múndro   wonderful, beautiful, fascinating (Athem. Adj.)

múrra   my, mine (before inflected feminine singular nouns)

múrre   my, mine (before plural nouns in the nominative and inflect-
                    ed plural nouns of both genders)

múrri   my, mine (before nominative singular feminine nouns)

múrro   my, mine (before nominative singular masculine nouns)

mursh (m.)   1) guy, fellow, man (not usually used to refer to Roma); 2)
                    male of the species (**o mursh thai e zhuvli** 'the male and
                    the female')

murtáno   tomcat

mútsa   female cat

mútsa-khandini (f.) skunk

muzíka   music

muzikánto   musician (especially if non-Romani)

N

na	no (in answer to a question. It also replaces **chi** (q.v.) in the subjunctive and infinitive moods. **Te na avel** 'May he not come')
nai (m.)	1) finger; 2) toe
nai	he/she, is not, they are not
naiyarel-pês	he bathes himself (past **naiyardyas-pês**)
nakh (m.)	nose
nakhel	1) it happens (past **nakhlo/nakhli. So nakhlo?** 'What happened?'); 2) he passes, gets past (past **nakhlo/nakhli**)
nas	he/she was not, they were not
nashavel	he makes to run, stampedes (past **nashadyas**)
nashel	he runs, flees, bolts, races, elopes (past **nashlo/nashli**)
nasul (f.)	evil, misfortune, sickness
nasul	bad, evil (Them. Adj. like **shukar**)
nasulimos (m.)	sickness
nasvalo	ill, sickly
nátsiya	nation
nav (m.)	name (contraction of **anav** (q.v.))
nayís-túke	thank you (to one person)
nayis-tumênge	thank you (to more than one person)
nêg	instead of
nevo	new (Them. Adj.)
nikerel	he carries, transports (past **nikerdyas**)
nipóta	1) niece; 2) granddaughter
nipóto	1) nephew; 2) grandson
nitála	even though
níva	field (North American-Kalderash)
núla	zero (numeral)
núma	but
nyáma	female relative
nyámo	male relative
Nyámptso	1) German man; 2) Germany
Nyámptsurya (m.pl.)	Germans
nyámurya (m.pl.)	relatives (including both genders)

O

o	the (before masculine nouns)
ófisa	office, reading parlour
Ói!	Oh!
Óide!	Oh!
opral	from above, over the top, from the top, upwards
opre	up, upwards
othe	there, right there
owêrish (m.)	day before yesterday
oxtáto	eighth (numeral)
ôxtó	eight (numeral)

P

pa	off, about, through
páchka	pack (**páchka kárti** 'pack of cards')
pai (m.)	water (variant of **páni** (q.v.))
pakyal	he believes (past **pakyáilo/akyáili**)
pal (f.)	plank, board
pála mizméri	after noon
pála	after, behind
pále	again
paleya (f.pl.)	floor (plural of **pal** (q.v.)
palorral	later, afterwards (usually with **mai** as in **mai palorral** 'later')
pálpale	back, back again (adverb. **Zhal pálpale** 'He is returning' (going back again))
páni (m.)	water
pansh chásurya	five o'clock
pansh	five (numeral)
pánshto	fifth (numeral)
papin (f.)	goose
pápo	grandfather
papúchi (f.pl.)	slippers
Parashtune	on Friday (adverb)
Parashtuvi	Friday
parintíya	ancestry, ancestors, parentage
parínto	male parent
parno	white (Them. Adj.)

parrno	barium sulfate (now used for cocaine), illegal hard drugs (barium sulfate is a toxic substance and was used by coppersmiths in their plating and tinning work)
parruvel	he trades, swaps, exchanges (past **parrudyas**)
pásha	near, close by, beside
pashal	nearby, close by
pásho	husband of wife's sister
páso	step, footstep
pastúxo	herdsman, cowboy
Patragi	Easter
pe	for, at, on (before feminine singular and plural nouns of both genders)
pe	variant of **pês** and **pên** (q.v.)
pecháta	1) spot, patch; 2) emblem, badge of authority
pekel	he cooks, bakes (past **peklas**)
pên	themselves (reflexive pronoun usually pronounced as **pe**)
pêngo	their own
perel	he falls (past **pelo/peli**)
pêrvo	first (numeral)
pês	himself, herself (used as a reflexive pronoun and usually pronounced as **pe**)
pêsko	his own, her own
phabai (f.)	apple
phabárdyol	he gets burned, incinerated (past **phabárdyilo/phabárdyili**)
phabarel	he burns, incinerates, heats up (past **phabardyas**)
phabol	he/she/it burns, heats up (past **phabulo/phabuli**)
phagel	he breaks, snaps, cracks (past **phaglas**)
phandayimos (m.)	confinement, detention
phandel	he closes, ties (past **phanglas**)
phari	pregnant (Them. Adj.)
pharo	hard, difficult, heavy (Them. Adj.)
pharravel	he shatters, smashes, demolishes (past **pharradyas**)
pharruvel	he explodes, disintegrates, falls to pieces (past **pharrulo/pharruli**)
phen (f.)	sister
phenel	he says, tells (past **phendyas**)
pherel	he fills (past **pherdyas**)
phey (f.)	sister (variant of **phen** (q.v.))
phirado	courted, wooed (past participle and Them. Adj.)

phiravel	1) he wears; (2) he courts (past **phiradyas**)
phirel	he walks, wanders (past **phirdyas**)
phral (m.)	brother
phurano	former, previous, older, ancient (Them. Adj.)
phúrdel	he blows, breathes (past **phurdas**)
phuri	elderly woman, matriarch
phuro	elderly man, patriarch
phuro	old (Them. Adj.)
phutêrdyol	it opens, becomes undone (past **phutèrdyilo/phutèrdyili**)
phutrel	he opens, undoes, unties (past **phuterdyas**)
phuv (f.)	earth, ground, soil
piramni	girlfriend, sweetheart, lover
piramno	boyfriend, lover
piyel	he drinks, smokes (cigarettes), absorbs (past **pilas**)
plácha	pleasure
plachal	it pleases (past **placháilo/placháili**)
plapóno	quilt, two quilts stuffed with goose feathers and sewn together like a modern sleeping bag
plócha	tile
po	on (before masculine nouns)
pódo	bridge
pokinel	he pays, pays for (past **pokindyas**)
polokorres	slowly (adverb)
polokorro	slow (Them. Adj.)
pomána	wake, period of mourning for a deceased Romani person (usually lasting one year with periodic feast tables every three months)
pômeníl	he arouses, awakens, makes aware (past **pômenisardyas**)
póno	1) plague; 2) typhus
ponyáva	carpet
pôrma	then
porrárro	pitcher, stein
porum (f.)	onion
posuki (f.)	pocket, pouch
pravarel	he feeds (animals) (past **pravardyas**)
pravarimos (m.)	fodder, food for horses, nourishment
práxo	dust
prekazhime	jinxed (Athem. past participle)
prindjarel	he recognizes, knows, is familiar with (past **prindjardyas**)

prinzharel	variant form of **prindjave** (q.v.)
prósto	common, ordinary, humble, contrite (Athem. Adj.)
prótivo	against, opposite, up against
pûnrró	foot
pûrr (m.)	stomach, entrails, guts
pushel	he asks, requests (with the ablative case of the object. **Pushlas mándar** 'He asked me'. Past **pushlas**)
pushimáta (m.pl.)	questions
pushimos (m.)	question
púshka	gun, firearm, revolver

R

rai (m.)	1) gentleman; 2) policeman
Raiyo	Heaven
rakli	non-Romani girl
raklo	non-Romani boy
ramol	he writes (past **ramosardyas**)
rani	gentlewoman, lady
rano	early (adverb)
rashai	priest, clergyman
ratyáko	at night
rêg (f.)	side
ródel	he seeks, searches, looks for (past **rodas**)
rovel	he cries, weeps (past **ruyas**)
rovli (f.)	stick, staff
rráka	crab
rrâkíya	whisky
rráko	cancer
rrándel	he shaves (past **rranglas**)
rrobíya	jail, prison
rroiyi	spoon
rroiyorri	teaspoon, tiny spoon
Rrôm baro	important Romani man, local leader
Rrôm	Romani man, husband if Romani
Rrom (m.pl.)	Roma, Romani men, people (North American variant of **Rroma**)
Rroma	Romani men, Romani people
Rromále!	Oh Romani adults! (vocative case)

Rromanes	like a Rom, like the Roma (adverb)
Rrómani shib	Romani language
Rromaníya	Romani culture, Romani environment
Rromano	Romani (Them. Adj.)
Rrômní	Romani woman, wife if Romani
rrugil	he beseeches, prays (past **rrugisardyas**)
Rumúniya	Romania
rup (m.)	silver
rupuno	having the colour of silver (Them. Adj.)
ruzhenil-pe	it rusts (past **ruzhenisáilo/ruzhenisáili**)
rúzho	red-hot, burning (Athem. Adj.)
ryat (f.)	night

S

sa	all
sábiya	sword, sabre
sam	we are
sáma	care, attention (**Le sáma** 'Take care')
sámas	we were, used to be
samuchi	almost, nearly
san	you are (singular and plural)
sánas	you were, used to be (singular and plural)
sano	slender, thin (Them. Adj.)
sap (m.)	male snake
sapni	female snake, viper
Sar mai san?	How are you?
sar	like, as
sar?	how?
sas	he/she was, used to be, they were, used to be
sastimus (m.)	health, wellbeing (North American- Kalderash)
sastipe (m.)	health, wellbeing (European-Kalderash)
sastri (m.)	iron
Sávato	Saturday
Savatone	on Saturday
savo?	which?
savorre (m.pl.)	everyone, everybody
sáyêkh	forever, always, eternally
serel	he reminds, remembers (past **serdas**)

shai	can, may, might (used with verbs. **Shai avel** 'He can or might come')
shav (m.)	variant form of **shávo** (q.v.)
Shavále!	Oh Romani youth! (vocative case)
shávo	Romani boy, youth, son
shax (m.)	cabbage
shêfto	business, work, deals (Central European-Kalderash)
shêl	hundred (numeral)
shêláto	hundredth (numeral)
sherand (m.)	pillow, cushion
shey	Romani girl, unmarried girl
shey-bari	eldest (oldest) daughter
shib (f.)	tongue, language
shîl (f.)	cold, flu
shilo	cold, aloof
shinel	he cuts, slices, slashes (past **shindyas**)
shkafedi (f.)	end table, coffee table
shkóla	school
shófto/shóvto	sixth
shon (m.)	1) moon; 2) month
shoro	head, top
shorr (m.)	beard
shoshoi (m.)	male rabbit
shov	six (numeral)
shtrafyaiyimos (m.)	lightning, lightning bolt
shtar	four (numeral)
shtaré-rêgèngo	square (compound Them. Adj.)
shtárto	fourth (numeral)
shtrángo	rope, thick cord, power cable for electrical instruments
shtrékya	strike, run of good luck in business
shudel	he throws, throws out, throws off, ejects (past **shudas**)
shudrimos (m.)	cold (opposite of heat)
shudro	cold (opposite of hot) (Them. Adj.)
shudrol	it grows cold (past **shudrilo/shudrili**)
shukar	beautiful, handsome (Them. Adj.)
shukares	beautifully (adverb)
shukarimos (m.)	beauty
shukarni	beautiful girl or woman
shûna	tyre (car, lorry, etc. **Pharruli pêski shûna** 'His tyre blew out')

shuri	knife, dagger
Shvedítska	Swedish (language)
si	he is, she is, they are
sikavel	he teaches, instructs, shows (past **sikadyas**)
sim	I am
símas	I was, used to be
síniya	table
sinzizáto	synthesizer (electrical musical instrument)
skamin (m.)	chair
skini (m.)	skinhead (the singular also serves as a plural)
skúrto	short (Athem. Adj.)
skutsome	sharp (as cutting edge of a knife. Past participle as Athem. Adj.)
sláva	feast, usually honouring a Saint
sluchayil-pe	it happens, is happening (past **sluchayisáilo/sluchayisáili**)
so?	what?
sóba	room
sóde?	how much?
sodya?	how many?
sogodi	whatever, whichever
sókra	mother-in-law
sókro	father-in-law
soldui (m. and f.pl.) both	
sórro ges	all day
sórro ryáto	all night
sórro	all (Them. Adj.)
sóstar?	why?
sovel	he sleeps (past **sutyas**)
stagi	hat
stánsiya	station
státo	statue, figure, body
stêngo	left (as a direction) (Athem. Adj.)
strázha	guard (**Gêló pe strázha** 'He was deported' (he went under guard))
súmnakai (m.)	gold
sumnakásko	made of gold (Them. Adj.)
sumnakuno	having the quality, colour of gold (Them. Adj.)
suno	dream
swágdar	always, eternally

swáko	each, every
swakorri	each female person
swakorro	each male person
swáto	word
swintáika	female saint
swínto	male saint
swínto	saintly, holy (Athem. Adj.)
swiyádêro	drill, pneumatic drill
sya	all (variant of **sa** (q.v.))

T

takimos (m.)	1) heat; 2) fever
Târánto	Toronto
tasavel	he drowns, sinks, smothers, suffocates, inundates (past **tasadyas**)
tasol	he drowns, sinks (past **tasulo/tasuli**)
tato	hot (Them. Adj.)
Tatrádji	Wednesday
Tatradjine	on Wednesday
taváno	roof, ceiling
taxdai (m.)	glass (as of water)
te	if (**Te dikhav lês phenav túke** 'If I see him, I'll tell you'.) Also subjunctive and optative particle. Since Kalderash-Romani has no infinitive, the particle **te** is inserted between two conjugated verbs to express the infinitive mood, for example, **Mangav te zhav** 'I want to go (I want that I go)', **Manges te zhas** 'You want to go (You want that you go)' etc. The optative particle expresses a wish: **Te avel tehára** 'May he come tomorrow')
tehára	tomorrow
tela	contraction of **telal** (q.v.)
telal	under, underneath
tele	down, downwards (**Besh tele** 'Sit down' (to one person))
televízhono	television
temnítsa	dungeon, solitary confinement
terno	young, inexperienced (Them. Adj.)
tha	and, also
thai	and also

than (m.)	1) place, spot, location; 2) bed in North American-Kalderash
them (m.)	1) country, kingdom; 2) people, humanity
thol	he puts, places (past **thodyas**)
thud (m.)	milk
thulo	fat (Them. Adj.)
thuv (f.)	smoke
tiburóno	shark
tilára	dollar (in North American-Kalderash)
tíra	your (before inflected feminine singular nouns)
tíre	your, yours (before nominative plural nouns of both genders and before inflected masculine singular nouns and inflected plural nouns of both genders)
tíri	your, yours (before nominative feminine singular nouns)
tíro	your, yours (before nominative masculine singular nouns)
tolmachimos (m.)	translation
tover (m.)	axe, cleaver, froe, bill hook
tradel	he drives (car etc. Past **tradyas**)
tradino	exiled, expelled (past participle as Them. Adj.)
trádyol	he is sent, deported from, forced to vacate, exiled (past **trádyilo/tradyili**)
tréla	trailer, travel trailer
trin	three (numeral)
tríto	third (numeral)
trobul	it needs, lacks (defective verb existing only in the present and continuous past tense third person singular in most dialects. Past **trobúlas**)
trushalo	thirsty (Them. Adj.)
tsálya (f.pl.)	clothes, clothing
tsêra	1) tent; 2) extended family
tsigára	cigarette
tsino	small, tiny (Them. Adj.)
tsírdel	1) he pulls, draws; 2) he endures, suffers (past **tsirdyas**)
tsírma	thread, strand (of material)
tsirra	a few, small amount of
tsóxa	skirt
tsûmpo	drumstick of a cooked fowl
tu	you (accusative pronoun, a variant of **tut** (q.v.))
tu	you (nominative personal pronoun)
tumáro	your, yours (pl.)

tume	a variant of **tumên** (q.v.) as a reflexive pronoun
tume	you (plural nominative pronoun)
tumên	you (plural accusative pronoun)
turbáto	wild, mad (Athem. Adj.)
tut	you (singular accusative pronoun)
tya	short form of **tíra** (q.v.)
tyára	plate
tye	your (short form of **tire** (q.v.))
tyi	your (short form of **tíri** (q.v.))
tyo	your (short form of **tíro** (q.v.))

V

vákto	time (Romanian-Kalderash)
vapóri (m.)	steamship, steamer
vára	female cousin
vash	for, for the sake of
véro	male cousin
vêska	because
vésolo	happy, joyous (technically athematic but many Romani speakers decline it as thematic)
vi-	prefix meaning 'too, also, even' (**Vi-tu zhanes** 'Even you know')
vitiyázo	hero, giant among men, physical giant
vítsa	Kalderash clan
volil	he loves (past **volisardyas**)
volime	beloved (Athem. Adj.)
vôrdòn (m.)	caravan (horse-drawn), station wagon
vôrdônútso	cart, little wagon, shopping cart, wheelbarrow
vryámya	time
vucho	tall, high (Them. Adj.)
vúni	some, a few

W

wárekai	somewhere, anywhere
wárekon	somebody, anybody
wáreso	something, anything
wast (m.)	hand

wêrsh (m.)	forest, bush
wo	he (nominative personal pronoun)
woi	she (nominative personal pronoun)
won	they (plural nominative personal pronoun)
wor	contraction of **wórka** (q.v.)
wórka	or, nor (**Chi me wórka tu zhanas** 'Neither you nor I know')
wórta	straight, straight ahead, right away, O.K.
wortáko	male partner, work partner
wuchitéli (m.)	teacher, mentor
wuchitêlka	female teacher, schoolteacher
wudar (m.)	door
wuloi (m.)	kerosene, heating oil
wúni	some, a few (variant of **vúni** (q.v.))
wunívar	sometimes, occasionally
wúrma (f.)	end, endmost, last
wushalin (f.)	shadow, shade
wushtyal	he ascends, rises, gets up (past **wushtilo/wushtili**)
wuzharel	he cleans (up) (past **wuzhardyas**)
wuzho	clean (Them. Adj.)

X

xabe (m.)	food (irregular oblique stem in **xabenes-**)
xal	he eats (past **xalyas**)
xalavel	he washes (past **xalad yas**)
xalavel-pês	he washes himself (past **xaladyas-pês**)
xanamik (m.)	father of a son or daughter's spouse, co-father-in-law
xanamíka (f.)	mother of a son or daughter's spouse, co-mother-in-law
xansi	less (usually as **mai xansi** 'less')
xanzhwalo	greedy, itchy (Them. Adj.)
xasarel	he loses, wastes (past **xasardyas**)
xaying (f.)	well, spring
xinel-pês	he defecates (past **xindyas-pês**)
xlútro	astute (Athem. Adj.)
xoli (f.)	anger, aggravation
xordo	small, small amount of (Them. Adj. **Xorde love** 'small change')
xóro	choir, band, music group
xoxavel	he lies, lies to, deceives (past **xoxadyas**)

xulai (m.)	host, master, landlord
xutel	he jumps, springs, leaps (past **xuklas** or **xuklo/xukli**)

Y

ya	yes (also **áva** (q.v.) and **va**)
yába	already, yet
yádo	hell
yag (f.)	fire, light (as with a match)
yakh (f.)	eye
yêkh	one (and sometimes 'a/an' as the indefinite article)
yekh-aver (m.)	each other
yêkh mai	one more
yertil	he pardons, forgives (past **yertisardyas**. **Yertisar man** 'Pardon me')
yilo	heart
Yoi!	Oh!

Z

zaharnítsa	sugar bowl
zaháro	sugar, sugar diabetes
zakóno	law, statute
zaloga	slightly (as an adverb), small amount, a little
zalogítsa	a little bit, to a small degree (**Grizhosardyas zalogítsa** 'He cleaned up a little bit')
zéleno	green (Athem. Adj.)
zéya	back (anatomical)
zor (f.)	power, strength
zoralo	powerful, strong (Them. Adj.)
zudo	wall
zurales	quickly (adverb)
zuralo	quick, fast (Them. Adj.)

ZH

zhal	he goes (past **gêló/gêlí**)
zhámutro	1) son-in-law, daughter's husband; 2) brother-in-law, wife's brother

zhanel	he knows (past **zhanglas**)
zhávo	sorrow
zhegáno	wild animal, man-eating beast
zhêkùn	until
zhene (m.pl.)	male persons, people as mixed gender group or all males (used mainly with numbers, for example, **pansh zhene** 'five people')
zheno	male person (used mainly with numbers, for example, **Chi dikhlem chi yêkh zheno** 'I didn't see even one person')
zhi-ka	until, up to, as far as
zhîpùn	unless
zhívina	creature, domesticated animal
Zhowine	on Thursday (adverb)
Zhóya	Thursday
zhukel (m.)	male dog
zhukli	bitch, female dog
zhutóri (m.)	lawyer (European-Kalderash)
zhútso	1) wire, steel guitar string; 2) wire service, newswire
zhuvli	woman, wife, female

Recommended reading

Recommended adjunct to this course

Lee, Ronald and Giannina Bottaccini. *E Zhívindi Yag: Homage to Kali Sara*, Ver-chères, Quebec, Canada, 2003. A CD featuring many of the songs in Romani dialects which appear in the course lessons.
Available from www.kopachi.com

Some useful works consulted

European Roma Rights Centre, Budapest. Articles in Romani in various issues of *Roma Rights* magazine and cassette tapes of radio broadcasts in various Romani dialects

Lee, Ronald and Waso Russel Demitro. *Lexicon of Canadian Kalderash Romani*, Unpublished, 1963

Lee, Ronald. *A Grammatical Analysis of Canadian Kalderash Romani*, Unpub-lished, 1970. This was used by Donald Kenrick to create the original *Learn Romani* course from which this present course was developed

Matras, Yaron. *Romani: A Linguistic Introduction*, Cambridge University Press, 2002. An excellent technical linguistic analysis of Romani dialects aimed at academic linguists and scholars

Sampson, John. *The Dialect of the Gypsies of Wales*, Oxford, Clarendon Press, 1923. While this dialect is now believed to be extinct, this work is an excel-lent source for students of Romani to determine etymology of words and has much useful material on other dialects of Romani and the evolution, phonetics and morphology of Romani

Sarău, Gheorghe. *Culegere de texte biblice în limba rromani*, Bucharest, Editura Kriterion, 2002. A collection of Biblical texts in Romanian Vlax-Romani

Sarău, Gheorghe. *Manual de alfabetizare în limba rromani pentru copii, tineri si adulti*, Bucharest, UNICEF Romania, Editura Vanemonde, 2002. A course in Romanian-Romani for children and adults

Zatreanu, Mihaela. *I Rromani Cib, O Trinto Bers*, Bucharest, Veritas Romania, 2002. A children's course book for learning Romanian-Romani

Materials for further study of Kalderash and related dialects

Edward Proctor

KALDERASH (also spelt Kalderaš, Kelderaš and Kêldêrašicka)

Kalderash dictionaries (English language)

ROMLEX Lexical Database http://romani.kfunigraz.ac.at/romlex/lex.xml
Free interactive dictionary of over 21,000 words. Currently translates to and from fifteen European languages and twenty-five Romani dialects (including Kalderash and Lovari). A scholarly project, but also practical and user-friendly.

**Cech, Petra, Christiane Fennesz-Juhasz et al., *Wörterbuch des Kalderaš-Romani. Teil I: Romani-Deutsch-Englisch. Teil II: Deutsch-Romani. Englisch-Romani* (Dictionary of Kalderash Romani. Part I: Romani-German-English. Part II: German-Romani. English-Romani). Graz/Wien: Romani Projekt, 2003. 168 pp. and 193 pp.
romani@gewi.kfunigraz.ac.at**
Massive, authoritative two-part Kalderash-German-English dictionary.

Demeter, R.S., P.S. Demeter, L.N. Cherenkov (eds.), *TSygansko-Russkii i Russko-TSyganskii Slovar: Kelderarskii Dialekt: 5,300 Slov* (Gypsy-Russian and Russian-Gypsy Dictionary (Kalderash Dialect) 5,300 words). Moscow: Russky Yazyk Publishers, 1990. 336 pp.
Russian and English also containing a "Gypsy-English Dictionary". Useful appendices include a systematic grammar, lists of personal names and illustrations of realia (the material culture of daily life) labelled in Romani.

Kalderash dictionaries (foreign language)

Calvet, Georges, *Dictionnaire Tsigane-Français: Dialecte Kalderash* (Gypsy-French Dictionary: Kalderash Dialect). Paris: L'Asiathèque, 1993. 464 pp. www.asiatheque.com
French text. Excellent lengthy dictionary, including grammatical outline, etymologies and illustrative sentences. Indian root words printed in Devanagari as well as Roman script.

Soravia, Giulio, "Vocabolario Kalderašitska" ("Kalderash Dictionary"). *Lacio Drom* (1985) 21 (5): 1-29. Reverse index (1985) 21 (5): 30-48.
Italian text. Brief word list of Italian-Kalderash.

Kalderash grammars (English language)

Gjerdman, Olof and Erik Ljungberg, *The Language of the Swedish Coppersmith Gipsy, Johan Dimitri Taikon*. Uppsala: AB Lundequistska Bokhandeln, Acta Academiae Regiae Gustavi Adolphi, 1963. 455 pp. http://home.swipnet.se/kgaa/publikationer.html
Outstanding scholarly study of Swedish-Kalderash (broadly similar to that spoken throughout Europe and America). The most detailed analysis yet published of any living Romani dialect. Complete grammar with forty pages of texts and translations. Dictionary of 3,600 words with English index. Essential for advanced study.

Hancock, Ian, *A Handbook of Vlax Romani*. New York: Slavica Publishers Inc., 1995. 178 pp. http://www.slavica.com
Analyses core features common to all forms of Vlax, highlighting similarities among Kalderash, Lovari and Machwaya. Grammar, vocabulary and pronunciation all discussed in a clear, easily-applicable manner. Useful for beginning students.

Ackerley, Frederick George, "The Dialect of the Nomad Gypsy Coppersmiths with Texts and Vocabulary". *Journal of the Gypsy Lore Society*, New [2nd] Series (1912-13), vol. VI no.4: 303-326; (1913-14) vol. VII no.2: 116-149; 161-214. UK: http://sca.lib.liv.ac.uk/collections/gypsy/journal.htm and USA: http://www.gypsyloresociety.org/jourlibrary.htm
First detailed English-language study of Kalderash. Good overview providing a great deal of useful information. In three parts: i) brief texts and translations of "extempore conversations", tales, songs, ballads and miscellaneous fragments; ii) systematic description of grammar; and iii) a fifty-page Romani-English vocabulary.

Bhatia, Rishi Gopal, *A Gypsy Grammar*. Thesis (PhD). Philadelphia: University of Pennsylvania, 1963. http://www.umi.com/umi/dissertations
Scholarly study of a Kalderash dialect representative of American-Romani in general. One of the few to draw attention to the existence of 'higher' and 'lower' (i.e. formal and informal) styles of speech. Four lengthy texts, followed by English translations and detailed line-by-line linguistic analysis. Romani-English vocabulary.

Barannikov, A.P., *The Ukrainian and South Russian Gypsy Dialects*. Leningrad: Publishing Office of the Academy, 1934. Translation of *Ukraïns'ki ta Pivdenno-Rosiïs'ki TSyhans'ki Diialekty*. 226 pp.
Classic study of Russian dialects (including Kalderash and Lovari). In two parts: i) detailed analysis of grammar and ii) large collection of songs and prose texts

with English translations. Out of print but available in major libraries.

Kalderash grammars (foreign language)

Boretzky, Norbert, *Romani: Grammatik des Kalderaš-Dialekts mit Texten und Glossar* (Romani: Grammar of the Kalderash Dialect with Texts and Glossary). Balkanologische Veröffentlichungen, Bd. 24 0170-1533. Berlin: Harrassowitz, 1994. 299 pp. http://www.harrassowitz.de/verlag
German text. Detailed, scholarly study of Kalderash as spoken in Serbia and Montenegro. Half grammar, half texts with a 100-page Romani-German glossary.

Matras, Yaron, *Untersuchungen zu Grammatik und Diskurs des Romanes: Dialekt der Kelderaša/Lovara* (Investigations into the Grammar and Speech of Romani: The Kelderash/Lovari Dialect). Balkanologische Veröffentlichungen, Bd. 26 0170-1533. Wiesbaden: Harrassowitz, 1994. 256 pp. http://www.harrassowitz.de/verlag
German text. Analysis of grammar and discourse style of a variety of Kalderash and Lovari originally from Transylvania, spoken in Poland, Germany and Sweden. Very useful for advanced students.

Kalderash phrasebooks and courses (English and foreign language)

Barthélémy, André, *Žanés Romanés?: Manuel de Conversation Tsigane (Dialecte Kalderaš)* (Do You Know Romani?: Handbook of Gypsy Conversation (Kalderash Dialect)). Paris: Études Tsiganes, 1982. 93 pp. plus two cassette tapes. http://www.etudestsiganes.asso.fr
French text. Seventy-lesson Kalderash-French phrasebook of a Parisian dialect heavily influenced by Russian. The tapes are extremely useful for beginners struggling to develop a good ear and proper pronunciation (especially helpful for those who have difficulty interpreting diacritical marks). Explanatory annotations but without a glossary or systematic grammar. The first forty lessons have been translated into English by the *Western Canadian Romani Alliance* (**celtrom@uniserve.com**).

Cioabă, Luminita Mihai, *Ghid de Conversatie Român-Tigănesc* (Romanian-Gypsy Conversation Guide). Bucuresti: Teora, 2001. 239pp. plus CD. http://www.teora.ro/
Romanian text. Substantial conversation guide with Kalderash and Romanian in parallel columns. Valuable accompanying CD.

Sarău, Gheorghe, *Curs de Limba Rromani* (Course in the Romani Language). Cluj Napoca: Editura Dacia, 2000. 254 pp. plus two cassette

tapes. minorities@mec.edu.ro
Romanian text. Well arranged textbook of "common Romani language"
("international standard Romani") similar to Kalderash. Easy-to-understand
format with tables of conjugations and declensions clearly laid out. Very
useful tapes.

Maximoff, Matéo, "Some peculiarities in the speech of the Kalderaš".
Journal of the Gypsy Lore Society, 3rd Series (1965) 25: 108–112. UK:
http://sca.lib.liv.ac.uk/collections/gypsy/journal.htm and USA:
http://www.gypsyloresociety.org/jourlibrary.htm
Useful introduction to idioms and proverbs and their social context by a
famous French-Roma author. In Kalderash with translations and explanations.

Romani reading material

Hill, Eric, _Kaj si o Rukun Amaro? / O Rukun Zal and-i Skòla / I Bari Lavenqi_
Pustik e Rukunesqiri (Where is Spot? / Spot Goes to School / Spot's
Big Book of Words). Centre Régional de Documentation Pédagogique
(CRDP) Midi-Pyrénées, 1995.
http://home.wanadoo.nl/holmesvr/Educate.htm
Romani, French and English text. Colourfully-illustrated series of children's
books useful for beginners, written in "standard" or "international" Romani
(similar to Kalderash).

Kurtiàde, Marcel, _Sirpustik Amare Chibaqiri_ (Our Language Book).
Toulouse: Than Rromane, Rodimatenqo (CRDP) Midi-Pyrénées: N.D.
(1992) (Rpt. 1994). http://home.wanadoo.nl/holmesvr/Educate.htm
French text. Primer in "standard" or "international" Romani. Teacher's
manual, _Sikavipen Sar te Siklon e Čhavorre e Sirpustikaça_ (_Learning How to
Teach Children with the Book_), available in several languages.

Lindgren, Astrid, _E'Pippi Lungo strinfa_ (Pippi Longstocking). Podium:
Sweden http://www.podium.nu/omp/about_podium.htm
Kalderash translation of the Swedish children's classic, _Pippi Långstrump._

Lundgren, Gunilla, Alyosha and Johan Taikon, _From Coppersmith to_
Nurse: Alyosha, the Son of a Gypsy Chief. Hatfield: University of Hert-
fordshire Press, 2003. 144 pp. http://www.herts.ac.uk/UHPress
English and Kalderash on facing pages. Fascinating life story with useful
grammatical notes and a brief glossary.

Kenrick, Donald and G. Puxon, _Bibaxtale Bersa_ [earlier edition _Bersša_
Bibahtale] (Years of Bad Luck). Madrid: Editoria Presencia Gitana, 1996.
164 pp. http://www.herts.ac.uk/UHPress/Spanish.html

Translation of *Gypsies under the Swastika* (a substantial revision of *The Destiny of Europe's Gypsies*) into "standard" or "international" Romani.

Kenrick, Donald, *Romengiro Drom: Indijatyr ke Maskiratuno Derjav* (Gypsies: From India to the Mediterranean). Hatfield: University of Hertfordshire Press, 2003. 69 pp. http://www.herts.ac.uk/UHPress/culture.html Translation into a dialect spoken in Belarus and Russia (with notes giving equivalents in several dialects and an English translation). Grammatical endings similar to Kalderash and Balkan dialects.

The Bible (English language)

Lists of translated portions are maintained by Bakker & Kyuchukov (see below), the *Romani Bible Network* http://home.wanadoo.nl/holmesvr/Bibles.htm and the *Global Recordings Network* http://www.gospelrecordings.com/catalog (which also sells cassette tape recordings and CDs and will soon be offering free streaming audio). A complete *New Testament* in Kalderash is archived online at http://web.archive.org/web/20040212014929/ http://www.rayida.org/RayidaNT.htm

DVDs, films and videotapes (English and foreign language)

***Angelo, My Love*. Columbia TriStar Home Entertainment, 1983. VHS. http://www.sonypictures.com** English and Romani (English subtitles). Several lengthy Kalderash dialogues. Good source of American-Romani.

***Gadjo Dilo*. (The Crazy Stranger). Princes Film, 1997. VHS and DVD. http://www.celluloid-dreams.com** French and Romani (English subtitles). Filmed in Romania, predominately in Kalderash (with a wealth of vivid maledictions).

***The JESUS Film*. The JESUS Film Project, 1979. VHS, DVD and streaming video. http://www.jesusfilm.org** Originally English, now dubbed into several dialects including Calderari (Kalderash) and Lovari and available in free streaming video http://www.jesusfilm.org/languages/index.html

LOVARI (also spelt Lovara and Lovāri)

Lovari grammars (English language)

Pobozniak, Tadeusz, *Grammar of the Lovari Dialect*. Prace Komisji

Orientalistycznej (Polska Akademia Nauk. Komisja Orientalistyczna) nr.
3. Kraków: Panstwowe Wydawn. Naukowe, 1964. 78 pp.
http://www.pan.pl
Good, concise overview of Lovari as spoken in southern Poland. Clearly laid-
out grammar and core vocabulary. No texts.

Lovari grammars (foreign language)

Cech, Petra and Mozes F. Heinschink, *Basisgrammatik. Arbeitsbericht 1a
des Projekts Kodifizierung der Romanes-Variante der Österreichischen
Lovara* (Basic Grammar. First Working Report of the Codification Project of the Austrian Lovara Variant of Romani). Wien: Verein Romano
Centro, 1999. 108 pp. http://www-gewi.kfunigraz.ac.at/romani/down-
load/files/l_ab1a.pdf
German text. Detailed scholarly analysis of Austrian-Lovari grammar.

Lovari dictionaries (English language)

Translator Lovara-Romani http://www-gewi.kfunigraz.ac.at/romani/cgi-
bin/trans-lov.cgi?lang=en&query=0&querytype=0&search_for=0.
Interactive 2,600-word Lovari-English-German and English-German-Lovari
dictionary.

Cech, Petra and Mozes F. Heinschink, *Wörterbuch der Romani-Variante
der Österreichischen Lovara. Lovari-Deutsch-Englisch* (Dictionary of
the Austrian Lovara Variant of Romani. Lovari-German-English). Wien:
Verein Romano Centro, 2002. 61 pp.
http://www-gewi.kfunigraz.ac.at/romani/download/files/l_ab3a.pdf
An up-to-date Lovari-German-English dictionary of an Austrian variant.

Cech, Petra, Christiane Fennesz-Juhasz et al., *Wörterbuch des Lovara-
Romani (Lovari). Lovari-Deutsch-Englisch. Deutsch-Lovari. Englisch-
Lovari* (Dictionary of Lovara Romani (Lovari). Lovari-German-English.
German-Lovari. English-Lovari). Graz/Wien: Romani Projekt, 2003.
186 pp. romani@gewi.kfunigraz.ac.at
Much larger Lovari-German-English dictionary which will undoubtedly
become a classic in the field. With German-Lovari and English-Lovari
indices.

Lovari reading material (English language)

Gjerde, Lars and Knut Kristiansen, *The Orange of Love and Other Stories:
The Rom-Gypsy Language in Norway*. Oslo: Scandinavian University
Press, 1994. 305 pp. http://www.universitetsforlaget.no

Delightful collection of tales, with Lovari and English on facing pages and helpful notes. Lovari-English vocabulary.

Lovari reading material (foreign language)

Cech, Petra, Christiane Fennesz-Juhasz et al. (eds.), *Lovarenge Paramiči* *taj Tekstura anda Österreich. Texte Österreichischer Lovara* **(Lovari** **Fairy tales and Texts in Austria. Austrian Lovara Texts). Wien: Verein** **Romano Centro, 1999. 155 pp. and 123 pp.** http://www-gewi. kfunigraz.ac.at/romani/download/files/I_ab2.pdf **and** http://www-gewi.kfunigraz.ac.at/romani/download/files/I_ab4.pdf
German text. Marvellous two-part collection of autobiographical fragments, fairy tales, poems and songs of Austrian Roma. In Lovari with German translations and helpful notes.

Cech, Petra, Christiane Fennesz-Juhasz et al., *Fern von uns im Traum.* *Märchen, Erzählungen und Lieder der Lovara. Te na Dikhas Sunend.* *Lovarenge Paramiči, Tertenetura taj Gjila* **(Far From Us in Dreams. Fairy** **tales, Texts and Songs of the Lovara). Klagenfurt: Drava Verlag, 2001.** **431 pp.** http://www.drava.at
Large collection of Lovari fairy tales, texts and songs with German translations.

Romani internet and electronic resources

Romanestan (Country of the Roma)
http://groups.yahoo.com/group/Romanestan
Roma-moderated listserv. Discussions usually conducted in English about Romani "to help each other to revive the language, no matter what dialect". Predominately Kalderash.

Romane Nevipena (Romani News)
http://groups.yahoo.com/group/Romane_Nevipena/
Moderated by a member of the International Romani Union "This announcement group is aimed to provide Romani (Gypsy) organisations and individuals with the international news on Romani language (Romanes)." Postings almost exclusively in Romani, with occasional English translations. Valuable for advanced students.

Romano Centro (Roma Centre)
http://romani.uni-graz.at/romani/rc/2001/rc2001-35.rom.shtml **(1993-2001) and**
http://www.romano-centro.org/publikationen_de.html **(2002-)**
Austrian. Quarterly magazine in German, English and Kalderash.

Romani audio resources

radiomultikulti 96.3 – Multikulti romanes (Multicultural Romani)
http://www.multikulti.de/ /sprachen_jsp/activeid=72.html
German and Romani. News, music and cultural programmes in Lovari, Arli
and Kovaci (Balkan dialects). The largest proportion of spoken language of
any of the Romani broadcasters.

Radio Romano Centro (Radio Roma Centre) http://www-
gewi.kfunigraz.ac.at/romani/rrc/index.de.shtml (Archived 1997–2000)
Austria. Broadcasts predominately in Kalderash, with occasional use of
other dialects.

Sarău, Prof. Ghorghe, *Curs Practic de Limba Rromani* **(Practical Course in**
the Gypsy Language). Bucuresti: Universitatea Virtuală Universității
din Bucuresti, 2004. http://www.edu.ro/lv/INDEXlv.HTML
Fifteen audio files in mp3 format. Part of an eLearning course in "common"
or "international standard" Romani, a strongly Kalderash-influenced version.

Sarău, Prof. Ghorghe, *Le Maj šukar Rromane Paramìčă thaj Svàtură. Cele*
Mai Frumoase Povestir si Pilde Rromani **(The Best Romani Fairy tales**
and Proverbs). Bucuresti: Pro Media Music – UPFR, 2001. Cassette tape.
Tape of tales and proverbs in Kalderash.

Guides to more material (English language)

Romani Media Address Book http://lists.errc.org/databases/media.shtml
Regularly updated database of magazines, journals, newspapers, radio and
television broadcasts in a wide variety of dialects.

Bakker, Peter and Hristo Kyuchukov, *Publications in Romani, Useful for*
Romani Language Education. **134 pp.**
http://fc.hum.au.dk/~peter_bakker/00D44EE2-0075824E.-
1/%20romedu-prefinal-november-20.pdf
A wealth of multi-dialectical resources. The most exhaustive listing available
of grammars, dictionaries, translations and texts. Intended for educators
teaching reading skills to Romani-speaking pupils.

Proctor, Edward, *Gypsy Dialects: An annotated bibliography of materials*
for the practical study of Romani. **Hatfield: University of Hertfordshire**
Press, January 2006. 224 pp.
A selection and evaluation of audio, broadcast, film, internet and print
sources (including journal articles) of use for learning Romani. Includes
detailed annotations of each item, and suggestions on how to begin, obtain
materials and keep in touch with future developments.